Disability and Development

Learning from action and research on disability in the majority world

Edited by

Emma Stone

The Disability Press

Leeds

First published 1999
The Disability Press
Disability Research Unit
School of Sociology and Social Policy
University of Leeds
Leeds LS2 9JT.

Output from disk supplied and printed by University Print Services, a division of Media Services at Leeds.

British Library Cataloguing in Publication Data
A catalogue record for this book is available from the British Library

Library of Congress Cataloguing in Publication Data
A catalogue record of this book has been requested

ISBN 0 9528450 3 2 (pbk)

Contents

The Disability Press

The Disability Press aims to provide an alternative outlet for work in the field of disability studies. The Disability Press draws inspiration from the work of all those countless disabled individuals and their allies who have, over the years, struggled to put this particular issue onto the political agenda. Its establishment is a testament to the growing recognition of 'disability' as an equal opportunities and human rights issue within the social sciences.

Funding for this fourth volume has been provided by the Disability Research Unit – which also provided funding for the UK Forum on Disability and Development in the Majority World, Leeds, April 1998. The editor also wishes to record her thanks to the School of Sociology and Social Policy at the University of Leeds for its continuing support.

Contributors

Alison Callaway finished a PhD at the Centre for Deaf Studies at Bristol University in 1998. Since then, Alison has returned to medicine and is practising as a doctor in Oxford. Her book, "Deaf Children in China", will be published by Gallaudet University Press shortly.

Peter Coleridge has worked in development for about twenty years in the Middle East, Horn of Africa and Afghanistan. He is the author of "Disability, Liberation and Development" (Oxfam 1993), a study of the social model of disability in selected countries in Africa, Asia and the Middle East. He is currently Programme Manager of a large CBR programme under UNDP (United Nations Development Programme) in Afghanistan.

Vic Finkelstein settled in the UK in 1968 as a political refugee from South Africa, and worked in the National Health Service as a Senior Clinical Psychologist. In 1975, he joined the Open University, where he was employed until 1997 as a lecturer in the field of Disability Studies. He has contributed to the social interpretation of disability and helped start several organisations of disabled people, including the Union of the Physically Impaired Against Segregation (UPIAS), London Disabilities Arts Forum (LDAF) and British Council of Organisations of Disabled People (BCODP). He represented the UK on the World Council of Disabled Peoples' International during its first 5 years.

Barbara Frost has been Chief Executive of Action on Disability and Development (ADD) for three years. ADD is an international development agency working in twelve countries in Africa and Asia. It supports the development initiatives of disabled people's organisations in their campaign for equal rights and opportunities.

Sally Hartley has worked for and with disabled people and their families mainly on the African continent over the past 30 years. She presently co-ordinates modules on Disability Services Strategies in low income countries and Communication Disability as part of the MSc Community Disability Studies programme at University College, London. She also co-ordinates the Disability Research and Training programme in Uganda.

Rachel Hurst is the Director of Disability Awareness in Action (DAA), the international information network on disability and human rights, and is the Vice-Chair for Human Rights of Disabled Peoples' International. She has been an activist in the development of the Disability Movement locally, nationally and internationally for over twenty years.

Hazel Jones worked for 5 years in a special school in Leeds, and has an M.Ed in Special Education from Manchester University. She worked for 3 years in Thailand with Voluntary Services Overseas (VSO) as an adviser in a special school. Hazel then worked with Save the Children (UK) as Special Needs Adviser in Ho Chi Minh City, Viet Nam. She has also worked with Save the Children (UK) in China and Myanmar. Hazel is currently a freelance consultant, living in York.

Ray Lang is currently undertaking doctoral research at the School of Development Studies, University of East Anglia, UK. Previously, he held the position of Disability Programme Co-ordinator at the Appropriate Health Resources and Technologies Action Group (AHRTAG), where he was responsible for the strategic development of the newsletter *CBR News*.

M. Miles has worked with Asian and African colleagues supposedly developing disability service resources. He studies (or invents?) the histories of social responses to disability in Asian, Middle Eastern and African countries. He lives in Birmingham with a wife and several small computers.

Susie Miles is the Co-ordinator of EENET (Enabling Education Network). Previously she worked in southern Africa for 12 years, initially as a teacher of Deaf children and later as Save the Children (UK)'s Regional Disability Adviser. In this role she supported the development of CBR and integrated education initiatives.

David Phillips is Senior Lecturer in Social Policy in the Department of Sociological Studies, University of Sheffield. He has undertaken research on the problems associated with transition from paediatric to adult services for disabled young people and is at present engaged in a research project on altruism, intergenerational relations and social welfare among Muslims in the UK.

Rebecca Saul has her doctorate in Social Anthropology and presently works on the Latin America and South Asia desk at CARE International UK. She has lived and worked in Nepal for more than three years. She specialises in social development issues related to gender, health, caste, and disability.

Emma Stone was until recently based at the Disability Research Unit, University of Leeds, where she completed her doctorate on disability in China, and also worked on the Snowdon Survey (on barriers to disabled people's participation in post-16 study in Britain). During fieldwork in China, Emma also worked with Save the Children (UK) and UNICEF-China. She is now Senior Research Manager on Social Care and Disability for the Joseph Rowntree Foundation.

Sue Stubbs has worked as the Disability Advisor in Save the Children (UK) since 1991. In her current post, her most passionate interest has been in relation to promoting 'lessons from the South', and developing the links between other issues of difference and discrimination. She was a co-founder of the Enabling Education Network and has been Co-ordinator of the International Disability and Development Consortium for several years. She now works part time for Save the Children to devote more time to a project enabling Northerners to learn from the South through workshops in India on music and Indian culture.

Majid Turmusani works for an umbrella non-governmental organisation in Jordan, operating in the field of disability and development. He is involved in disability issues at both national and international level. Majid was a founding member of the International Association for Cross-Disability Research. He has published several papers on disability and development issues.

Sheila Wirz, who has worked for and with disabled people and their families throughout her career, became interested in issues of disability and development in the late 1980s. For the past 6 years she has been course director of the MSc in Community Disability Studies at the Centre for International Child Health, and heads the disability research group of seven staff members who are working on 6 different projects in India, Uganda, Sri Lanka and Zimbabwe.

CHAPTER 1

Disability and development in the majority world

Emma Stone

> Across the world, disabled people are struggling for access to education, jobs and housing, for the right to express their sexuality and to have children, to participate in political and social life, and in the development of our communities. However, the world is a disabling place, and millions of us experience the effects of it every day of our lives.
> (Leonard Williams 1995, President of the Disabled Persons Rehabilitation Association, Solomon Islands.)
>
> While people in the rich world are talking about Independent Living and improved services, we are talking about survival.
> (Joshua Malinga, leading disabled activist from Zimbabwe and Chair of Disabled Peoples' International, in Beresford 1996, p.560.)

INTRODUCTION

This book covers' such a wide range of topics and perspectives that it is almost impossible to write a short introduction. What makes this task even harder is the hope that those who read this book will come from very different backgrounds. Some readers will come from a disability studies background and will know a great deal about western theories of disability, but much less about the issues facing disabled people and their allies in the rest of the world. Others will have a strong knowledge of international development research and practice, perhaps working for (or hoping to work for) a non-governmental organisation that strives to combat global poverty. There will be readers who are already involved in working with disabled people in some of the poorest regions of the world; and others who are thinking about getting involved in the future. Given such a wide target audience it feels more appropriate simply to set out some issues, highlight other sources of information, and give a feel for what this book can and cannot offer.

WHAT IS "DISABILITY"?

Who defines disability? Who is disabled and who is not disabled? Does disability mean the same thing across cultures and across time? What exactly is disability? Is it a physical or mental condition? Or is it the response of society and culture to people with that condition? Your answers to these questions will have a direct impact on how you approach disability and development in the majority world.

In any book on disability, especially one with a global perspective, definitions are hugely problematic. For a start, there is the inevitable tension between the need for internationally shared meanings that enable cross-cultural information exchange and, on the other hand, the need to recognise cultural differences. There are also tensions between those who fight for the power to define what disability is. Historically, the power to define disability has been held by professionals – mostly western, mostly medical, educational or administrative. But recent decades have seen new and challenging definitions coming from disabled people themselves – albeit mostly western, white and educated disabled people. (See Oliver 1996, Finkelstein 1991 and contributions to Barnes & Mercer 1996 on debates surrounding disability definitions.)

In Britain and elsewhere, disabled people and their allies have developed the "social model of disability" as a radically different way of thinking about disability. In the social model, the problem is not located in the individual, but in a society (economy, culture) that fails to meet the needs of people with impairments. *Impairment* is the term used for an individual's condition (physical, sensory, intellectual, behavioural). *Disability*, in complete contrast, is social disadvantage and discrimination. The social model message is simple and strong: if you want to make a difference to the lives of disabled people, you must change society and the way society treats people who have impairments. That change must begin with full recognition of disabled people's civil rights, the full involvement of disabled people themselves in planning and policy that is about their lives, and a commitment to removing *disabling barriers* that prevent disabled people's participation in society. Hence the slogans: "RIGHTS NOT CHARITY" and "NOTHING ABOUT US WITHOUT US".

The social model of disability has many critics. For some, the social model might be right for politicised disabled people in the west, but it should not be transferred beyond the west. That would be more like imperialism than empowerment (see Miles 1992, 1996; Stone 1997). On the other hand, the evidence from many disabled people who live in the majority world is that the social model makes sense across cultures and countries. Letters and stories printed in *Disability Tribune* (newsletter of Disability Awareness in Action) give strong evidence that disabled people worldwide are forming their own organisations to bring about rights-based change.

It would be wrong to downplay the significance of this movement, although it is equally important to recognise how much still needs to change. In Britain, home to many disabled people's organisations, the "individual model" or "medical model" of disability (which sees the individual as the problem, victim, object of charity, and object of professional intervention) still rules. There is a long way to go before the social model is the basis on which policies are made, services are provided, and lives are lived.

Most of the contributors to this book adopt the social model to a greater or lesser degree – although many do not use the 2-fold distinction, tending to use "disability" for both impairment and disability. No editorial changes have been imposed here. It is probably important to make clear, however, that fully adopting a social model of disability does not mean that there is no place for medical or other professionals. As Vic Finkelstein argues in the next chapter, the social model means that existing professions, services and ideologies need to be transformed in ways that promote disabled people's self-empowerment and real social change. Professionals should be allied to disabled people and the community, not allied to medicine or administration.

WHAT IS "DEVELOPMENT"?

Development is another problematic, although less often problematised, word. Think about the terms "developing countries" or "underdeveloped countries".

Implicit in these terms is the concept of a ladder of development, with the west occupying the highest rungs while the rest of the world is balanced on the rungs below. Those at the very bottom of the ladder are often referred to as LDCs – the Least Developed Countries, with the longest way to go before they approach western standards.

It is the value-laden nature of the term "developing" that has led to my personal and political preference for "majority world" (developing countries, the South, the Third World) and "minority world" (the west, the North, industrialised countries). The majority world is the world that the vast majority of the world's people live in, yet they have access to a fraction of the world's wealth and power. In contrast, the richest countries of the world with a minority of the world's people exploit the lion's share of global resources. (Again, use of these terms has not been imposed on contributors.)

The term "majority world" also gets away from geographical notions about wealth and power. There are pockets of great deprivation in countries of the North, and pockets of incredible wealth in countries of the South. This is particularly relevant when talking about disability since, worldwide, disabled people are often among the most marginalised people in a community.

Finally, using the word "majority world" also enables a clear separation between western-dominated notions of progress, and the workings and study of processes of development where "development" is shorthand for change – social, economic, political, cultural, for better and for worse, complex and contradictory. It is in this second sense of the word that "development" becomes a useful and critical focus for understanding disability in the majority world and in global perspective, just as it has been for disability theorists and activists focused on the minority (western) world.

MAKING CONNECTIONS BETWEEN DISABILITY & DEVELOPMENT

The most frequently made connection between disability and development (and the connection has been made many times) is actually the link between poverty and impairment in the majority world (see Beresford 1996, Coleridge 1993, Boylan 1991 for example).

People with impairments in the majority world are more likely to be poor for two reasons. First, because the root causes of impairment in majority world countries – malnutrition, poverty, landmines, lack of services, etc. – hit the poorest people hardest (Chambers 1983). In fact, a considerable proportion of impairments in the majority world are a direct result of poverty, injustice, and exploitation by the minority world.

- Over 100 million people have impairments as a result of malnutrition.
- 250,000 children go blind every year through lack of Vitamin A.
- 800 million people are at risk of preventable learning difficulties through lack of iodine.
- 100,000 women in Africa acquire impairments through childbirth complications.
- 40% of hearing loss in children in the majority world would be preventable by early identification.
- There were 100,000 new cases of polio in 1994.
- Six million people worldwide are affected by leprosy.

Sources: *New Internationalist* (1992); Tiroler in *CBR News* (1995).

Secondly, people with impairments worldwide are more likely to be poor because of the disabling barriers that prevent them from getting an education, a job, access to appropriate support and services, and so forth. Some of these barriers are rooted in local attitudes and responses to impairment. Others are rooted in the broader structural processes of poverty and injustice that produce disability as well as impairment.

> The question still remains: how can disabled people have equal opportunities in developing countries in the face of rapid cultural change, worldwide recession, armed conflicts, continued imbalance of trade, structural adjustment and the ongoing rapid technological advances of the modern world? (Kisanji 1995, p. 199, in Zinkin & McConachie).

Here we move from connections between poverty and impairment to the connections between disability (as defined by the social model) and development.

In western disability studies, leading theorists have linked the social construction of disability in the west to western development (e.g. Finkelstein 1991, Oliver 1990, Albrecht 1992, Bickenbach 1993, Stone 1984, Barton 1996, Davis 1997). Whilst different theorists put forward very different analyses, there is a general argument that runs through all: disability is socially constructed, a product of western development processes and the dominance of certain professional élites. Urbanisation; industrialisation; the rise of medical and rehabilitation professions; the creation of a welfare state premised upon divisions between disabled and non-disabled people; western concepts of "normalcy"; western concepts of charity; the creation of ever larger mechanisms of social control; and so forth. These are just some of the processes that have been used to explain the construction of disability in the minority world.

Whether or not you agree with these theorists, it is surely indisputable that social and economic development processes will impact on the lives of disabled people. How can they not?

Several within the disability/development field have started to argue for a more critical approach to disability in the majority world that incorporates political, social and economic factors. For example, Momm & König (1989) suggest the following framework for collecting data prior to undertaking any disability projects:

- geographical, organisational, economic, political, social, linguistic, tribal and other community characteristics;
- socio-economic modes of organisation and production with an understanding of the impact of socio-economic change;
- relations between the community and the outside world, from a neighbouring village to national government; and
- the nature and impact of outsider interventions whether through trade, aid, services, or tourism.

Few have met Momm & König's expectations. Nonetheless, the message seems to be seeping through that global and local factors impact on perceptions of and responses to impairment and disability. Take (and I use one example only) Nicolaisen's (1995) study of disability among the Punan Bah of Borneo.

In the closing paragraphs of her account, Nicolaisen considers the impact of extensive logging on the Punan Bah economy and society. The large extended households that once facilitated the integration of individuals with impairments are now breaking up into smaller units with decreased capacity to provide support. Increased reliance on waged labour has undermined the role of many people with impairments in economic production. Meanwhile, expectations and attitudes to beliefs and rituals are changing, to be "more in tune with the capitalist Western values that imperceptibly permeate [the] Punan Bah view of themselves and the world"...

> This may save the life of children impaired like the spirit boy, but it may well make the lives of many others considerably less fulfilling and more difficult (Nicolaisen 1995, p. 54, in Ingstad & Whyte).

The point is important. Change is not only complex but may also be contradictory. Where some members of a household or community may benefit from new economic opportunities, others find previous social roles removed or redundant, or are set apart for special intervention where once they were integrated. Benefits may accrue such as literacy, mobility aids or the organisation of community groups, but they accrue at the risk of undermining previous forms of social accommodation, weakening the role of the extended family as the main source of social security, threatening local strategies and healing systems, and creating a class of "disabled" people that did not exist prior to outsider involvement in rehabilitation, surveys or research (see Burck 1989, contributors to Ingstad & Whyte 1995 for example).

The impact of "development" must not be ignored when considering disability in the majority world. Yet most who write on disability in the majority world fail to explore these issues to sufficient degree. Governments, television, newspapers, professionals, ideologies, institutions, structures, schools, modes of production, disability policies and state-social definitions of disability do not exist in the west alone. Many majority world countries have institutional and ideological legacies that stretch back over millennia. All of these will have an impact on perceptions of and responses to impairment (and thus the social construction of disability). All of these are subject to processes of rapid and often skewed under/development. Now more than ever.

THE GLOBALISATION OF DISABILITY

Globalisation has been the buzzword of the 1990s. We live in a global society: MacDonalds, Coca Cola and the Internet are the hallmarks of a global culture; the United Nations, World Bank and multinational corporations like Glaxo and Microsoft wield more economic and political power than most national governments. Development can only be understood in global context. And there is ever growing demand to think about disability in a global context too.

1981 was the International Year of Disabled Persons. The United Nations Decade of Disabled People (1982-1992) followed. During that decade and in the years since, there have been successive waves of new initiatives targeted at disabled people living in the majority world. Some of these initiatives have been developed specifically for the majority world, often by western or western-trained professionals. Community Based Rehabilitation (CBR) is a good example. The concept of CBR was originally championed by the World Health Organization with the aim of making rehabilitation services available to grassroots communities in a cost-effective way. It has spread like wildfire and has been adopted, adapted, contested and reworked to cover a wide range of projects in an even wider range of settings. It is one example among many. None of this is new or surprising. What is happening in the 1990s is simply an updated, less obviously imperialistic, version of what missionaries were doing in the 1890s. Well-meaning, but not always carefully considered, sensitively implemented, or appropriate to local practices and perceptions.

New initiatives require funders, planners, implementers and evaluators. The emergence of CBR (and other outsider-led interventions) has fostered the emergence of CBR training programmes, training manuals and professional trainers, not to mention CBR workers, managers and evaluators. There are growing numbers of western or western-trained professionals working in disability and development, facilitated by international circuits and international journals.

The past two decades have also seen a dramatic increase in organisations controlled by disabled people. Local, national and international organisations of disabled people have taken a strong role in promoting social change based on their own analysis of disability and society. There are international networks and newsletters here too – such as Disabled Peoples' International (the international umbrella organisation for disabled people's organisations, see Driedger 1989) and Disability Awareness in Action (a project led by disabled people to increase networking among disabled people and their organisations worldwide). Minority world disabled people and their organisations have generally been the key players, given greater access to resources.

Researchers have played their part too. There is a small but growing body of reports and publications that explore disability in the majority world. For the most part, these are practitioner-led and practice-based. The focus is on interventions (social, rehabilitation, education, income generation, etc). At best, this literature offers useful evaluations of processes and outcomes, but little space is generally left to explore wider issues such as attitudes, life chances, local strategies and responses, beliefs, social expectations, cultural perceptions. Fortunately, that is beginning to change. There are now a handful of studies that look behind interventions to consider local meanings of impairment, and to identify ways in which local (and global) values and structures disable people who have impairments. (A proper literature review is beyond the scope of this chapter, but useful texts are listed at the end of this chapter.)

Is the globalisation of disability good or bad? Where activists, academics and practitioners are from or trained in the minority world, working in or with people in the majority world, there will always be risks. Whose agenda dominates? Whose ideology is put into practice? Whose definition of impairment or disability rules? Whose cultural or religious values? Whose social systems? Whose ways of working?

On the other hand, the long overdue recognition that most disabled people live in the majority world, in poverty and without access to appropriate support, must be welcomed. So too the emergence of professionals who are real allies to disabled people and communities, and researchers who deepen our understanding of the issues. For, at the end of the day, the globalisation of disability must be seen in the context of the continuing marginalisation of disability issues and disabled people in international development work.

THE MARGINALISATION OF DISABILITY AND DISABLED PEOPLE

There is little that can be done to stop the globalisation of disability. If anything, more should be done to support it. After all, the field of disability and development in the majority world is woefully under-resourced. The comparatively few professionals that are committed to working with disabled children and adults are themselves marginalised in the mainstream of development organisations and development studies. Disability is not a "sexy" subject. Indeed, it is often labelled as a "specialist" subject, for medical or special education professionals only. The challenge, then, is how to raise the profile of disability issues in development programmes, research and on policy and practice agendas whilst minimising the risks that this carries.

The best way to do this is to follow the suggestions made by Rachel Hurst (Chapter 3) and others in this book to support the development of disabled people's own organisations, and to learn from disabled people's analysis and strategies for social change. There is also an urgent need for development organisations and funders to get their own houses in order and take disability on board as an equal opportunities issue (as with gender and ethnicity). Why shouldn't all development programmes and initiatives be required to involve disabled people? Or be subjected to a critical analysis to ensure that they do not compound the marginalisation of disabled people and their families? (See Hastie 1997, Coleridge 1993, and contributors in this book.)

It is also important to enable a deeper understanding of disability issues by those involved in the development field, and of majority world issues by those involved in the disability field. At the moment, the situation in Britain is that disability studies courses are mostly western-focused, while development studies courses seldom include anything about disability. This has to change.

Finally, there is a need to promote more networking and information sharing among those who are already involved in both disability and development in the majority world. The UK event on which this book is based is one small example of how that can be done.

WHY THIS BOOK?

In April 1998, 25 people were invited to participate in the first UK Forum for Information Exchange on Disability and Development in the Majority World. It was a one-day event, hosted by the Disability Research Unit at the University of Leeds, with an ambitious agenda.

The event aimed to "straddle divides" between activists, academics and practitioners with an interest in disability in the majority world. This was to be achieved through creating a space for networking and for sharing information about new initiatives and new research.

A lack of funds meant it was not possible to support the participation of disabled activists, academics and practitioners who live in the majority world (or, indeed, anywhere outside Britain). One of the presenters and some of the participants were from the majority world, but working in Britain. Even so, the absence of people from the majority world was keenly felt and remains a serious weakness in this book.

The Forum underlined the value of creating spaces for sharing information. It became clear that there was a real need to disseminate the information more widely. Hence this book.

WHAT THIS BOOK OFFERS

This book draws on the experiences of people who have been actively involved in disability in the majority world. Many contributors have spent significant periods living, working and researching in the majority world. Some are key figures in the disabled people's movement. Others have amassed considerable experience in planning and implementing disability-related development projects. A few are undertaking or have recently completed doctoral research on disability in the majority world. All share a commitment to removing disabling barriers.

Not surprisingly, then, the contributions span a huge range of interests and geographical areas – from empowerment to community-based rehabilitation, and from Afghanistan to Jordan. Among other things, the contributions offer:

- Ideas about practical action to bring about social change and remove barriers facing disabled people in the majority world.
- Honest discussions about the difficulties and dilemmas that those researching disability or working in disability-related development work have encountered.
- Analysis of what happens when western ideas and practices migrate to non-western settings – whether brought by western professionals, or bought into by western-influenced professionals.
- Insights into the ways that different cultures and societies respond to impairment and construct disability.
- Discussions of difficult issues, such as: the role of professionals and outsider organisations; cross-cultural transfers of ideas and practice; ways of working with local disabled people; whether or not all development projects should include a disability focus.

WHAT THIS BOOK CANNOT OFFER

This book is not a "how to" guide on "doing disability and development in the majority world". In common with other books that seek to straddle divides and promote marginalised issues, this book is more about stimulating discussion than providing solutions. More importantly, anyone who reads this book must be aware of three weaknesses.

First, this book represents minority world perspectives on majority world realities. Where the perspectives of disabled people and their allies in and from the majority world are set out, they are often "second-hand" voices and views, mediated (distorted) by western or western-trained professionals. This book cannot offer the personal experiences and collective analyses of disabled people who live in the majority world.

Secondly, the fact that the contributors write from a huge range of backgrounds and experiences is a weakness in so far as the contributions vary widely in style, content, and sometimes in core assumptions (although this can also be seen as a strength).

Thirdly, this book is part and parcel of the globalisation of disability and rehabilitation mentioned above ... and therefore it must be subject to careful and critical reading.

PLAN OF THE BOOK

The contributions in this book have been divided into four groups.

- Challenges from Disabled People
- Programmes and Partnerships
- Evaluating Interventions
- Researching Disability

This has the less than ideal effect of recreating divides, but it does at least break the book up into more manageable chunks. Each group is preceded by a preface that includes an "Overview of the Contributions" and "Discussion Points" to aid discussion and a more critical engagement with the assumptions and messages that are presented.

"Challenges from Disabled People" sets out the perspectives of disabled people who have long been involved in disabled people's movements, locally, nationally and internationally.

"Programmes and Partnerships" is written from the perspective of minority world professionals who work with and for development organisations, like Save the Children UK, or universities. The contributors set out their aims, ways of working, core assumptions, and some of the dilemmas and difficulties faced when doing disability-related development work.

"Evaluating Interventions" goes even deeper into the difficulties involved in disability-related development in the majority world, especially where the nature of interventions has been steered by western ideologies and practice. Importantly, the evaluations in this section consider processes and contexts as well as outcomes.

"Researching Disability" moves away from thinking about specific interventions and considers the meaning and construction of impairment, disability, and disability services in different contexts and using different data sources (including historical records, language, fieldwork interviews, newspapers, etc). The final chapter sets out personal experiences of doing disability research and reiterates the importance to look critically on everything written on disability in the majority world.

WHO SHOULD READ THIS BOOK?

This book is aimed at those who are currently involved, or thinking about getting involved, in disability in the majority world – whether as activists, students, researchers, practitioners, consultants, aid and development planners or funders. It is also hoped that the book will be a useful resource for lecturers and students of Disability Studies and Development Studies. It is time for mainstream Disability Studies and Development Studies courses in the west to take proper account of the important and difficult issues relevant to disabled people in the majority world.

REVIEW

This book is full of strong challenges and practical suggestions for action and research. At times, these may read more like a wish-list, but the importance of building a shared vision should not be underestimated. The different experiences shared by contributors confirm that this is not an easy area in which to get involved, and that particular dilemmas and difficulties arise where minority and majority worlds meet, and conflict. But that should not stop us from moving forwards, and from wrestling with the practical and conceptual difficulties that abound in disability action and research in the majority world.

USEFUL READING

A) Disability and Development in the Majority World

BOYLAN, E. (1991), *Women and Disability*, London: Zed Books.

BURCK, D. (1989), *Kuoma Rupandi: The Parts are Dry: ideas and practices concerning disability and rehabilitation in a Shona Ward*, Research Report no. 36, Leiden: African Studies Centre.

CHAMBERS, R. (1983), *Rural Development: putting the last first*, Harlow: Longman. (A key text on development issues).

COLERIDGE, P. (1993), *Disability, Liberation and Development*, Oxford: Oxfam.

DISABILITY & SOCIETY (1996), *Special Issue: Disability, Development in the Changing World*, Vol. 11 (4), December 1996.

- BERESFORD, P., "Poverty and Disabled People: challenging dominant debates and policies", pp. 553-567.
- MILES, M., "Community, Individual or Information Development? Dilemmas of concept and culture in South Asian disability planning", pp. 485-500.
- MILES, S., "Engaging with the Disability Rights Movement: the experience of community-based rehabilitation in southern Africa", pp. 501-518.
- STONE, E., "A Law to Protect, A Law to Prevent: contextualising disability legislation in China", pp. 469-483.

DEVLIEGER, P. (1995a), "From Self-help to Charity in Disability Service: the Jairos Jiri Association in Zimbabwe", *Disability & Society*, Vol. 10(1): pp 39-47.

DRIEDGER, D. (1989), *The Last Civil Rights Movement: Disabled Peoples' International*, London: Hurst & Company.

FLETCHER, A. & HURST, R. (1995), *Overcoming Obstacles to the Integration of Disabled People*, London: Disability Awareness in Action.

FINKENFLÜGEL, H. (ed) (1993), *The Handicapped Community*, Amsterdam: VU University Press.

HASTIE, R. (1997), *Disabled Children in a Society at War: a casebook from Bosnia*, Oxford: Oxfam UK and Ireland.

HELANDER, E. (1992), *Prejudice and Dignity: An Introduction to Community-Based Rehabilitation*, UNDP Report E93-III-B.3, New York: UNDP.

INGSTAD, B. & WHYTE, S.R. (1995) (eds), *Disability and Culture*, Berkeley: University of California Press.

- BRUUN, F. J. (1995), "Hero, Beggar, or Sports Star: Negotiating the Identity of the Disabled Person in Nicaragua".
- DEVLIEGER, P. (1995b), "Why Disabled? The Cultural Understanding of Physical Disability in an African Society".
- NICOLAISEN, I. (1995), "Persons and Nonpersons: Disability and Personhood among the Punan Bah of Central Borneo".
- HELANDER, B. (1995), "Disability as Incurable Illness: health, process, and personhood in Southern Somalia".
- INGSTAD, B. (1995a), "Public Discourses on Rehabilitation: From Norway to Botswana".
- INGSTAD, B. (1995b), "Mpho ya Modimo – A Gift from God: Perspectives on 'Attitudes' toward Disabled Persons".

- SENTUMBWE, N. (1995), "Sighted Lovers and Blind Husbands: Experiences of Blind Women in Uganda".
- TALLE, A. (1995), "A Child is a Child: Disability and Equality among the Kenya Maasai".
- WHYTE, S. R. (1995), "Constructing Epilepsy: Images and Contexts in East Africa".
- WHYTE, S. R. & INGSTAD, B. (1995), "Disability and Culture: An Overview".

JAYASOORIA, D. & OOI, G. (1994), "Disabled Peoples Movement in Malaysia", *Disability & Society*, Vol. 9 (1): 97-100.

KALYANPUR, M. (1996), "The Influence of Western Special Education on Community-based Services in India", *Disability & Society*, Vol. 11 (2), pp. 249-270.

LANG, R. (1998), "A Critique of the Disability Movement", *Asia Pacific Disability Rehabilitation Journal*, Vol. 9 (1): 4-8.

MALLORY, B., NICHOLLS, R., CHARLTON, J. & MARFO, K. (1993), *Traditional and Changing Views of Disability in Developing Societies: causes, consequences, cautions*, Monograph No. 53, Durham, NH: IEEIR.

MILES, M. (1992), "Concepts of Mental Retardation in Pakistan: toward cross-cultural and historical perspectives", *Disability, Handicap & Society*, Vol. 7 (3): 235-255.

NEW INTERNATIONALIST (1992), "Disabled Lives: Difference and Defiance", No. 233, July 1992 (special issue).

O'TOOLE, B. & McCONKEY, R. (1995) (eds), *Innovations in Developing Countries for People with Disabilities*, Chorley: Lisieux Hall.

PETERS, S. (1993) (ed), *Education and Disability in Cross-Cultural Perspective*, London: Garland.

SAVE THE CHILDREN FUND (1995), *Disability and Integration in Morocco: In our own words*, London: SCF (UK).

SCHEER, J. & GROCE, N. (1988), "Impairment as a Human Constant: Cross-Cultural and Historical Perspectives on Variation", *Journal of Social Issues*, Vol. 44 (1): 23-37.

SHIRLEY, O. (ed) (1983), *A Cry for Health: poverty and disability in the Third World*, Frome: Third World Group & AHRTAG.

STONE, E. (1997), "From the Research Notes of a Foreign Devil: Disability Research in China", *in* Barnes, C. & Mercer, G. (eds), *Doing Disability Research*, Leeds: The Disability Press.

THORBURN, M. & MARFO, K. (eds) (1990), *Practical Approaches to Childhood Disability in Developing Countries: insights from experience and research*, Canada: Project SEREDEC and Spanish Town, Jamaica: 3D Projects.

TIROLER, G. (1995), "Learning about the Links", *CBR News*, No. 21, pp. 4-5.

United Nations (1983), *World Programme of Action Concerning Disabled Persons*, New York: UN.

WERNER, D. (1987), *Disabled Village Children*, Palo Alto: Hesperian Foundation.

ZINKIN, P. & McCONACHIE, H. (eds) (1995), *Disabled Children & Developing Countries*, Clinics in Developmental Medicine No. 136, London: MacKeith Press.

- AINSCOW, M., JANGIRA, N.K. & AHUJA, A. (1995), "Education: responding to special needs through teacher development".
- CHAUDHURY, G., MENON-SEN, K. & ZINKIN, P. (1995), "Disability Programmes in the Community".
- KISANJI, J. (1995), "Growing up Disabled".
- McCONKEY, R. (1995), "Early Intervention in Developing Countries".
- WILLIAMS, L. (1995), "Rights not Charity".

B) Key Texts and Readers on Western Disability Studies

ALBRECHT, G. (1992), *The Disability Business: Rehabilitation in America*, London & Newbury Park CA: Sage.

BARNES, C., MERCER, G. & SHAKESPEARE, T. (1999), *Exploring Disability: A Sociological Introduction*, London: Polity Press.

BARNES, C. & MERCER, G. (1996) (eds), *Exploring the Divide: Illness and Disability*, Leeds: The Disability Press.

BARTON, L. (ed) (1996), *Disability & Society: emerging issues and insights,* Harlow: Addison Wesley Longman Ltd (especially chapters by Paul Abberley, Colin Barnes and Mike Oliver).

BARTON, L. & OLIVER, M. (eds) (1997), *Disability Studies: Past, Present and Future*, Leeds: The Disability Press.

BICKENBACH, J. E. (1993), *Physical Disability and Social Policy*, Toronto: University of Toronto Press.

CAMPBELL, J. & OLIVER, M. (1996), *Disability Politics: Understanding our Past*, Changing our Future, London: Routledge.

DAVIS, L. (ed) (1997a), *The Disability Studies Reader*, New York: Routledge.

FINKELSTEIN, V. (1991), "Disability – an administrative challenge? (The health and welfare heritage)", in Oliver, M. (ed), *Social Work: disabled people and disabling environments*, London: Kingsley.

GARLAND THOMSON, R. (1997), *Extraordinary bodies: figuring physical disability in American culture and literature*, New York: Columbia University Press.

HIRST, M. & BALDWIN, S. (1994), *Unequal Opportunities: Growing Up Disabled*, London: HMSO.

HUNT, P. (1966), "A Critical Condition", in Hunt, P. (ed), *Stigma: The Experience of Disability*, London: Geoffrey Chapman.

MORRIS, J. (1993), *Pride Against Prejudice: A Personal Politics of Disability*, London: The Women's Press.

MORRIS, J. (ed) (1996), *Encounters with Strangers: Feminism and Disability*, London: The Women's Press.

OLIVER, M. (1990), *The Politics of Disablement*, Basingstoke: Macmillan.

OLIVER, M. (1996), "Defining Impairment and Disability: issues at stake", *in* Barnes, C. & Mercer, G. (eds), *Exploring the Divide: Illness and Disability*, Leeds: The Disability Press.

STONE, D. (1984), *The Disabled State*, Philadelphia: Temple University Press.

SWAIN, J., FINKELSTEIN, V., FRENCH, S. & OLIVER, M. (eds) (1993), *Disabling Barriers – Enabling Environments*, London: Sage Publications with The Open University.

C) Useful International Journals on Disability Issues, Action and Research

ActionAid Disability News (newsletter of ActionAid India)

Disability International (newsletter of Disabled Peoples' International)

Disability Tribune (newsletter of Disability Awareness in Action)

Disability & Society (international journal on disability studies)

Disability Studies Quarterly (international journal on disability studies)

Also useful are the Information and Resource Kits produced by Disability Awareness in Action. These are available in English, French and Spanish, in English Braille, tape, ASCII on computer disk and via e-mail and in large print in all three languages. Most DAA material has been translated into national and regional languages (see List of Useful Organisations in this book).

There are also several international journals which are primarily aimed at practitioners in different fields (e.g. rehabilitation, education). The contributions vary widely in how far they are based on a disability rights perspective, or on a more individualising and medical model of disability. Examples include: *HealthLink* (formerly *CBR News*, focused primarily on the majority world); *International Rehabilitation Review; International Journal of Rehabilitation Research* and similar journals in the field of special education.

Challenges from Disabled People

From the Solomon Islands to Sweden, disabled people have been organising and campaigning for equal rights and citizenship. Local, national and international organisations controlled by disabled people lead the struggle to make the world a less disabling place. From the Organisation for Revolutionary Disabled in Nicaragua to Greater Manchester Coalition of Disabled People in Britain, disabled people are pushing for change. Change in the way that disabled people are viewed and treated by non-disabled people. And, fundamentally, change in the way that societies (labour markets, services, cultures) operate.

At the heart of the struggle is the social model of disability, which takes the "problem" of disabled people <u>out</u> of the individual and <u>into</u> society. From a social model standpoint, it is time to stop pitying disabled people as victims. It is time to uphold disabled people's rights as citizens.

There is a long way to go before disabled people's vision of a less disabling world is realised. As with any struggle for civil rights, there are vested interests and obstacles to change. Service providers, professionals, charities and development organisations – no matter how well meaning – have often been seen as part of the problem (i.e. a barrier to rights) rather than part of the solution.

In this section of the book, Vic Finkelstein and Rachel Hurst challenge professionals and development organisations to do things differently: to take the lead from disabled people and their organisations about ways of working and ways of bringing about real social change.

OVERVIEW OF CONTRIBUTIONS

"A Profession Allied to the Community: The Disabled People's Trade Union"

Vic Finkelstein has long been involved as an activist in disabled people's organisations and as a theorist in the field of disability studies. Here,

Finkelstein offers a short but powerful critique of "professions allied to medicine" and welfarist notions of service. Finkelstein puts the case for PACs: Professions Allied to the Community. Finally, he warns of the dangers inherent when minority world professions and professional ideologies (rooted in a culture of care, cure and expertise) migrate or are transferred to majority world contexts.

"Disabled People's Organisations and Development: Strategies for Change"

Rachel Hurst, Director of Disability Awareness in Action, also writes as a disabled person with a long record of activism in local, national and international organisations of disabled people. Hurst sets out the importance of learning from disabled people's organisations – about disability, social development and rights-based change. Hurst challenges development funders to invest more resources in building the capacity of disabled people's organisations. She also challenges development organisations to put their own houses in order, and to ensure the inclusion of disabled people in all aspects of social development work.

DISCUSSION POINTS

- Do you agree with the notion of an "international disability movement"? Why, or why not?
- Do you think that the social model of disability is relevant in the majority world, or just in the minority world? Why, or why not?
- What would you list as the key characteristics of PACs – Professionals Allied to the Community?
- Can you give examples of minority world (western) ideologies, practices or definitions that have been transferred to majority world countries? How are they transferred? Are such transfers always wrong? Who decides and how?
- What can those involved in social development learn from disabled people's organisations and their strategies?
- What action should development organisations take to ensure the inclusion of disabled people and disability issues in social development work?
- Do you agree or disagree with the statement that disability is a human rights issue, and a development issue? Why?
- Do you agree or disagree with the view that all development projects should take disability on board in ways similar to being "gender aware" or "child focused"?

CHAPTER 2

A Profession Allied to the Community: The disabled people's trade union

Vic Finkelstein

A HISTORICAL PERSPECTIVE

Human beings, by nature, structure their social relationships in order to assist each other to attain the necessities of life and to enhance the quality of their lifestyles. During the historical development of societies, this has taken many forms, with different groups at different times dominating the shape, meaning and accessibility of social assistance.

This process has embraced the design and provision of helping, or assistive, devices. For example, the invention of the printing press is an assistive device (a special aid) for "the sighted" to exchange information. The growing importance of this invention and proliferation of printed material, however, and the inability or unwillingness of sighted people with abilities to recognise the legitimacy of equivalent forms of information exchange for people with visual impairments, provides a critical context for defining the social meaning of "blindness" and excluding this particular group from the facilities and mainstream events of society.

Control over the shaping and reshaping of social assistance has not only enabled specific social groups to dominate others, but has also enabled them to define what is "normal" and, in so doing, label all assistance required by other groups as "special" and "compensatory". Consequently, people with abilities have come to see access to *their* forms of assistance as an essential aspect of a normal lifestyle. Deviations from this *ability*, then, are not only seen as tragic, requiring interventions which aim at "curing" or "caring", but have added a "vulnerable" label to the social invention of non-normal individuals. Where there is not as yet an effective cure, and the provision of care threatens to become a curtailing burden on their own lifestyles, people with abilities have sought to shape the deviant and vulnerable as much as possible in their own image of normality.

PROFESSIONS ALLIED TO MEDICINE

It is in this context that people with abilities have invented exclusive professions to cure the deviant, care for the vulnerable and to control perception of appropriate human attributes and desirable personal and social environments. The result is a National Health Service dominated by professions allied to medicine (PAMs) who work in cure or care services and Social Services dominated by a culture of welfare provision for the "vulnerable". Around this development, people with abilities have created an elaborate "normative" language and culture. This is the language of the health and community care services. In this language, disabled people are seen as having "special needs" that require special expertise; while people with abilities remain totally unaware that the roads, public transport, telephones, television, retail shops, restaurants, etc., created by themselves for themselves, are also examples of special assistive devices and services.

PROFESSIONS ALLIED TO THE COMMUNITY

The growth of the world-wide disability movement has shaken this comfortable cultural dominance. Disabled people in organisations *of* disabled people (our *vehicles* for change) have begun to express their human nature by re-defining themselves and inventing their own forms of assistance in *this* image. In so doing, disabled people have begun a process of engaging in the transformation of the disabling society. There are three things to say about this development for our relationship to the majority world.

- First, the development of our own approaches to assistance not only requires an unpacking of the version imposed on us by people with abilities, but the creation of our own "normal" forms of assistance. Our constructing of systematic forms of help according to our own social model of disability will generate new services and service providers – professions allied to the community (PACs). I believe that these workers will constitute our own trade union. It is these trade unionists, truly immersed in a disability culture, who will be a vital *engine* for social change. They will have a crucial role in promoting the national and international criticism of the dominant health and community care ideology that is not wanted by disabled people.

- Secondly, we can be sure that the elaborate culture, language, policies of medicalising health (seeking to "cure" disability), community care policies, community-based variations of rehabilitation, and obsession with assessing and labelling us (such as the latest World Health Organization's ICIDH-2: International Classification of Impairments, Activities and Participation) will be vigorously defended by people with abilities whose careers are shaped within the framework of able-bodied chauvinism. As the struggles of disabled people to create a barrier-free world according to our own image of human functioning advances, we can expect the PAMs and welfare workers' defence of their philosophy (based on the individual and administrative models of disability), and the associated expertise, to be exported to places where they are less likely to be challenged.

- Thirdly, the migration of the cure or care culture and expertise (e.g. as in the "community-based rehabilitation" ideology and the WHO ICIDH) are important tools for advancing the able-bodied work ethic of the minority world to the majority world. Maintaining that the marginalisation of disabled people is due to our personal inadequacies (our disabilities) sustains the view that the disabling society is not responsible for creating the barriers that impoverish us. Providing PAMs and welfare workers for our special needs enables the disabling societies of the minority world to further their control of the international economy – free of criticism from the majority world whose established supportive social relationships are being dismantled.

FURTHER READING

FINKELSTEIN, V. (1980), *Attitudes and Disabled People*, New York: World Rehabilitation Fund.

FINKELSTEIN, V. and STUART, O. (1996), "Developing New Services", in Hales, G. (ed), *Beyond Disability: Towards an Enabling Society*, London: Sage.

FINKELSTEIN, V. (1998), "The Biodynamics of Disablement?", Paper presented at the Disability and Rehabilitation Systems Research workshop, Harare, Zimbabwe (29 June 1998).

FINKELSTEIN, V. (1998), "Re-thinking Care in a Society Providing Equal Opportunities for All", Discussion paper for the World Health Organization.

CHAPTER 3

Disabled People's Organisations and Development: Strategies for change

Rachel Hurst

INTRODUCTION

There is no country in the world where disabled people's rights are not violated. The discrimination, oppression, violence and abuse faced by disabled people does not respect national boundaries, national wealth or national poverty. As a result of our direct experience, and our articulation of our own situation, disabled people have a unique understanding of what constitutes "development" and the social change that is required to ensure our equalisation of opportunities and the enhancement of rights. This unique understanding has shown us that strategic change cannot happen on one front alone. To ensure the empowerment and inclusion of disabled individuals in the development of their own communities and states, strategies for change must be devised to:

- develop, strengthen and resource disabled people's own organisations;
- give disabled people control and choice in their lives and also over the policies and services that directly affect them;

- build a shared understanding that disability is a rights issue and should be defined in the social context;
- ensure that there are significantly improved information networks to raise awareness of the situation of disabled people and of appropriate solutions for change management; and
- recognise and support disabled people as full and equal participants in mainstream activities.

To put all that in simple terms, it is my contention that the development and empowerment of disabled people cannot happen unless the Disability Movement is at the forefront of bringing about social change.

THE DISABILITY MOVEMENT

The Disability Movement is unique among civil rights movements since it is the only movement which has a democratically-organised international structure as well as structures at national and local levels. Whether it be through the cross-disability national assemblies within Disabled Peoples' International, or through single-impairment organisations such as Inclusion International, the World Federation of the Deaf, the World Blind Union or the World Federation of Psychiatric Users, disabled people at the grass-roots have a mechanism through which they can have a voice, through which they can be understood and supported. Of course, these structures are not perfect and have varying degrees of strength and effectiveness – but at least they are there, to be used as the main instrument through which development takes place.

The history of the Disability Movement worldwide and in the UK has been well-documented (Driedger 1989, Campbell & Oliver 1996), so I focus here on just three points. First, disabled people's own organisations happened as a direct action against the oppression of the medical and rehabilitation professionals and social workers, and their assumption that they 'owned' disability and, by inference, disabled people. Secondly, the movement happened because disabled people with leadership qualities from all over the world had the opportunity to come together and share experiences. And thirdly, disabled people needed to have a united voice to be heard. It was vital that our voice was listened to, that we ceased to be the "silent emergency" as once described by the UN Secretary-General Perez de Cuellar, and became instead the shouting, loud-mouthed demanders of civil rights.

We had this whole plethora of people who were speaking for us, keeping us as children, not allowing us to make decisions for ourselves. There were our families and friends who were shocked and guilty at our presence, and would keep us hidden away or over-protected. There were the medical and rehabilitation professionals who thought that they knew all there was to know about us as individuals because they had some technical knowledge about our impairments. There were the charities set up by righteous individuals to help us, never recognising that they were patronising and disempowering us. And then there were the policy makers, the aid and development agencies and the general public who did their utmost to ignore us, leave us out of their plans and programmes, except when they could find expensive "special" projects for us.

It is vital that our voice is heard at last. Though, because progress is so slow, I often wonder whether our voice really is being heard ... whether we are shouting loudly and clearly enough. Whether we are getting our messages across.

LEARNING FROM DISABLED PEOPLE'S ORGANISATIONS

Our understanding of development has moved a long way on from the old saying that "give a man a fishing rod and he will feed himself for life; give him a fish and he will be hungry again tomorrow". That approach to development was an improvement on throwing money at poverty, but it has still not brought about sustainable development or social equity for oppressed and marginalised groups.

It is now increasingly recognised by development professionals and social scientists that the social change necessary to support diverse groups in a society based on rights and equal opportunities will only be brought about by the actions of the groups themselves. So, strengthening the leadership, empowering the grass-roots membership and giving equal status to these social groups and movements is the only effective way to achieve real social development. It is here that the experiences and perspectives of disabled people and their organisations are so important – not just for disabled people...

In 1995, at the World Summit on Social Development, the disability international non-governmental organisations presented a position paper based on their direct experience in empowering and developing themselves through their own organisations: *The Disability Dimension, A Joint Statement to the World Summit on Social Development* (DPI *et al* 1995). The main thrust of the paper was that development should start with the people. They said:

> The World Summit on Social Development is an important event which provides an exciting opportunity for a shift in attitudes to and implementation of social policy and development. But changes will only come if new approaches are examined and debated and the people concerned are at the forefront of those approaches and discussions. Development and policy that is not made in full collaboration with the people is never effective. And it is particularly important that disabled people are fully involved in all the World Summit discussions. We have a unique experience and have, over the years, found cost-effective, integrative solutions to our development which are relevant to everyone and should form a basis for the outcome of the World Summit (*The Disability Dimension* 1995).

The position paper went on to set out solutions and strategies for social change:

> In any situation, people find the best solution for themselves. And disabled people have come up with solutions, the solutions of advocacy, independent living, income generation and self-help within our own organisations. All these solutions are based on the principles of integration and equalisation of opportunities and the implementation of our human rights. We know from our own direct experience that it is through these two solutions that disabled people can become participating, contributing members of our own societies. And it is those solutions which should be thoroughly debated and examined by the World Summit.
>
> These solutions are all effective, low-cost and do not require setting-up tiers of professionals to run then. They do not include expensive buildings that have to be maintained and re-furbished. They are the grass-roots solutions that can be applied everywhere — in rural and urban areas — which will benefit everybody and which include everybody. They are solutions that not only apply to all disabled people but to the rapidly growing numbers of elderly people, to children, to the poor, to refugees, to ethnic minorities. They apply to all these groups because disabled people form a part of these groups and it is disabled people themselves, from their experience of extreme deprivation and isolation, who have come up with the solutions.

> We have to get this message across. Our solutions work and have been seen to work. If our experience is ignored, then social development will remain what it so often is — politicised charity — and a great opportunity will be lost (*The Disability Dimension* 1995).

We still have not got these messages across. The barriers of prejudice and ignorance are so strong that those engaged in aid, development and social policy are finding it hard to break them down and to change entrenched ways of behaviour. Although disability did get on to the World Summit agenda and was mentioned in the final Declaration, there was no recognition that our unique experience might underpin broader discussions of social policy and social development. We were still seen as separate. Our voice was not really heard.

DOES DEVELOPMENT EQUAL CHARITY?

Certainly for disabled people, aid and development programmes can remind us quite forcefully of the disability projects of rehabilitation professionals and charitable organisations. Programmes which involve sending workers from a rich country to poor countries to give money (sometimes in ways that make the rich country even richer), to show what clever things we do in rich countries, and to show the poor how to behave – these are clear parallels with the work of disability charities in the west. Meanwhile, a whole language has been built up around aid and development work which is very similar to the language adopted by social workers when "dealing with" their clients: animation, training, support, care, concern, victims, assimilation, sustainability, marginalised, behaviour patterns. Words like rights, empowerment and participation have only recently begun to be part of the language of development.

As a result, and despite good intentions, development programmes have not achieved what was intended. The numbers of people in poverty remain much the same, health levels are only slowly creeping up in some countries, education is still only available to the relative few, while for the majority, employment means earning just enough money to feed a small family. The gap between rich and poor is widening and in places where there is political upheaval, war or civil strife, the poor do not earn enough to eat. Women remain oppressed, without equal rights, doing two-thirds of the world's work for half the money – if they are lucky. People who have different political or religious views or who do not fit the "norm" suffer constant discrimination. So what is going wrong? And what should we be doing to ensure real sustainable development?

HUMAN RIGHTS AND SOCIAL CHANGE PARTNERSHIP

We must recognise clearly and strategically that real sustainable development cannot take place outside the paradigm of human rights and social change working in partnership. If you develop one without the other, effective change will not result. The ineffectiveness of social change without human rights is demonstrated clearly in many dictatorships.

The inherent ineffectiveness of trying to implement human rights without social change has been less obvious to aid and development agencies. Millions of pounds are spent every year through the British government and non-governmental organisations on grass-roots projects which aim to ensure human rights for a particular group or village. And many of those projects often seem to be very successful and to help the people concerned. However, initial success is no guarantee of sustainable success. Take a project that aims to teach farmers new irrigation techniques to increase crops and improve the local economy. At first, the results are good, but a few years on, some outside political force or natural disaster eradicates those gains and the achievements are not sustained. Consider what would have happened if, alongside developing new irrigation techniques, the project had sought to empower local people to speak for themselves, to work co-operatively in changing farming techniques, and to join together to ensure that the national government supports the new techniques through appropriate policies. The result: the initial project becomes sustainable through changing the social context and supporting the human rights of the individual. The lesson: development at the grass-roots is not sustainable unless it goes hand-in-hand with social change implemented at the national level.

It is comparatively recent that development strategists have understood that the support of women's self-advocacy, organisation-building and leadership training as well as specific projects on health, income-generation etc. are all essential for sustainable development and the empowerment of women. But so far they have failed to extend and apply that understanding to working with disabled people and their organisations.

THE CHALLENGE TO DEVELOPMENT AND AID AGENCIES

If disability is to be included on the mainstream social development agenda, as it must be if social change and empowerment are to happen, then development and aid agencies will have to revise their approaches accordingly.

Funding and Supporting Disabled People's Organisations

When the disability movement first started, aid and development agencies did support organisations of disabled people. In fact, the concept of organisations of disabled people was so novel that they were clearly seen as a useful development tool and therefore worthy of financial aid. As a result those organisations have grown – in size, experience and effectiveness. They are now running grass-roots projects which not only empower disabled individuals but also widen the membership and enlarge the pool from which potential leaders can be drawn. However, the funding situation has changed and now the only way these organisations can get funding is through running projects – particularly those projects that the funding agencies think are appropriate. Funding for networking, leadership support, or for the straightforward "core costs" of running an organisation is not available. Whilst in those areas where organisations of disabled people have not developed yet, there is no recognition that the only way to promote self-organisation is through networking, leadership training and learning from others.

Funders, it seems, need to feel that they are seen to be directly helping the poor, suffering individual, and directly relieving that poverty and suffering. Spending public money on supporting organisations, whose leaders now seem to be dismissed as the élite, is not considered acceptable. This funding approach is partly driven by market attitudes and the ethos on which charitable giving is based, whereby the haves give to the have-nots directly and on an individual basis. But it is time that funders and development professionals recognised that this ethos does not promote sustainable development. We all have to play our part in getting over the message of human rights and social change partnership, even if this is not an easy message to convey from a "pulls at the heart-strings" – and therefore purse strings – perspective. In the final analysis, what is the point of giving support to a particular grass-roots project if the organisation of disabled people running that project cannot sustain themselves? The project may succeed in the short-term but it is unlikely to succeed in the long-term, and the number of people who benefit will be minimal and unsustainable.

I am not suggesting that funders should not put money into grass-roots practical projects. But I do want to make the point – as clearly and loudly as I can – that only putting money into those projects, and ignoring the need to develop and sustain the self-advocacy rights movement as well, will put the whole development strategy into jeopardy. And as the disability international non-governmental organisations made clear at the World Summit of Social Development in Copenhagen – what works for the Disability Movement also works for all other socially excluded groups.

Disability Equality Training and Development Agencies

Whatever strategies and policies we agree for including disabled people on the development agenda, there will need to be a change of attitude to back up the change of behaviour that such policy and legislation require. It is not enough for an aid or development organisation to have an equal opportunities policy if the individuals in the organisation do not know what such a policy means or how to implement it in practice.

There is an issue about how to get the message of equal opportunities across to aid and development agencies and professionals. Is it appropriate that non-disabled people should be the message-bearers? Should it only be disabled people who give the message? These and other questions have exercised the minds of many people in relation to training on sexism and racism, and the issues are no less important when it comes to disability equality training. There are also doubts in some people's minds as to the efficacy of equality training. Is it preaching to the converted? Is it possible to change the entrenched attitudes and behaviour of someone in a day or two of training? Probably training only tickles the surface of attitudinal change, but it can be a positive step towards a more inclusive society and social development culture – as long as the trainers fully understand and have direct experience of the issues, know how to convey the messages, and how to help people "own" the message. At the end of the day, there is no doubt that disabled people's own organisations are the essential messengers of disability as a rights issue.

Including Disabled People in All Development Programmes and Planning

One of the most important parts of a sound development strategy must be to ensure that policies are in place which recognise the need to include socially excluded groups in all stages of development work.

Most aid and development agencies have employment equal opportunities policies and many have specific gender policies, aimed at ensuring that gender issues are taken into consideration through all the working and funding practices of the organisation. There may even be a specific percentage of funding for women's programmes. But the number of development agencies who have similar policies for disabled people as employees and as recipients of funding and programmes, can be counted on the digits of a two-toed sloth.

The inclusion and mainstreaming of disability in all social development work is an important strategy. It is also difficult to implement. The habit of excluding us or seeing our programmes as "special" has a long history. Less than a year ago, the head of a major aid agency articulated his firm belief that disability should not be part of his organisation's policy on the basis that disability was a "special issue and had to be dealt with by specialists". Most people are so frightened by anything to do with disability that their reaction to including it on any agenda is inevitably one of rejection. There is also the stereotyped attitude that believes that disabled people are unable to participate in mainstream life. Proponents of this view do not comprehend that we are quite *able* to participate, but are *disabled from participating by others' attitudes and social barriers.*

A welcome example has been set by the government of the United States – the only government that has decided to ensure that foreign policy is included in comprehensive non-discrimination legislation. The new policy will state that a percentage of overall funds should go to disability projects, that disabled people should be included as participants in all other development projects funded by the government, and that all buildings, including embassies, should be accessible to disabled people. In short, and to echo the words of US Secretary of State Madeleine Albright, the United States has decided to implement the Americans with Disabilities Act in its foreign policy (Albright 1997).

In summary, there are disabled people in every section of society, and in every part of the world. To *include* disabled people and their organisations in all development programmes makes good development sense. To *exclude* disabled people and their organisations from any development programme is to discriminate against them. Moreover, the strength of their empowerment, their self-advocacy and their accountability to a grass-roots membership can only enhance the learning and experience that disabled people's organisations have to offer. It is therefore crucial that disabled people's organisations should *always* be involved in planning and policy-making for aid and development work, as well as in setting the parameters for training. This is not a new concept. It has always been assumed that women's groups and ethnic minority groups must be directly involved in setting policy and training agendas that affect them. The same logic and learning must now be applied to disabled people and our organisations by those professionals and agencies who are active in the world of international development work.

CONCLUSION

Development leads to (or should lead to) empowerment – of a nation, of a group, of an individual. Empowerment cannot happen without the full involvement of the nation, the group and the individual. A nation will not be fully empowered unless its citizens are empowered. A group will not be empowered unless their peers are empowered. Nor can an individual's empowerment take place in isolation from others. Moreover, empowerment cannot and will not happen without social change. Social change can create the circumstances that allow empowerment. Empowerment can also create the circumstances that allow genuine social change and sustainable development.

The history and comprehensive nature of disabled people's exclusion in society is such that radical and far-reaching social change is necessary if empowerment is ever to be real for disabled people. The empowerment of disabled people which follows will then produce another social change: the creation of a society which recognises the unique contribution that can be made by disabled people. It is a contribution that no "developed" society or world should be without.

REFERENCES

ALBRIGHT, M. (1997), Address to the International Leadership Forum for Women with Disabilities, Washington, D.C.

CAMPBELL, J. & OLIVER, M. (1996), *Disability Politics: Understanding our Past, Changing our Future*, London: Routledge.

DISABLED PEOPLES' INTERNATIONAL, INCLUSION INTERNATIONAL, WORLD BLIND UNION, WORLD FEDERATION OF THE DEAF (1995), *The Disability Dimension, A Joint Statement to the World Summit on Social Development*, Copenhagen 1995.

FURTHER READING

BARNES, C. (1991), *Disabled People in Britain and Discrimination: A Case for Anti-discrimination Legislation*, London: C. Hurst & Co. (Publishers) Ltd.

BERTHOUD, R., LAKEY, J. & McKAY, S. (1993), *The Economic Problems of Disabled People*, London: Policy Studies Institute.

CROSSLEY, R. & McDONALD, A. (1980), *Annie's Coming Out*, London: Penguin Books Ltd (reprinted 1989).

COLERIDGE, P. (1993), *Disability, Liberation and Development*, London: Oxfam Publishing.

DEGENER, T. & KOSTER-DRESSE, Y. (eds) (1995), *Human Rights and Disabled Persons: Essays and Relevant Human Rights Instruments*, The Netherlands: Martinus Nijhoff Publishers.

DRIEDGER, D. (1989), *The Last Civil Rights Movement: Disabled Peoples' International*, London: C. Hurst & Co. (Publishers) Ltd.

DORKENOO, E. (1994), *Cutting the Rose: Female Genital Mutilation – the practice and its prevention*, London: Minority Rights Group.

FLETCHER, A. & HURST, R. (1995), *Overcoming Obstacles to the Integration of Disabled People*, London: Disability Awareness in Action.

FOLEY, C. & PRATT, S. (1994), *Access Denied: Human Rights and Disabled People*, London: British Council of Disabled People and Liberty.

GOODE, D. (ed) (1994), *Quality of Life for Persons with Disabilities: International Perspectives and Issues*, Cambridge, USA: Brookline Books.

MANN, Jonathan *et al* (eds) (1993), *AIDS in the World: A Global Report*, London: Harvard University Press.

QUINN, G., McDONAGH, M. & KIMBER, C. (1993), *Disability Discrimination Law in the United States, Australia and Canada*, Dublin: Oak Tree Press.

RIESER, R. & MASON, M. (1992), *Disability Equality in the Classroom: A Human Rights Issue*, London: Alliance for Inclusive Education.

Programmes and Partnerships

Disabled people's organisations are usually much smaller and less resourced than other key players in the disability and development field. There are the United Nations agenices like the World Health Organization, International Labour Organization, UNICEF (child focus) and UNESCO (education, science and culture focus). There are governmental development agencies like DfID (Department for International Development, Britain) or SIDA (Swedish International Development Agency). There are major international and national non-governmental organisations (NGOs) with a global development focus like Save the Children and Oxfam. There are international and national organisations with a disability-related focus – most of which are not controlled by or democratically accountable to disabled people at the grassroots (e.g. Rehabilitation International, Leonard Cheshire Foundation International, SENSE). And that is not to mention the host of smaller organisations that are involved in development and/or disability worldwide.

The impact of disabled people as activists, as professionals, and through their own organisations on these other key players has varied widely – not just between but also within different organisations. At best, development professionals are forming real partnerships with disabled people's organisations, supporting them to undertake the work they have identified as important. At worst, development professionals continue to function in "charity mode" or "expert mode" or "rescuer mode".

Working with disabled people at the grassroots, and working in the field of disability and development generally, is not straightforward ... especially when you want to work in ways that fit (more or less) with a social model standpoint. In this section of the book, you will learn something of the experiences that development and disability professionals have faced in trying to do just that.

OVERVIEW OF CONTRIBUTIONS

ADD: Working with Disabled People's Organisations in Developing Countries

Barbara Frost sets out the vision, aims and objectives of Action on Disability and Development (ADD), why it was set up, and its modes of operation. ADD works exclusively with and through disabled people's organisations in the majority world, to promote change and human rights. Frost also outlines some of the difficulties that ADD has faced in its 12 years as a development organisation focused on disability – including difficulties relating to: which disabled people to work with; and how to work in ways that give more power to local people, when it's the western organisation that has access to the resources.

Integrating a Disability Perspective into Mainstream Development Programmes: The Experience of Save the Children (UK) in East Asia

Hazel Jones tackles the difficult issue of whether it is better to set up development projects that have a specific disability focus, or to integrate a disability perspective into all mainstream development projects. The issue is illustrated using examples (good and not so good) from Save the Children's work in Lao, China and Viet Nam. Jones also offers a "Framework for Integrating a Disability Perspective" with some practical suggestions on how to implement this.

Creating Conversations: The Evolution of the Enabling Education Network

Susie Miles writes about the Enabling Education Network. EENET promotes international networking and information exchange to support the inclusion of all marginalised groups in education. Miles outlines EENET's aims, ways of working, and some of the difficulties encountered so far. Along the way, Miles considers: the concept of inclusion (versus integration); issues of global power imbalances in information production, control and access; and the need for professionals in the minority (western) world to listen to and learn from initiatives that are happening in the majority world.

Challenges for Universities of the North Interested in Community Based Rehabilitation

Sheila Wirz and Sally Hartley draw on their experiences in research, training and practice at the Centre for International Child Health in London to inform their discussion of the role that universities of the minority world might play in disability research and service provision in the majority world – through training, partnerships, research links, etc. Wirz and Hartley also consider the transfer of western approaches and professions to other countries; the dangers of "professional fashions"; and the potential mutual benefits of North-South partnerships.

DISCUSSION POINTS

- Should all development organisations take disability issues on board? If so, how?
- Is it better to include disability issues and disabled people in <u>all</u> development projects, always? When, if ever, is it better to have a project that is <u>only</u> focused on disabled children or disabled adults?
- What are the benefits of working, as ADD does, with organisations led and controlled by disabled people in the majority world? Are there any dangers?
- What practical steps can be taken to support the development of disabled people's organisations worldwide, at local as well as national levels?
- Do you think students and practitioners from the minority world have anything to learn from research and practice in the majority world? If so, what? Would western practitioners really listen to people from the majority world?
- What do you think about the transfer of ideas and ideologies like "inclusive education" to majority world settings?
- Should westerners and western-dominated organisations be involved in disability issues in the majority world at all? Why, or why not?

CHAPTER 4

Action on Disability and Development: Working with disabled people's organisations in developing countries

Barbara Frost

INTRODUCTION

Action on Disability and Development (ADD) is a UK-based non-governmental development organisation, working in Africa and Asia to promote the equal opportunities of disabled people (especially disabled people in poverty) and the development of the disabled people's movement. ADD believes that disabled people should be included in all aspects of overseas development work, and that the issue of disability should be a cross-cutting theme, as gender has become in recent years. ADD is a relatively small agency with 68 staff worldwide. In 1997, ADD had an income of £1.6m.

The paper explains why ADD was established. It goes on to describe ADD's vision, aims, operational objectives, ways of working. I also outline some of the key issues and dilemmas which we have encountered within our organisation and in our operations overseas over the past 12 years. Issues related to governance, resource management and fund-raising are not included here, but are covered in ADD's Five Year Strategic Plan (ADD 1998).

ADD: THE BACKGROUND

ADD was set up in 1985 by Chris Underhill, who had been inspired by the work of the disability movement in Zimbabwe, where organised self-advocacy by disabled people's organisations was having an impact on attitudes and policy.

During the mid-1980s, other international non-governmental development agencies had identified disabled people as being among the poorest people in the majority world. However, disabled people's needs were all too often viewed from a medical perspective, related only to their impairment. As a result, interventions by development agencies generally took the form of specialist services, provided by medical professionals, and with little involvement by disabled people themselves. In short, the services and approach were premised on a view of disabled people as "different", with very "different" needs from the rest of the population. In fact, the priorities for most poor disabled people were no different from the priorities of their non-disabled neighbours: food, clean water, shelter, health care, schooling for their children, and the means to make a livelihood.

Many non-governmental organisations (NGOs) claimed to be doing "integrated" development work: by this, NGOs meant a focus on the holistic needs of poor people. However, the vast majority of these NGOs had not even started to consider a fully *inclusive* approach to working with and supporting *all* poor people. Gender issues were beginning to be raised, but still disabled people (men, women and children) were generally excluded from grass-roots development programmes.

Clearly there was a need for an organisation which would target poor disabled people and help build the capacity of disabled people's organisations to push forward their demands for equal opportunities and socio-economic inclusion. It was with this in mind that ADD was established in 1985, as a development agency working with disabled people's organisations in developing countries, and with a specific development focus on issues of poverty and exclusion.

ADD positioned itself alongside other international aid and development agencies working towards the reduction of poverty through self-help initiatives, and was also keen to align itself with the growing international disability movement (e.g. Disabled Peoples' International). ADD was not established as an organisation *controlled by* disabled people, although it has established an affirmative action policy in choosing staff and trustees (at least 50% should be disabled people), on the basis that a personal understanding of the negative attitudes, oppression and discrimination experienced by disabled people themselves is vital to the organisation if it is to work effectively.

ADD remains the only British-based development agency supporting development work *exclusively* with groups and organisations of disabled people in Africa and Asia.

VISION AND AIMS

ADD's vision is a world where all disabled people are able to participate fully at every level of society. We believe that all people have the same fundamental rights to determine their own futures and to control decisions that affect their lives.

ADD aims to promote the human rights agenda of disabled people in the developing world and believe that disabled people are their own most powerful advocates. More specifically, our aim is to work in partnership with groups of disabled people in some of the poorest communities in the world to support their campaign for the rightful inclusion of disabled adults and children in society. We aim to achieve this by promoting disabled people's organisations to work with their members and other disabled people (to build the confidence of local disabled people in their own worth, abilities and rights); to set up self-help initiatives to improve their own standards of living; and to take control of their own lives.

OPERATIONAL OBJECTIVES

There are six main operational objectives which are reflected in the rolling five year plans and activities of all ADD's programmes and partners, all of which are achieved through supporting the activities of disabled people's organisations (ADD 1998):

1. *Building Strong Associations of Disabled People*

- To work with disabled people's organisations (DPOs) to develop democratic effective organisations with plans which will allow them to raise the social status of their members and to lobby effectively for equal opportunities.
- To assist DPOs to link up with, or join, existing movements of disabled people.
- To support DPOs who are tackling issues of attitude, power and control in an endeavour to challenge the causes of their oppression.
- To assist disabled women and children to organise themselves and pursue initiatives to improve the quality of their lives.
- To develop partnerships with groups of disabled people who are most marginalised within their societies e.g. people with mental illnesses, learning difficulties or hearing impairments and look at innovative ways of working with them.

2. *Self-Advocacy and Influence*

- To assist disabled people to advocate effectively at national level for laws which guarantee disabled people's rights and compliance with the UN Standard Rules.
- To work at district and regional levels with disabled people's organisations in lobbying for equal opportunities.
- To influence policy makers, development agencies and NGOs to adopt an inclusive approach to working with disabled people.
- To assist disabled adults and children to be involved in decision making about activities designed to benefit them e.g. HIV/AIDS messages, community based rehabilitation, mobility aids, health, transport and educational services.

3. *Access*

- To ensure that local institutions and services e.g. transport services or schools are accessible.
- To support organisations which are providing appropriate mobility appliances or aids to disabled people.

4. *Economic empowerment*

- To provide information and training to disabled people in managing their resources effectively.
- To lobby local financial service providers to include disabled people.
- To assist disabled people to gain access to vocational training.
- To provide training for disabled people in setting up their own small businesses, and provide start up capital for revolving funds.

5. *Information and Education*

- To ensure that development messages and information are accessible to disabled people, e.g. AIDS messages in Braille or sign language, to overcome any sensory or physical barrier to communication.
- To provide information on, for example, mobility aids, good health, HIV/AIDS, entitlements to schooling or other state services.
- To help disabled people and their communities to become aware of the causes of different impairments and encourage parents, for example, to have their children immunised against polio.
- To support literacy and numeracy work.
- To encourage Governments and schools to take on an inclusive approach to education by adopting suitable curricula and training for teachers.

6. *Recreation, Sport and Cultural Activities*

- To support recreational, sporting and cultural activities chosen by disabled people.
- To encourage drama, dance etc. to raise awareness, disseminate information and provide a basis for disability culture (ADD 1998).

WHAT WE DO & WHAT WE DON'T DO

The way in which ADD carries out its operational objectives is crucial. In our ways of working, we adopt the social model of disability, whereby the onus is on society to change and become more inclusive of diversity, including disabled people.

Solidarity with Disabled People

ADD works through establishing partnerships with disabled people's organisations either through country programmes or directly from the UK. We work with organisations or groups who share our aims, values and beliefs and who have been established along democratic lines to seek equal opportunities for all disabled people. ADD also partners groups who work towards the inclusion of disabled children in society and education. We believe that disabled children's rights are often advocated most effectively by parents and carers organisations.

In terms of best practice, we feel that solidarity with disabled people is crucial. If development initiatives concerning disabled people are not in solidarity with them, there is little sense of ownership and the project collapses as soon as funding ends. Initiatives which are planned, carried out, managed and evaluated by disabled people themselves are likely to be more sustainable in the long-term.

Partnership Agreements

We believe in the concept of "partnership", while acknowledging that this can only occur when a level of trust is built. To help build this trust, ADD sets up agreements with partner organisations, which state clearly mutual expectations, obligations and duration of support.

Support for Self-Help

ADD believes in backing self-help initiatives which have been planned by disabled people themselves. ADD supports a community development approach with disabled people's groups identifying and tackling the causes of their poverty and oppression. In this way, development is part and parcel of an on-going process of self-empowerment and liberation. This approach respects the rights of disabled people to determine their own futures.

Support for Capacity Building

Much of our work focuses on building the capacity of organisations through training and support in organisational development. This may take the form of "direct" capacity-building – such as building the management capacity and skills in a disabled people's organisation; or it may be "indirect" – such as supporting disabled people's organisations to achieve their operational objectives.

ADD tries to be responsive to the plans and priorities of the various organisations it works with. Often it is appropriate to maintain support to initiatives and organisations operating at different levels within a country. For instance, in supporting a National Federation of Disabled People, the priority might be an understanding of effective advocacy and lobbying techniques. For a village-level group, the priority might be gaining access to livelihoods and income-generating opportunities. At regional and district level, ADD's support might be geared towards membership development programmes or local awareness raising.

What We Don't Do: Relief Work and Rehabilitation

ADD does not get directly involved in emergency or relief work, although we recognise that such disasters often increase the numbers of disabled people in any community. However, we do accept a responsibility to influence aid and development agencies which provide emergency relief: those agencies must plan for the needs of disabled people, who are often severely disadvantaged and tend to be excluded from mainstream aid and relief work.

In relation to rehabilitation, including community-based rehabilitation (CBR), ADD sees its role as complementing the work of CBR programmes and relevant agencies and, crucially, influencing them to take on the social model of disability. In some countries, we do support disabled people's organisations who produce low-cost appropriate prosthetic appliances and train disabled men and women as technicians.

ORGANISATIONAL CULTURE & EQUAL OPPORTUNITIES

ADD believes that in order to establish effective relationships with our programme staff and partner organisations, we need to make our values, beliefs and ways of working explicit and consistent with our approach to community development. We also want to build an organisation which is constantly learning, reflecting and improving practice; and which reflects the values which inspire and drive our work:

We aim for a culture which is decentralised, trusting, empowering, informal, and flexible. While accountability must be paramount, we will aim for an ethos which emphasises freedom, initiative and humour (ADD 1998).

ADD has an Equal Opportunities policy which aims to ensure we recruit the best person for the job while guarding against inappropriate discrimination. We have an affirmative action policy with regard to the appointment of disabled people: wherever possible, disabled people are recruited. Accessible premises, suitable equipment and fittings, part-time positions and flexible working hours are provided to facilitate this.

WHERE ADD WORKS

ADD has six well-established and staffed programmes in Africa. These are located in Uganda, Sudan, Tanzania, Zambia, Ghana and the "West Africa" programme which covers Burkina Faso, Mali and Côte d'Ivoire. In Asia, there are two staffed programmes in Cambodia and Bangladesh. In addition to staffed programmes, ADD provides support to partner organisations in Zimbabwe, South Africa and India, including to a sister organisation, ADD India, which has an independently constituted board.

KEY ISSUES & DILEMMAS

In this final section of the paper, I set out some of the key issues and dilemmas that ADD has faced in its work in Africa and Asia. These relate to: partnerships; influence and self-advocacy; gender issues; HIV/AIDS issues; financial services and income generating projects; learning and evaluation. ADD does not have all the solutions to these problems, but believes that it is important to reflect on the weaknesses – as well as the strengths – of our work.

Partnerships

Partnerships are much easier said than done. In ADD's work, we have come up against several difficult issues and questions. These questions are discussed in turn.

- Does ADD only work with cross-impairment groups?

As a general rule, ADD does not work with single impairment groups concerned with service provision. In some countries, however, only impairment-specific organisations exist. In these circumstances, ADD may support such organisations whilst encouraging the formation of a single disability organisation. One of the reasons why we prefer to work with cross-impairment organisations is that, from our experience, governments and policy makers are more likely to listen to a single unified voice representing the interests of all disabled people.

- How representative are the disabled people's organisations that ADD supports?

ADD tries to support groups that are genuinely democratic, involve women as well as men, and involve a cross-section of disabled people in their work. However, as with all organisations, disabled people's organisations may be dominated by the most powerful individuals within the disability movement, while the more marginalised may not gain a voice. Leaders are often physically disabled men which, given the young age of the disability movement in most countries, is not surprising. People with learning difficulties, leprosy, epilepsy or mental illness rarely gain equal access to these cross-impairment groups (largely because their impairments are surrounded by more myths and misconceptions than those of other disabled people).

The marginalisation of disabled women is another major concern. ADD encourages discussion of gender issues and women's participation and exploitation. That said, ADD also acknowledges that challenging gender dynamics has to come from within the society and culture. ADD's dilemma is how to promote discussion on gender issues and increased representation of disabled women *without imposing western views*. As much as we may seek to promote better representation of women, it is disabled women themselves who must lead this struggle. And disabled women are doing precisely that. In Sudan, I recently heard a young deaf women declare to another friend: "What good will a husband be? It is skills and an income that we need".

- What happens when disabled people's organisations compete?

Again, as with all community-based groups, power struggles and breakdowns between elected boards and staff occur, and ADD has to be careful about how to deal with these dynamics. In some countries we have made a deliberate decision to concentrate our work in rural towns where there are fewer disabled people's organisations, rather than in the capital city where political rivalry between the more and less established organisations may make it very difficult to decide who to support.

- How equal can any partnership with ADD really be?

As stated in an earlier section, ADD recognises that partnership requires trust – therefore partnership agreements are used. However, given the colonial history of many of the countries in which we work, building trust takes time and understanding. Moreover, any partnership with ADD is inevitably based on an unequal distribution of resources: ADD accesses the funds, and therefore ADD holds power. Whatever we strive to do in creating partnerships, we must also recognise the inherent inequalities.

- Doesn't ADD's accountability to other donors compromise ADD's partnerships?

Since ADD is almost entirely dependent on project grants to finance its work, we are therefore subjected to rigorous accountability and monitoring requirements by our donors. These requirements are consistent with operating an effective NGO, but they also lead to conflict when (as has happened) increasing amounts of time are spent on improving documentation, planning and monitoring, with less and less time spent actually carrying out the work and working directly with disabled people's organisations. This works against the development of partnerships when it appears that we are making heavy demands on a group and, perhaps, not fulfilling our obligations.

A Local Presence?

In our experience, the absence of a local or country presence makes it harder to work closely with disabled people's organisations to help in their organisational strengthening and development. Therefore, in most countries in which we work a small country programme office has been established (an office and a small team of development and support workers with a programme manager overseeing the work). The drawback to a local presence is the danger that in building an ADD structure (by setting up a country programme office), the local ADD office will come to be seen as the power base, rather than the disabled people's organisations. There are also difficulties relating to employing disabled people to work for ADD in the country programme offices. Disabled people may leave their own advocacy organisations to join the ADD team, as the pay and conditions are comparable to other NGOs and therefore better than most local organisations can afford to offer.

In countries where no office is established, ADD's ability to work closely with disabled people's organisations in capacity-building is more limited. Our role is likely to become one of a funding agent that relies heavily on other local agencies to provide training and support. Certainly, this can be a workable model for supporting disabled people's organisations that are more established and that therefore require little more than financial support from ADD. However, since ADD also aims to support less established, more marginalised disabled people's organisations, this way of working can have severe limitations. ADD has to continually redefine its role as an agency working to strengthen the capacity of all levels of the disability movement, supporting smaller, more isolated groups to link into the wider movement, and also building lobbying skills at central level.

Influence and Self-Advocacy

ADD is not an organisation of disabled people and therefore is not in a position to advocate directly for disabled people. Self-advocacy skills are critical for disabled people's organisations if they are to achieve lasting social change.

In developing ADD's strategic plan, a "visioning" exercise was carried out with all stakeholders (disabled people's organisations, country programme staff, UK-based staff and trustees). All felt it was important for ADD to take a proactive role in influencing policy makers to adopt an inclusive approach to their work. We believe that our credibility to do this relies on constantly building on our accumulated experience in working with disabled people's organisations.

In addition to supporting local and national disabled people's organisations in developing countries to lobby power-holders and policy-makers in their own country, ADD has been in dialogue with the Department for International Development (DfID) in Britain regarding the revision of their technical note on disability as applied to NGOs working with disabled people. We have called for a complete revision of this to reflect the social model of disability. We have also called on the British government to establish a policy of including disabled people in all bilateral-funded aid programmes as well as NGO activities. ADD has also tried to facilitate the inclusion of disabled people's organisations on World Bank consultative committees which involve development organisations from the South.

ADD takes every opportunity to ask development agencies and development professionals how they are including disabled people in their work: we are continually amazed at the low-level of awareness, and the absence of a disability equality perspective. Taking account of gender issues is now a requirement of several funding, aid and development agencies (including DfID); we would like to see disability and access requirements treated in the same way.

HIV/AIDS Issues

ADD is aware that malaria still kills far more children in Africa than die from illnesses related to HIV/AIDS. Yet the impact of HIV/AIDS on the countries where we work is something that we cannot underestimate. It is clear that ADD must take a position on this, since very few of our present programme plans include support to activities related to HIV/AIDS.

There are issues regarding disabled people's access to health messages. Also, disabled women may constitute a particularly high-risk group. We have encountered many disabled women who want to find a husband and have children. However, there may be strong social prejudices which prevent them from marrying. Sometimes the wish and pressures to have children may outweigh the risks of contracting HIV/AIDS. Also, women who are seen as less marriageable may also be seen as less likely to be HIV positive, and thus become more likely to be sexually abused.

ADD has a duty to raise awareness and provide support to our own staff on HIV/AIDS. We also have a role in supporting disabled people's organisations to assess their own position regarding HIV/AIDs and to provide contacts with NGOs and service providers active in HIV/AIDS-related work.

In Peter Coleridge's book *Disability, Development and Liberation* (1993), he likens the liberation struggle of disabled people to that of other civil liberty movements. The struggle against stigma, prejudice and exclusion which people with HIV/AIDS face is another liberation struggle which many have yet to join. There would appear to be many experiences that the growing disability movement and the embryonic movement of groups of people with HIV/AIDS could share.

Financial Services and Income Generating Projects

Overcoming poverty is clearly a priority for most of the disabled people ADD works with and we want to support disabled people in their endeavours to improve their standard of living. Disabled people face additional obstacles in establishing income generating activities due to lack of education, mobility constraints and limited access to credit through the normal channels. Building the capacity of disabled people's organisations to deal with credit and to establish sustainable income generating projects requires specialist skills, so wherever possible ADD tries to work in partnership with other NGOs who specialise in this.

Where ADD is directly supporting credit work a grant is normally made to the disabled people's organisation, which then disseminates this as repayable loans to create a revolving fund. Before credit is given out it is important that the recipients understand the expectations and repayment requirements. If it is to be used for income generation, then training is provided in conducting a feasibility study and formulating a basic business plan.

There is a danger that if local organisations see ADD as a credit fund provider, the operation of a credit scheme will become the main aim of the disabled people's organisation, instead of the organisational development work which ADD considers most important (from the perspective of building strong local organisations capable of promoting opportunities for all local disabled people).

An additional dilemma relates to donors, and the types of credit schemes that they find acceptable. Most donors want to support sustainable revolving loan schemes. This often puts credit beyond the reach of some of the poorest individuals and households. ADD's experience is that credit management can assist disabled people to gain the respect of their communities. To paraphrase Jim Wolfensohn (head of the World Bank), the key issue is less about "being credit worthy", and more about "engaging in society". The opportunity to "engage" is exactly what disabled people are seeking to achieve. The demonstration of disabled people receiving small-scale credit can achieve much in terms of attitudinal change.

It is often assumed that anyone can run a small income-generating activity if capital and training are provided. We know from the high failure rates of small enterprises the world over that this is unlikely to be true. Therefore we are currently reviewing ADD's experience and lessons learned.

Learning and Impact Assessment

Our aim is to consolidate our learning and document this for internal and external use. However, this requires time and resources which – for a small agency dependent on project grants – is not always easy to do without letting operational activities slip, and without letting "indicators, targets and evaluation processes become the newspeak of the age, often substituting for the facts of power relations, exploitation and poverty" (Zadek 1996).

We want to encourage partners and programme staff to exchange information and create learning groups, and have planned to hold a meeting of all our Programme Managers in Uganda to launch this process. Improved impact assessment will also feed into this process, so that we can plan what to do with a better understanding of current impact and value for money. Social impact is not a short-term goal and meaningful indicators have to be developed with local organisations, at the outset. It is important to build a learning organisation which reflects on its experiences, shares the lessons learned, whilst not sinking under a pile of bureaucracy and paperwork.

CONCLUSION

In the recent Government White Paper on *Eliminating World Poverty: A Challenge for the 21st Century* (1997), the importance of "encouraging democratic structures which can hold government accountable and give the poor a voice" was highlighted. ADD views the development of the disabled people's movement as an example of such a structure – and one which has had notable success in influencing policy. For example, the National Disabled People's Union in Uganda has successfully lobbied the Ugandan government to bring about constitutional change with six disabled people being voted into parliament. In South Africa, as a result of links between the African National Congress and the disabled people's movement, a legislative environment has been created which requires that disabled people must be treated equally and affirmative action policies have been implemented. (Here, it is interesting to note that the legal protection for disabled people in a number of African countries is far ahead of anything achieved so far in the UK.) Supporting and working in partnership with disabled people's groups and organisations, at all levels and worldwide, is crucial for change.

Until fundamental legislative changes are realised disabled people are unlikely to realise equal opportunities. Until all development and aid agencies (governmental and non-governmental) make their programmes fully inclusive of and accessible to disabled people, development work will continue to marginalise. Taking account of gender as a cross-cutting theme is now a requirement of many aid and development agencies (including DfID); we would like to see disability issues treated in the same way.

REFERENCES

ADD (1998), *Action on Disability and Development Five Year Strategic Plan 1998-2002*, Frome: ADD.

COLERIDGE P. (1993), *Disability, Liberation, and Development*, OXFAM.

The Secretary of State for International Development (1997), *Eliminating World Poverty: A Challenge for the 21st Century*, London: The Stationery Office.

ZADEK S. (1996), "Comparison and Calculation" in Sogge, D. (ed), *Interlude: Looking Back from 2010*, Photo Press.

FURTHER READING

ADD (1997), "ADD Paper to Comic Relief", Frome: ADD.

ADD (1997), "ADD Inputs to DFID Policy Review: Working with Disabled People", Frome: ADD.

ADD (1997), "ADD Submission to the Select Committee on International Development", Frome: ADD.

ADD (1990), "Disabled People in Development: Challenging Traditional Attitudes" *in* ADD, *Critical Choices for the NGO Community: African Development in the 1990's*, Frome: ADD.

CHAPTER 5

Integrating a Disability Perspective into Mainstream Development Programmes: The experience of Save the Children (UK) in East Asia

Hazel Jones

INTRODUCTION

It is now almost two decades on from the inception of community-based rehabilitation, and yet one of the most pressing issues for the majority of the world's disabled people – those who live in rural areas of the majority world – is still how to get access to any kind of services at all. To this end, the concept of *integrating a disability perspective into mainstream development programmes* has begun to attract debate among development organisations which work in countries of the majority world.

There is, however, a lack of clarity about what this new concept means: it is currently used to refer to a variety of approaches and activities, by a variety of development organisations and professionals. Accordingly, the main aim of this paper is to make a contribution to current debate, primarily through outlining and reflecting on the experience of Save the Children (UK) in five disability-related development projects in East Asia. These five projects highlight a range of approaches which are relevant to the concept of integrating a disability perspective.

In this paper, the current disability strategy of Save the Children (UK) (hereafter SCF) is outlined first, and is followed by a brief discussion of the rationale that underpins the strategy. Then five projects supported by SCF in East Asia are described, with a view to learning about the strengths and weaknesses of different approaches to disability-related development work. Finally, and on the basis of lessons learned by SCF and also by ActionAid, some guiding principles are proposed which might help others working in the majority world who want to integrate disability into mainstream development, whilst also ensuring that all the needs of disabled children (and disabled adults) are met.

SAVE THE CHILDREN'S DISABILITY STRATEGY

Disability has been part of SCF's work since it was first founded in 1919. Over the years, and in line with the development of SCF's work generally, the underlying ethos of SCF involvement in disability has changed significantly. Initially, direct delivery of specialist services was viewed as the best way to support disabled children – this clearly reflects the dominance of segregated special educational or medical models of disability in Europe at that time. Since then, there has been a gradual shift towards supporting community-based, integrated educational work, with a clearer focus on advocacy and rights. For information, a detailed account of this changing focus is provided in a history of an SCF disability programme: *In our own Words: Disability and Integration in Morocco* (SCF/UK 1996).

SCF now recognises the basic principles of the "social model" of disability: that disabled people are disabled not so much by their individual impairments but more by the external barriers – physical, psychological, institutional – which exclude them. In line with the "social model", the main aim of SCF's current work is to address the barriers and constraints that face disabled children, whether those barriers lie in the family, in the physical environment, in the system, or in the attitudes of others. This is done to ensure that the rights of disabled children will be realised, that their basic needs will be met, and that they will no longer be prevented from participating fully in the life of their families and communities.

The shift towards a rights-based approach has been boosted by the United Nations Convention on the Rights of the Child. Using the Convention as a starting point, SCF's Policy on Disability aims to:

> support, promote and develop activities which enable disabled children to enjoy full lives, be self reliant and independent and ensure their active participation in their respective communities (SCF/UK 1998a).

SCF's Global Disability Strategy identifies eight key issues. The second of these issues states that:

> SCF will integrate disability into its programme and advocacy work starting with pilot country programmes within regions to implement disabled children's integration into regular programme and project work (SCF/UK 1998b).

SCF's rationale for integrating a disability perspective into mainstream programmes is based on the following beliefs and convictions:

- Disabled children are first and foremost children.
- The rights and needs of disabled children are the same as the rights and needs of *all* children, and include: rights to the love and care of their family, the opportunity to develop and learn, and to belong to and contribute to their family and community.
- Most of these rights and needs *can* and *should* be met through mainstream services and programmes, which have a responsibility to provide for *all* children, *including* disabled children.

- The onus should therefore be on the service-provider to justify the exclusion of a child, rather than on the family to petition for their child's inclusion, as is often the case.

All of the above statements are embedded within the UN Convention on the Rights of the Child. Here, it is important to note that Article 23 is commonly – and wrongly – seen as the only article which covers disabled children's rights. In fact, *all* Articles of the Convention apply *equally to disabled and non-disabled children*. Article 23 refers only to those needs that disabled children may have *in addition* to the common and shared needs that all children have ("the right of handicapped children to special care, education and training designed to help them achieve greatest possible self-reliance and to lead a full and active life in society").

Finally, I should also note that SCF is only one of several organisations that is moving towards more inclusive development work. For example, ACTIONAID India have made a "strategic decision to integrate disability work [mostly community-based rehabilitation] with mainstream development project initiatives" (Rao 1997).

INTEGRATING DISABILITY INTO MAINSTREAM DEVELOPMENT: ISSUES

Integrating a disability perspective into mainstream development work, as outlined in SCF's Policy on Disability and the Global Disability Strategy, will not be easy to put into practice. Barriers to implementation can be identified in the views and practices of development professionals generally, and of disability/development professionals also; in the attitudes of local communities, local professionals and local families; as well as in the pressures of time and resources which are commonplace among development organisations.

In my experience, most colleagues who work in other (non-disability) development sectors openly recognise the problems facing disabled children and disabled adults. They are invariably open to the idea of mainstreaming disability in development work, but they face constraints in putting the idea into practice. It can be difficult for those responsible for implementing development programmes to give disability the attention it deserves, especially when faced with increasing demands to make their programmes sensitive to a whole range of marginalised groups – women, children, ethnic minorities as well as disabled people.

There is also the problem that many development professionals see disability as a "specialist" issue, and one for which they lack the necessary expertise and experience.

Unfortunately it is often we "specialists" who inadvertently contribute to this misconception. In the pursuit of advances in treatment and therapy, we create the impression that the best approach to the problems faced by disabled people is to focus on what is different about them, and therefore the best solution lies with securing the help of more specialists. However, it is much more important and productive to focus first on what is shared (what children or communities have in common) rather than on the usually minor differences.

The view that specialist and/or medically-oriented services are the best solution may also be shared by other stakeholders in a community and in a development programme ... by local families, for example. From my experience in East Asia, it seems that a disabled child is often seen in terms of her disability, rather than as a child who happens to have a disability. As a result, getting treatment is the overriding priority of the family.

Where specialist services are available, many families spend an inordinate amount of time and resources in search of treatment alone; in the process, their child's other needs are put to one side. I have met many parents with a child of school age with a physical impairment, who believe that once their child is "better", *then* they will then start to teach him to look after himself, let him play with other children, and send him to school.

Where there are no specialist services available locally (as is the case in most parts of rural East Asia), it is quite common to find some disabled children attending their local primary school. These tend to be children with mild physical impairments, or with learning or sensory impairments which may not have been detected. However, in these areas local education personnel often see this form of casual integration as unsatisfactory, since many of these children are unable to keep up with their classmates and eventually drop out of school. There are also many disabled children who cannot attend school for other reasons: because they cannot get there, because of poverty, because the curriculum is unsuitable for their needs.

The standard solution to the problem of educating disabled children has been – and still is – to establish special schools or centres. But is this the best and most appropriate solution? On closer scrutiny, it becomes clear that many of the factors preventing disabled children from attending school in poor rural areas are actually the same factors that prevent many non-disabled children from going to school. Poverty, poor nutrition, bad roads or no roads, flooding, poorly resourced health centres and schools, lack of trained staff, lack of information, a curriculum with limited relevance to children's lives and futures ... all of these are major constraints that face the rural population as a whole, not just disabled children.

It surely follows that much more could be achieved in the lives of disabled children (and disabled people generally) by focusing on how to improve the living conditions of the rural population and local communities *as a whole*, rather than setting up 'special' facilities for a minority. The logic is clear: if schools improve their facilities, teaching methods and curricula in a way that benefits *all* children, then access to education for disabled children will automatically become easier.

All of this sounds straightforward, but the reality is very complicated – and is partly linked to views and processes of "development". For example, SCF's experience in Viet Nam indicates that in *rural* areas, disabled children are more easily accepted into a local school because it is the only option, the only school around. The view is that "it's best if they are with their friends" (quote from a primary school teacher). In contrast, and paradoxically, casual observation in *urban* areas with better resources indicates that disabled children may be *more* likely to be refused by mainstream schools than might be the case in rural areas.

One possible explanation for this is a knock-on effect caused by "development": rising standards of living lead to rising parental expectations and hopes for their child's education. In turn, parental demands on teachers increase, and teachers respond by discouraging children who are more likely to "fail" and who require more teacher input. At the same time, specialised schools and services are developed and it becomes easier for mainstream schools to pass responsibility for *all* disabled children to special schools – including disabled children who have no difficulty learning. All too often, demand for special school places outstrips available places, thereby compounding educational exclusion.

We need to guard against assumptions that "development" (as defined by the majority in rural and urban areas, in the minority and majority worlds) will automatically bring improvements for disabled people and other marginalised groups. "Development" is equally likely to lead to increased polarisation between those who are well-placed to take advantage of new opportunities and those who may have to wait a very long time to reap the benefits. Of course, in a better world, marginalised and vulnerable groups would be involved in defining what "development" should be.

EXAMPLES OF SCF'S DISABILITY WORK

In this next section, I draw on SCF experience in disability-related development work in rural areas of East Asia. Some of the projects are described in more detail than others – this reflects my own familiarity with those particular projects, and is in no way a comment on the relative quality of the projects. The five projects fall into two broad categories, which are explored in turn. First, "specific" disability projects; secondly, mainstream projects which integrate a disability perspective.

"Specific" Disability Projects

In SCF's specific disability projects, disabled children are the main target beneficiaries, and the project focus is on improving opportunities for disabled children to develop their full potential, and to participate in the life of the family and community. Some specific disability projects involve specialist provision; many projects aim to promote the access of disabled children to *mainstream* services, such as local schools and nurseries.

Two projects are described in this section. The first is an integrated education project (in China) and the second is a care in the community project (in Viet Nam).

Integrated Education Project, China

Anhui Province is one of the poorer provinces of south-east China. In the 1980s, Anhui's Provincial Education Commission began to consider how to improve kindergarten provision (for 3-6 year olds) and, at the same time, how to respond to new national legislation and targets which promoted "Education for All" (all rural children, all girl children, all disabled children, etc.). A link was established with SCF and, in 1988, a pilot project was started with SCF support. The aim of the pilot was to integrate children with mild learning disabilities into two kindergartens.

From the outset, a key focus has been on changing the rather formal teaching approach used in the kindergartens. The pilot project introduced a more flexible teaching methodology, involving small group teaching and learning through play, which encouraged more active, creative learning. At the same time, one or two children with mild learning disabilities were integrated into each class of three-year olds. As the project developed, it was recognised that not only did many of the disabled children make good progress, but in fact the education of *all* children in the kindergartens had improved (Holdsworth 1994). The integrated education programme has now expanded to 68 kindergartens, and aims to reach every county in the Province. Anhui Provincial Education Commission is now thinking about how to include children with other types of impairment in the project.

A strength of this project has been its impact on teaching methodology – including in kindergartens and schools which have not been formally included in the project. This has happened because teachers and parents have recognised the benefits that new approaches can bring to all children. A weakness of the project, and an issue of great concern, has been the lower than expected number of disabled children who have been enrolled in kindergartens participating in the project. SCF project staff expected to see one or two children with learning disabilities in each class. Instead, there are many instances of only two or three in each kindergarten.

There are various possible explanations for this low enrolment rate, including: poor identification procedures, over-narrow acceptance criteria, or reluctance on the part of parents to admit their child has learning difficulties. But there is also a possibility that the project mission has been compromised by adopting a wider "benefits for all" approach. In other words, the pilot project was conceived with an initial focus on disability and disabled children. It then gained widespread appeal because it brought benefits to non-disabled children too. These wider benefits were used – by the project staff and the Education Commission – to promote the adoption of the new, more inclusive, teaching methodologies. Gradually, the interests of the majority (non-disabled children and their parents) became the main focus, while disabled children and their interests became marginalised once again. It seems likely that this has been happening in the Anhui integrated education project.

Care in the Community Project, Viet Nam

The Care in the Community (CiC) project for disabled children was started in 1995 by the Committee for the Protection and Care of Children, with support from SCF. It was initially based in one ward of Ho Chi Minh City, and has now expanded to 12 wards (urban) and communes (rural) in four Districts. For information, there are 24 Districts in Ho Chi Minh City, each with a population of 250-300,000 people.

The aim of the project is to provide support to families with a disabled child, in order to help the child develop and participate fully in the life of the family and community. A team of local volunteers, some of whom are parents, receive basic training on children's needs, on attitudes to disability, types of disability, listening skills and problem-solving. They then visit families with disabled children to find out about their situation and any needs they may have. Using their local knowledge and experience, the volunteers act as intermediaries (link-workers) to help families gain access to existing services, resources or information in the community. The range of needs is broad. Some families need support to enrol their child in the local school or in vocational training. Some families need guidance to get appropriate health treatment for their child. Other families face economic hardship and need support to apply for a loan. For the most part, local mainstream services can meet many of the needs identified. However, there will also be some children who need extra support or specialist advice which is not locally available. To this end, further training with a more technical focus is provided for volunteers and parents (e.g. basic physiotherapy, teaching children with learning or communication difficulties).

As in the Anhui programme, the overall aim is not to set up a separate special service, but to improve access to existing mainstream services. This is done by co-ordinating with relevant agencies and service providers (Education, Health, Women's Union, etc.) to raise awareness of their responsibility to *all* children, and to support them in responding to the needs of disabled children *as part of their regular activities*.

This approach works well in locations where there is good teamwork between volunteers and officials from different sectors and backgrounds, and where the participation of family members of disabled children is welcomed. In these contexts, information about the CiC project tends to be well-disseminated among local agencies, and that in turn enables smooth access to services and resources when needed.

The story has not been so good in other areas. Some local officials still do not see the importance of using existing local resources and services to meet the needs of disabled children and their families. Instead, they imagine that the role of the CiC project is to provide everything, from money for poor families, to sending disabled children overseas for treatment. The reasons for this lie in attitudes and perceptions: not only attitudes to disability, but also perceptions and expectations of the role of "social development programmes" and development organisations (like SCF and their partners) in general. These attitudes, perceptions and expectations intersect with each other, and produce a situation in which families, volunteers and officials may feel disappointed by the project and the development workers; a situation in which the project is implemented as a "charity", not a "development" programme.

- Family Expectations

  Many families are unable to understand the CiC project from any perspective other than the dominant social view of disabled children as "poor and unfortunate", and therefore deserving of pity and charity (rather than rights).

- Expectations of Project Volunteers and Partners

  Some project workers are unfamiliar with the new CiC approach to disabled children and services. They are also uncertain of their role in relation to the family. In order to secure family participation, and to feel more confident about their own role, some volunteers and development workers may adopt the more familiar "charity" approach.

On top of this, it is a time-consuming process to discuss with relevant officials (especially if you are not very clear yourself) about gaining access to resources and services under the control of other agencies; whereas it is much easier to ask the CiC project to provide funds to organise something separate.

It seems, then, that there are both internal and external obstacles to implementing this kind of project: internal problems such as weak management and a lack of understanding on the part of project staff about the thinking behind the approach; external problems such as negative attitudes to disability and a misunderstanding of the role of the project itself.

Mainstream Projects with a Disability Perspective

SCF has found that, if attitudinal barriers are recognised and addressed, many of the needs of disabled children can be met by mainstream services and existing local resources. The next logical step, therefore, is to move towards development work which focuses on including disabled people in mainstream development programmes. In this section, three projects from Lao, China and Viet Nam are described. The common feature is that all these projects are essentially *mainstream* projects, but disabled children are included among the other target beneficiaries.

Mainstream Education with a Disability Perspective, Lao PDR

In 1989, SCF became involved in supporting teacher-training programmes in the pre-school and primary school sectors as part of a Lao Ministry of Education initiative to improve the quality of pre-school and primary education. The aim was to develop and implement a new curriculum and teaching methodology underpinned by a more child-centred approach to teaching and learning.

In the course of developing the programme, attention was turned to the high number of children who were "failing" (repeating or dropping out), and also to those children who were not enrolled at all. As a result, an integrated education pilot project started in 1993 in one school.

Five years on, 34 kindergartens and primary schools are now integrating children with disabilities and special needs into their regular classrooms. This has been made possible by the teachers' greater understanding of child development, and the new flexible and child-focused teaching methodology. At the same time, the "failure" rates in many of these pilot schools are gradually being reduced (Holdsworth 1997).

Guangde Child Welfare Home, China

In 1995, SCF began support to Guangde County Civil Affairs in Anhui Province to improve the quality of care for rejected (sometimes abandoned) children, specifically those living in the Guangde Child Welfare Home. Over 50% of these children were disabled. It is important to state that this project was not designed as a disability project (in fact, SCF was not aware of the large number of disabled children in the welfare home when the first links were made with local officials). However, at all stages of project implementation, disabled children have, on principle, been included. They have been included as children first, with the same needs as other children "and then extra" (Brookfield 1998).

An important phase of the project has been the reorganisation of children into small family groups within the Welfare Home, followed by the relocation of two of these family groups into ordinary houses in the local township. During the planning and negotiation stages of the second phase, the initial suggestion was that the "best" children should be moved into the community first. This idea was resisted, and instead, the principle of selecting a cross-section of age, gender, disability was established, to reflect the differences commonly found among members of a family.

The most striking benefit of the small group arrangements is that staff now see all the children in their group, including the disabled children, as individuals (rather than as a group of 5 year-olds, for example). As a result, they now pay more attention to the individual needs of each child, and have also started taking pride in the personal development of "their" children. The children, meanwhile, have become more lively, healthy and active. Importantly, anecdotal evidence suggests that the move of two groups from the Welfare Home into the local community has helped to overcome some of the stigma of the Welfare Home and has had a positive impact on community attitudes. Contrary to initial fears, neighbours have been supportive and helpful to both the staff and the children who have moved into houses in the community.

Constraints are still considerable, however. In China, rejected children, disabled are not, tend not to be accorded the same worth as children living in families. Disabled children in the care of the Civil Affairs bureau are therefore a marginalised group in an already marginalised population. This helps to explain an apparent lack of interest in their development and quality of life. These attitudes inevitably make working with disabled children in a mainstream context more difficult. There are also significant constraints in terms of the lack of specialist skills, knowledge and services related to disability. Children in the Welfare Home who have a cleft-lip or cleft-palate, for example, are only considered for an operation if they survive beyond the age of 5.

Credit and Savings Programme, Viet Nam

In the poor North Central region of Viet Nam, a credit and savings programme is being implemented by the Women's Union with support from SCF. It aims to help poor women with children under the age of 15 to improve the living conditions of their families. Since the programme began four years ago, more than 6,000 women have taken out loans. As a result, they have improved their families' economic situation, and their families are better fed and clothed. Children also benefit educationally, since a percentage of the interest paid on loans goes to an education fund to provide stipends to disadvantaged children (including children of non-borrowers) who might otherwise drop out of school.

During a review of the project in 1996, SCF identified the need to make the programme more child-focused (to ensure that children were clear beneficiaries). At the same time, discussions were taking place within SCF about disability as a cross-cutting theme in all development work. Prompted by these thoughts and debates, SCF proposed to integrate a disability perspective in relation to the credit and savings programme.

The idea was welcomed by District officials. Local perceptions indicated a high prevalence of disability in the district, spread among people of all ages. A large proportion of the adult population fought in the American war, which exposed them to toxic chemicals: this factor is perceived to be a major cause of disability in the area.[1] It was decided to pilot the approach of "integrating a disability perspective". The first step was a study of the situation of disabled people in the project area, and the extent to which disabled women and children did or did not benefit from the existing credit and savings programme (Jones 1997). It was important to identify barriers to benefit, and ways to remove those barriers. The study produced the following findings:

- Disabled people are not excluded from the programme: a few disabled women are borrowers, and some borrowers have a child or other family member with a disability.
- The local primary school accepts some disabled children (as a teacher told me: "If a child can get here then we don't refuse him").
- Disabled children were seen playing with their friends, with very little discrimination.
- Disability or chronic sickness were major factors in *not* taking out a loan among the poorest families who were non-borrowers. In many cases, local officials had tried to persuade these families to take loans, but the families were too afraid of being unable to repay.

Another reason for non-borrowing among these families might be the "borrower-group format" – a common feature of credit and savings programmes, whereby a group of six borrowers is formed, and only two members in the group can borrow at any one time. Only when the previous loans are repaid can other members take out a loan. In such cases, borrower-groups may exclude those whom they perceive to be more likely to default on repayment (thereby reducing other members' chances of accessing future loans).

The findings showed that more could be done to improve access and increase benefits for disabled women and children. Therefore a short awareness-raising workshop was organised with the Women's Union, at which some practical ideas were proposed which local women could carry out without training or specialist advice. These included: prioritising education scholarships for disabled children; prioritising loans requested by women with disabled children; and encouraging Women's Union members to contact local schools and persuade them to accept disabled children. The impact of these activities on disabled children has been reviewed regularly, with the following results:

- A marked increase in the number of disabled children receiving educational scholarships.
- 97 families with disabled family members have received loans.
- Four disabled children, previously left at home, have been accepted at their local school, while eight others have been encouraged to return after dropping out.
- Two communes provided free health examinations for the disabled children in the area, and free medicine as needed; while four children received a subsidy from the Women's Union for cleft-lip/palate operations, and one for eye treatment.
- Several families with disabled family members have received assistance with their harvest.

These results indicate that, after only two short awareness-raising sessions to introduce a low-tech social perspective on disability, local people have achieved significant benefits for disabled children in their communities.

Clearly more could be done, however. After all, if two communes can provide free health treatment, what is stopping the other nine? That said, the evidence from communes which have done as much as they can suggests that there is a limit to what local people can do with only scarce local resources, before there is a need for input from more specialised services. So, for example, the District

Women's Union have repeated their request for support for operations for children with cleft-lip/palate, and for education and vocational training for the many unemployed blind people in the District.

This approach to integrating a disability perspective was subsequently initiated in a second credit and savings project, located in an even poorer District. The activities and benefits were similar. However, in a further SCF supported project (run by the Education Service for children of ethnic minority background) apparent interest at the outset has resulted in no significant activity. A reason for this could be the existing barriers for non-disabled children: scattered hamlets, inaccessible mountain paths, language barriers, severe poverty. It might therefore be expected that disabled children are low on the list of priorities (even though the issue is one of access to existing provision rather than creation of new provision). Yet, experience also tells us that poverty is seldom the *key* barrier: mainstream projects with a disability perspective have also run successfully in areas where living standards are very poor.

Experience from these projects also suggests that the implementing partner and their perception of their role and responsibilities are crucial determinants of success. For example, the District Women's Union have more contact with women and their families, so their priorities are likely to be closer to those of local women and children. In contrast, education officials tend to work within a bureaucratic system, where the policies, guidelines and targets are often valued more than children's educational needs.

DISCUSSION: DRAWING OUT THE WIDER LESSONS

This brief overview of five SCF projects in East Asia has revealed strengths and weaknesses in both the approaches used.

Specific disability projects can highlight the individual needs of disabled children, and demonstrate effective activities with clear benefits. Participants in these specific projects gain not only skills and experience (thereby providing a potential resource for mainstream programmes), but also a strength and confidence from working together (thereby resulting in more effective advocacy and lobbying for rights and access). A major risk, however, is that the good results of a disability-focused project are used by mainstream service providers to justify the delegation of responsibility for disabled children to specialist providers. Clearly, emphasising the different nature of disabled children through a specific disability project runs the risk of compounding the marginalisation of disabled children.

In comparison, the strength of mainstream programmes with a disability perspective lies in their emphasis on what disabled and non-disabled children have in common, rather than what is different about disabled children. Often, these programmes highlight the benefits that can potentially be achieved for disabled children at little extra cost, and with no specialist input. The methods used may not be as high-tech as a specialist programme, but the approach suits the "here and now" needs and resources of local communities.

Mainstream programmes with a disability perspective also have drawbacks. Inevitably, disabled children are always the minority in a mainstream programme. Their differing needs are at risk of being buried under the seemingly more pressing needs of the majority. It is this risk that makes specific disability programmes necessary for a while longer yet. There is still a significant minority for whom specialist services (corrective surgery, physiotherapy, appropriate equipment, etc.) make a huge difference to their lives.

I would argue that until and unless the "integrating a disability perspective" approach develops activities which improve access to these "specialist" services, all that will happen is that the division which previously separated disabled and non-disabled children will be replaced by a new division – between those who can be integrated, and those who cannot. In conclusion, the question is not whether or not there is one "right" approach, but rather how to maximise the strengths of both approaches: the expertise and capacity to meet particular unmet needs that is the strength of specific disability programmes; and the low-cost, large-coverage local solutions that are the strength of mainstream programmes with a disability perspective.

A FRAMEWORK FOR INTEGRATING A DISABILITY PERSPECTIVE

I would like to propose a framework for integrating a disability perspective into mainstream development programmes – a framework which sets out a range of available options. My aim is to provide both disability specialists and mainstream development professionals with an accessible framework of graded activities. Many of these activities will be well within the mandate and capabilities of existing mainstream programmes.

The process of implementation will depend on the programme context, level of awareness, and available resources. So, while the framework is presented as a developmental step-by-step process, with the gradual introduction of increasingly specialised activities, there is actually nothing to prevent any programme taking any of the activities as a starting point.

The activities set out are examples only, and have been selected from two SCF programmes in Viet Nam (since these are the programmes I am most familiar with).

❒ **Disabled people are welcomed, consulted and actively included in all regular project activities, for example:**

Design a checklist of minimum standards to aim for when including disabled people (SCF/UK 1992)

Invite a disabled representative to be a member of the project steering committee

Disaggregate project data to reflect the situation of disabled people.

❒ **Regular programme activities pay extra attention to addressing issues of disability, for example:**

Make education scholarships available to disabled children.

Ensure that existing programme materials include information related to disabled children (e.g. breast-feeding information includes advice on children with feeding problems; teacher training includes information on how to help children who develop slowly, or have sensory or physical difficulties).

❒ **Extra activities are initiated with disabled people in mind but which are of benefit to all, for example:**

Parents and teachers make low-cost educational equipment or toys for the primary school, to support and encourage them to continue integrated education.

A youth group organises play activities suitable for a disabled child, but which non-disabled children also enjoy and benefit from.

Neighbours contribute to mending the path leading to the house of a disabled child who uses a wheelchair, which makes it safer and more accessible for everyone.

❒ **Improved access gained to existing specialist services, for example:**

Provide clear information and co-ordinated support for free corrective surgery.

Invite physiotherapists from the city hospital to the village to give advice to parents.

❒ **New activities are initiated with a specialist disability focus, for example:**

Train local people (health workers, parents, disabled people) in specialist skills, such as physiotherapy, teaching children with learning disabilities, etc.

Support a Braille teaching programme led and run by blind teachers.

Help set up a workshop to produce wheelchairs, hearing aids, Braille materials, etc.

Support Deaf people set up sign language clubs for deaf children and their families.

Finally, it is vital to make *explicit* the inclusion of disabled children when designing and implementing a mainstream programme that is intended to be inclusive. If this is not explicit from the outset, then local officials, partners and project workers may automatically (if unwittingly) exclude disabled children and disabled adults from project participation. The following constructed exchange (based on conversations I have had with local officials throughout East Asia) provides a good illustration of why this is so important:

Q: In this district, what percentage of school-age children attend school?

A: 100%.

Q: 100% of *all* children?

A: Yes, of all children.

Q: So where are all the disabled children?

A: Oh, you mean including disabled children?

CONCLUSION

It is the responsibility of those of us involved in disability issues to communicate with colleagues in mainstream development programmes using the common language of rights, access and participation. Save the Children (UK), ACTIONAID India, and many other NGOs are making a start in piloting the inclusion of a disability perspective in mainstream development work, with the added aim of demystifying and desegregating disability issues.

We need to persuade those organisations which are responsible for planning, funding and establishing criteria for development programmes (especially where children are target beneficiaries) to ensure that *all* development work benefits the *whole* community, and not only the majority. NGOs must also work to ensure that the lessons from these inclusive programmes are documented in accessible formats, and widely disseminated to governments, major donors and mainstream development organisations.

It is vital that steps are taken to ensure that all aid and development programmes explicitly include a disability perspective, with adequate provision (human and financial resources, training, awareness-raising) to put it into practice. In the long term, it is only through mainstream programmes that most disabled children will ever achieve equal rights and equal opportunities.

END-NOTES

[1] Outsider, official and local definitions of "disabled" do not always coincide. Men disabled as a result of fighting in the war are grouped separately as "war invalids" (*thuong binh*), for the purpose of receiving benefits under a specific War Invalids policy. The criteria of this policy are broad, ranging from severe disability through to mild discomfort from an old wound. In any other context, not all war invalids would be considered disabled. The category "disabled" (*khuyet tat* or *tan tat*) does not include war invalids, and I have heard this group also referred to as "congenitally disabled" (*khuyet tat bam sinh*). Disabled people themselves resist any suggestion that war invalids might also be *khuyet tat*, as they are a more privileged group – they benefit from favourable government policies, and are treated better by society.

REFERENCES

BROOKFIELD, K. (1998), personal communication, Hefei, China.

HOLDSWORTH, J. (1994), "Integrated Education Project, Anhui Province", in *Making it Happen: Examples of Good Practice in Special Needs Education and Community-Based Programmes*, Paris: UNESCO.

HOLDSWORTH, J. (1997), *The Uses of 'Managed Experience' and the Limitation of Training: Lessons from the Lao Integrated Education Programme*, Discussion Paper No. 2, SEAPRO Documentation Series, Bangkok: Save the Children (UK) South-East, East Asia and the Pacific Regional Office.

JONES, H. (1997), "Integrating a Disability Perspective into a Credit & Savings Programme: First Steps", Cam Xuyen District, Ha Tinh Province, Viet Nam: SCF (UK).

RAO, V. (1997), "Orientation Workshop for Programme Executives on CBR", *ACTIONAID Disability News* 8(1), p.6.

SCF/UK [Save the Children (UK)] (1998a), *Policy on Disability*, London: SCF(UK).

SCF/UK (1998b), *Global Disability Strategy*, London: SCF(UK).

SCF/UK (1996), *In Our Own Words*, London: SCF(UK).

SCF/UK (1992), *Equal Opportunities: a Guide to Ensuring Good Practice in Disability in UK Fieldwork*, London: SCF(UK).

CHAPTER 6

Creating Conversations: The evolution of the Enabling Education Network

Susie Miles

INTRODUCTION

The Enabling Education Network (EENET) was set up to establish an information-sharing network to support and promote the inclusion of marginalised groups in education worldwide. EENET aims to provide a networking opportunity for those involved in educational programmes which enable individuals to participate in, and contribute towards, an inclusive society – where gender, poverty, ethnicity, class, behaviour, HIV and TB status, and disability do not mean exclusion; and where education is not confined to schools.

In this chapter the concept of inclusive education and current international trends towards promoting inclusive education policies are discussed. The rationale for establishing EENET, the key players and the underlying values and principles are then outlined. This is followed by an account of EENET's activities in its first year of existence and a discussion of the type of network EENET aspires to be. Two examples of the kind of networking which has already taken place are provided; these also illustrate the way in which responsibility for information dissemination can be devolved to key partner organisations. Finally, some of the main challenges facing EENET are discussed.

TRANSITIONS FROM SEGREGATION TOWARDS INCLUSION

In countries of the industrialised North, the dominant approach to children and adults with impairments has been the provision of expensive, segregated and institutionalised provision for separate categories (with categorisation based primarily on impairment). In the last two decades, however, large numbers of children have been integrated into their local schools. Sadly, the successes of integration remain limited in Britain and elsewhere in the North. A large proportion of children continue to be marginalised within and from education systems, or, at best, accepted on a conditional basis ... conditional on the extent to which the child adapts to the school. Meanwhile, a significant minority of disabled children continue to be educated in separate, segregated provision. Attempts to adopt a more inclusive policy have generally been hampered by a long legacy of exclusion, which ties up resources and creates enormous bureaucratic and attitudinal obstacles to the process of inclusion.

The concept of "inclusion", as distinct from "integration", describes a process whereby schools, education structures, systems and methodologies are required (and enabled) to change so that they can cater to the individual needs of *all* children, including all disabled children. By contrast, the focus of "integrated" education is on disabled children who are brought into mainstream schools. In integrated education, adjustments are made to the individual child so that s/he fits into the particular school. By implication and with a degree of inevitability, the regular school stays the same.

The distinction between these two concepts of inclusive and integrated education is absolutely critical. In essence, the distinction is analogous to that between the medical (individual) model of disability and the social model of disability. The focus on "fixing" the individual is replaced by an attempt to change the environment and (in the case of education) to change the context in which children are expected to learn. The following definition of inclusive education was developed for a seminar held in Agra, India (IDDC 1998).

Inclusive education:

- Acknowledges that all children can learn;
- Acknowledges and respects differences in children: age, gender, ethnicity, language, disability, HIV and TB status, etc.;
- Enables education structures, systems and methodologies to meet the needs of all children;
- Is part of a wider strategy to promote an inclusive society;
- Is a dynamic process which is constantly evolving (IDDC 1998).

It is important to make clear that promoting inclusive education does not deny the diversity of children's needs and abilities in learning. Certainly, including disabled children in mainstream schools and trying to get away from the distinction between so-called "normal" and "disabled" children (so characteristic of segregated educational provision) is important. But a denial of the differences would be naïve and dangerous. Many, including EENET, are aware of the need to maintain a balance between working towards better education for all children and recognising the very real life challenges which face severely disabled children. Individual differences should be recognised and celebrated as part of the inclusion process. Support and encouragement for self-help groups and the involvement of positive adult role-models, ex-pupils and children themselves in the education process are essential for the promotion of positive identity in disabled children and other marginalised groups. We need to move towards a more holistic view of disability to promote a stronger understanding of inclusion.

In countries of the South, where there has been relatively little investment in segregated educational provision for disabled children, inclusive education programmes tend to be more successful. In fact, wealthier nations have arguably created greater, more insurmountable obstacles to inclusion because of their relatively vast material resources. In the South, by contrast, the rehabilitation and special needs industry is much smaller and less powerful, and human resources can be harnessed to bring about inclusion. Here, implementation of inclusive education may simply involve the positive reinforcement of well-established, community-based and inclusive attitudes and practices.

In some areas, it would never even occur to teachers working in remote rural areas that a child disabled by polio, for example, should be educated anywhere other than the local school. This has been described as "casual integration" by Miles (1989). This form of casual integration is clearly widespread and deserves to be recognised and documented. However, casual integration tends to happen on an *ad hoc* and individual basis, rarely impacting on the system as a whole. Thus, even where casual integration is evident, it remains likely that many children will continue to be excluded unless efforts are made to include them.

In both North and South, inclusive education is a dynamic process which is still evolving. The concept inevitably means different things to different people. Some of those differences will depend on the context and stage of development in a particular setting. Problems also arise in language and translation: in many countries it may be difficult to find appropriate and different words for integration and inclusion, thus making it harder to differentiate clearly between the two concepts. Meanwhile, many practitioners may not be aware of the theoretical analysis and thinking that underpins the two concepts. This is not to say that these concepts have limited use. They can and have proved useful to many individuals (professionals and non-professionals, western and non-western) who are engaged in re-thinking the "educational task". The key to effective re-thinking in line with an inclusive approach is to ask: "How can we prepare schools so that they can become places that deliberately reach out to all children?" (EENET 1997).

INTERNATIONAL TRENDS

Most large development organisations employ an adviser or expert on one or more of the many issues which relate to difference (e.g. gender, race, ethnicity, age). But only rarely are the commonalities between marginalised groups explored. Sadly, awareness and equal opportunities training in any one issue does not guarantee awareness in relation to all issues. A person may be race-aware and gender-aware, but completely disability-unaware (Stubbs 1995). Inevitably, this has worked against the promotion and acceptance of inclusive education as a strategy for responding to diversity. Despite this barrier, recent years have seen an increasing focus on, and debate about, the potential for inclusive education.

Inclusive education is gaining impetus globally. Sometimes the impetus comes from a rights perspective: "Disabled children and other marginalised groups have a right to be educated alongside their peers". Sometimes it comes from an economic perspective: "We cannot afford or sustain segregated 'special' education, and so inclusion is the only option". Generally a combination of these two approaches prevails.

The United Nations' world conferences on "Education for All – meeting basic learning needs" (Jomtien, Thailand in 1990) and on "Special Needs Education: access and quality" (Salamanca, Spain in 1994) added to this impetus by emphasising that many children are excluded or are not benefiting from current systems, such as disabled children, street children and children from ethnic minorities. Contributors to these conferences highlighted the importance of taking another look at existing systems, structures and methods within schools, with a view to creating a schooling system that benefits and includes all children in the particular community. Moreover, a clear link was made between inclusive education, and initiatives aimed at school improvement and effectiveness, since these initiatives share the same aim of providing a better educational environment for all.

An outcome of the Salamanca conference was the *Salamanca Statement and Framework for Action* (UNESCO 1994). This has been and is currently used to support policy changes in many countries, North and South. Another invaluable UNESCO product is the *Teachers Education Resource Pack* (UNESCO 1993), produced as part of a long-term initiative to help schools develop more inclusive practices. The "Special Needs in the Classroom" project began in 1988 with the aim of producing and disseminating a resource pack of pre-service and in-service teacher training materials. This initiative subsequently developed into a broader analysis of educational transformation and the management of change. The pack, available from UNESCO in fifteen languages, has led to initiatives in over 50 countries.

In the light of this international activity and interest, the establishment of EENET is very timely. EENET is essentially a post-Salamanca initiative which aims to broaden the concept of inclusive education beyond the classroom to include community-based strategies; and to promote the dissemination of useful and relevant information in accessible formats throughout countries which have limited access to basic information and/or financial resources.

WHO IS INVOLVED IN EENET?

The initiative for EENET came from the International Disability and Development Consortium (IDDC): a group of international non-governmental organisations working to promote disability and rehabilitation issues, primarily in the countries of the South. For information, IDDC was set up in 1994 and does not have an organisational infrastructure.

Save the Children Fund (UK), which acts as IDDC's lead agency on inclusive education, identified the need for a network which would both share experience and help produce low-cost training materials relevant to the needs of the South. It was also felt that there was a need for a more independent body that would look at inclusion in its broadest sense and supply simple, useful and relevant information to the field. UNESCO gave full support to the idea, since it recognised the need for such a network but lacked the capacity to develop one. Several IDDC members pledged minimal funding for the establishment of EENET and, in mid-1997, a part-time co-ordinator was appointed.

The day-to-day administration of EENET is carried out by the part-time co-ordinator with support from staff and students at the Centre for Educational Needs, University of Manchester. So far, students from Ethiopia, Palestine, Brazil, Kenya and Cyprus have taken a great interest in the development of EENET and have given generously of their time in carrying out a variety of tasks, such as designing the database and mailing newsletters. Their comments and suggestions have been very valuable in the process of thinking through how to create an international network which will benefit people in countries of the South as well as the North. The students have also provided names to add to EENET's mailing list, and will continue to publicise EENET and provide valuable feedback when they return to their home countries.

Although membership is open to individuals and organisations in all countries of the world, EENET gives priority to the needs of countries in the South. There are over 600 individuals and organisations in over 100 countries on the mailing list so far, with an enormous range of professional and personal interests, including: parents and parents' organisations, teachers, teacher trainers, academics, community development workers, policy-makers, disabled people's organisations and ex-pupils of special schools.

EENET is possibly unique in the way it makes connections between academics and a wide range of practitioners on the issue of inclusive education. EENET is based in an academic institution, but has strong links with UNESCO and the major international NGOs working on disability and development issues. Thus, EENET has great potential to reach a large number of relevant individuals and organisations.

RATIONALE FOR EENET

At the grassroots level, practitioners have limited access to relevant information and lack opportunities to network with each other. There is a severe shortage of relevant and appropriate resource materials in local languages. It was primarily in response to these very basic needs for useful information that EENET was established.

Inclusive education programmes in the South are often more successful at being fully inclusive and community-based than those which operate in the North. Even so, seminars and publications are invariably biased towards the North, because when it comes to processing and disseminating information – the crucial resources are mostly held in the North. Yet there is a tremendous need to share the experiences of the South in promoting and practising inclusion ... and to share these experiences with others in both South and North. So, EENET aims to create space for sharing experiences.

The distorted ways in which much information about the South is processed, and the ways in which those in the North set the agenda for what is and is not processed about those in the South, are also cause for concern. International research, literature and conferences tend to be dominated by a Northern perspective with the result that pioneering examples of good practice in the South go unrecognised or unvalued. The flow of information goes from North to South. These imbalances increase the likelihood of the uncritical and sometimes inappropriate export of Northern (western) debates and practices to and by the South. Therefore, EENET aims to create space for people in the South to set their own agendas and present their own experiences, and for more critical reflection of Northern practices.

Finally, EENET also aims to influence the policy and practice of major donor agencies who continue to invest large amounts of money in projects which are modelled on practice in the North, without any awareness of projects which are innovative, inclusive and underway in the South, and with little thought to issues about transferring practice from North to South. EENET is anxious not to reinforce the negative deficit model of developing countries (Stubbs 1994), but instead to recognise and publicise examples of good practice in inclusive education, often in the absence of material and financial resources.

UNDERLYING VALUES & PRINCIPLES

By creating conversations between members of a participatory information network, EENET aims to be far more than just an information service. It is extremely difficult to process information without bias, and therefore EENET tries to be as explicit as possible about its own underlying values and principles, and its own bias. With this in mind, the underlying values and principles of EENET are set out below.

EENET:

- Believes in the equal rights and dignity of all children;
- Prioritises the needs of countries which have limited access to basic information and/or financial resources;
- Recognises that education is much broader than schooling;
- Acknowledges diversity across cultures and believes that inclusive education should respond to this diversity;
- Seeks to develop partnerships in all parts of the world.

In conducting its work, EENET:

- Adheres to the principles of the Salamanca Statement;
- Believes that access to education is a fundamental human right;
- Recognises the intrinsic value of indigenous forms of education.

EENET is committed to:

- Encouraging the effective participation in IE of key stakeholders, such as disabled people; children of different ages and gender; people from ethnic and other minorities;
- Engaging with the difficulties caused by the global imbalance of power;
- Encouraging a critical and discerning response to all information and materials circulated.

WHAT DOES EENET OFFER?

"Enabling Education", EENET's newsletter, is the major focus in the short-term for the dissemination of stories and articles by practitioners, information about useful publications and video training packages, and the development of international conversations about inclusive education. The first issue of the newsletter was published in December 1997 and a limited number of Braille copies were produced as part of EENET's commitment to disseminate information in a variety of accessible formats. The newsletter was translated into Portuguese at the initiative of a reader. The style of the newsletter is deliberately non-academic and participatory. The newsletter aims to be an accessible vehicle for sharing and disseminating up-to-date information, ideas and experiences of inclusive education.

EENET's website was established within the first few weeks of the appointment of the co-ordinator. It acts as a bibliographic database for key documents produced by EENET (e.g. the newsletter) or by practitioners (e.g. a manual, produced in Lesotho, to accompany a video training pack for teachers; a Child-to-Child training pack on inclusion produced in Palestine). There are also several documents produced by Save the Children (UK) which analyse their experience of moving from integration towards inclusion. References for relevant UNESCO documents are also listed. Already information available on the web site has been used by intermediaries who in turn have established direct contact with grassroots teachers and community development workers. All of this frees up the co-ordinator's time to concentrate on the needs of practitioners who do not have access to the world wide web.

EENET also runs seminars. The first EENET seminar was held in July 1997 in Manchester and was attended by 20 participants from 13 countries and organisations. Discussions at the two-day seminar helped to formulate EENET's values and principles and contributed to the development of the strategic plan. The first meeting of EENET's steering group took place at this seminar. The steering group is deliberately small: seven people who represent the major funding agencies, the University of Manchester and countries of the South. This meeting was short and primarily discussed financial issues relevant to the initial establishment of EENET.

In June 1998, a longer meeting of the steering group took place which reviewed EENET's first year and discussed the nature of the network and how it should develop. It was felt that connections *between* organisations rather than through EENET should be prioritised, in order to avoid setting up parallel structures. The danger of falling into the trap of building a small UK-dominated NGO network was also discussed (see below).

In March 1998, EENET played a major collaborative role in the preparation for, and the facilitation of, a South-focused international seminar on inclusive education. This was held in Agra, India. The ongoing and ever-increasing need for useful, relevant information was highlighted by the 50 participants – all of whom pledged to publicise and participate in EENET. The seminar reinforced three key lessons (IDDC 1998):

- A recognition that the main barrier to inclusion is the prevalence of negative attitudes and not a lack of resources, as is often assumed.
- There is a need for effective school-based support through the empowerment of all involved.
- Inclusive classrooms are unlikely to work in isolation, they require community support and participation.

A PARTICIPATORY INFORMATION NETWORK

EENET aims to be a participatory information network, rather than a dissemination machine.

EENET's main aim is to disseminate useful and relevant documents and training materials in a variety of formats to practitioners in the field who normally find it difficult to access information. EENET will only produce additional documentation where no other such material exists. In order to do this as cost-effectively as possible and with maximum participation from interested parties, conversations have to take place so that information can be shared as widely, and in as many different formats, as possible. Conversations have been initiated through the newsletter, correspondence and seminars. By providing a platform for practitioners who would not normally share their ideas and experiences with a wider audience, the vision of a participatory information network should become a reality.

National and regional organisations which share similar principles are encouraged to take responsibility for information collection, translation and dissemination. In this way, there should be maximum participation from the beginning, so that EENET can grow slowly and sustainably on a relatively small budget. The word "decentralisation" was initially used to describe a major aspect of EENET's strategy in relation to the establishment of a participatory network. However, "decentralisation" implies that there is a substantial "centre" from which information and ideas emanate, and which exercises some control over the activities of sub-centres. But EENET cannot afford to exercise too much control if it is to succeed in reaching those individuals and organisations who have previously been "hard to reach", and thus excluded. Central (and Northern) control is *not* what EENET is about.

In the interests of sustainability, the newsletter and other documents will only be translated if there is sufficient interest and commitment by a partner agency to allocate resources for that purpose. Translation issues, after all, should not be seen in isolation. Once documents appear in other languages there will inevitably be correspondence in those languages and perhaps a desire to develop regional versions of the newsletter in the appropriate languages. This would overload EENET's minimal infrastructure in the UK, and would be more efficiently dealt with on a regional basis.

Finally, one of EENET's key roles is to develop ways of documenting experiences which otherwise would not be documented because of difficulties with translation or with written language, and to make them as widely accessible as possible. Sharing these experiences through the website would be just one of the methods of dissemination, as the vast majority of people in the South will continue to use other, more traditional methods of communication. Guidelines for running workshops to explore a wide variety of methods of communication, including writing, will be developed. These will focus on the particular issues of inclusive education with a wide range of stakeholders, including children. It is hoped that the workshops will both build skills in a given community and produce useful documentation of inclusive education experience which can be shared.

SHARING EXPERIENCES

EENET recognises the danger and nonsense of transplanting educational practices across cultures and instead supports the idea of using local practice and thinking as the foundation for development activities (Ainscow 1998). In essence, this is about "making the familiar unfamiliar" by encouraging practitioners to stand back from their own situation, and take a fresh look at their own work in the light of experiences from another part of the world. It is still too early in EENET's development to be able to quote many examples of this process in action, but the following vignettes illustrate the type of networking which has already taken place.

A Vignette from South Africa

Saajidha, a lecturer at a distance education teacher training college in South Africa, is involved in developing a new course on special needs in education. She is nervous about using the term "Inclusive Education" as she is "weary of feeding the students too much too fast and then losing them". The term "Inclusion" has only recently been discussed as part of the government's National Commission on Special Needs Education. Furthermore, the majority of Saajidha's students speak English as their second language and come from peri-urban and disadvantaged rural communities.

Saajidha is in regular correspondence with EENET to share ideas, enquire about opportunities for further study for herself, and to comment on the range and usefulness of the documents on the website. She says: "Introducing something as new and as significant as this [inclusive education] is challenging". She desperately needs teacher education materials. The video training package recently produced in Lesotho, "Preparing Teachers for Inclusive Education", is an example of the locally produced and appropriate materials which EENET is able to provide at low cost. It is likely that Saajidha will act as a dissemination point in South Africa for that training package.

This is an example of the kind of conversations that have been created so far – conversations which combine sharing experience and ideas, feedback on EENET's information provision, and concrete offers of help to disseminate training materials. As a result of these conversations with Saajidha and others, it is hoped that a partner agency will emerge through which EENET can channel information relevant to southern Africa and South Africa (thereby regionalising EENET).

A Vignette from Portugal

Ana works in the Ministry of Education's Institute of Educational Innovation in Portugal and, through her involvement with UNESCO's "Special Needs in the Classroom" project, networks with large numbers of primary schools in Portugal. She received the first copy of the EENET newsletter, "Enabling

Education", in late December and emailed back immediately offering to arrange for its translation into Portuguese. This very spontaneous translation was promptly arranged and in early February a photocopy of "Promovendo a Educacao" arrived in the EENET office. Dissemination in all Portuguese-speaking countries in Africa is now possible; and dissemination in Brazil has begun through a Brazilian student based at the Centre for Educational Needs in Manchester University.

The development of such pro-active partnerships in key regional and sub-regional centres in the world will enable EENET to share information and create conversations with inclusive education practitioners, policy-makers and researchers in large parts of the South, with minimum financial commitment and administrative responsibility. It is essential to forge partnerships with experienced networking agencies already committed to the principles of inclusion.

CURRENT DIFFICULTIES

EENET is already facing up to several difficult challenges. In this paper, mention has been made of some of the difficulties inherent in implementing a participatory information network – especially how to make the network *truly* participatory, and how to avoid domination by Northern professionals and organisations.

Mention has also been made of issues of translation and regionalisation. These link directly with another key issue: globalisation through technology. EENET was set up amid an information revolution. This brings advantages; but it also carries risks. The information industry is changing rapidly. Access to information has never been as quick or as easy, and it is set to become even faster and more accessible as telephones, fax machines and televisions all become linked to the World Wide Web. In this context, it is not surprising that the decision to establish a website was one of the first decisions made when EENET was set up.

The dilemma for EENET is how to balance these increasingly rapid, high-tech forms of communication which proliferate in the North with the needs of the most excluded and marginalised people in the South, whose communication systems continue to be orally-based. It is likely that a variety of communication methods will be employed in order to reach as many people as possible. Homeless International supports local NGOs in India and South

Africa which provide support to organisations of slum and pavement dwellers (Homeless International 1998). Regular exchange visits take place, while "backyard emails" provide regular news updates. Individuals in both countries also enter into email correspondence, with literacy support provided by their local NGOs. This illustrates the possible ways in which high-tech forms of communication can complement face-to-face exchanges of experience. It points the way forward for EENET to explore all possible methods of disseminating information and creating conversations.

Perhaps the greatest and most exciting challenge is to develop partnerships with children, and emerging organisations of children and young people, on the issue of inclusive education. Discussions about how to empower young people with learning difficulties have begun to take place among parents' organisations in Africa; EENET will maintain close contact with this new development through two steering group members who are centrally involved. In addition, writing workshops (referred to above) will seek to involve children in the analysis and documentation of their own experiences, alongside policy-makers, teacher trainers and other interest groups. It will be essential to develop appropriate methods and materials to ensure that children fully participate in workshops and feel safe to express their opinions. It will be equally essential to guard against tokenistic involvement.

CONCLUSION

EENET's core function is to provide basic information about inclusive education, primarily for practitioners in the South, and to encourage the sharing of ideas, information and experiences by a wide range of practitioners in the field. The majority of individuals and organisations on EENET's mailing list so far are concerned with inclusive education as it relates to disabled children. Increasingly, though, as the understanding of inclusion broadens to include all children, EENET will focus on the need for quality and equity in education as a whole. Maintaining a balance between the specific needs of marginalised groups and the need to challenge structures and systems to become more inclusive is one of the many challenges facing EENET. The other major challenges can be summarised in a series of questions as follows:

- How do we reach the "hard to reach"?

- How do we overcome barriers to communication?
- How do we avoid Northern domination?
- How do we encourage South-South conversations?
- How do we involve children and young people?

EENET will continue to grapple with these issues while building a sustainable and participatory network. EENET welcomes suggestions for further development and offers to share ideas and information that could be of use to colleagues around the world who are working to develop education for all.

REFERENCES

AINSCOW, M. (1998), "Reaching out to all learners: some lessons from experience", Keynote address made at the International Conference on School Effectiveness and Improvement, Manchester, January 1998.

EENET (1997), "Towards inclusion: the role of information", A report of EENET's inaugural seminar, Manchester, July 1997.

IDDC (International Disability and Development Consortium) (1998), *Inclusive Education: Making a Difference.* A report of an international seminar, Agra, India (printing arranged by SCF Delhi).

HOMELESS INTERNATIONAL (1998), personal communication.

MILES, M. (1989), "The role of special education in information based rehabilitation", *International Journal of Special Education* 4(2), pp. 111-118.

STUBBS, S. (1994), "A critical review of the literature relating to the education of disabled children in developing countries", Unpublished MEd paper, University of Cambridge.

STUBBS, S. (1995), "Avoiding issue overload: Core principles and diverse discrimination", Unpublished paper, London: Save the Children (UK).

UNESCO (1994), *The Salamanca Statement and Framework for Action on special needs education*, Paris: UNESCO.

UNESCO (1993), *Teacher Education Resource Pack: Special Needs in the Classroom*, Paris: UNESCO.

CHAPTER 7

Challenges for Universities of the North Interested in Community Based Rehabilitation

Sheila L. Wirz and Sally D. Hartley

INTRODUCTION

In this paper, we reflect on our experience at the Centre for International Child Health, University of London, with a view to exploring the challenges that face universities of the North as they continue to contribute to disability-related work and service provision in countries of the South. This paper argues that universities of the North have a role as facilitator based upon strong partnerships with colleagues in the majority world. This partnership, as well as enabling creative North-South links, can enable South to South links and, equally importantly, can raise awareness among professionals and professional educators in the North about CBR (Community Based Rehabilitation) and appropriate services in the South. This paper will discuss how Western disability literature impacts upon CBR definitions and planning; it will then present an educational and research agenda for universities of the North. (For information, the term "majority world" in this paper refers to the 80% who have household incomes of less than $7,500 per year, referred to by Robert Chambers, 1997, as "global middle and global under classes".)

SOME HISTORICAL CONTEXT

Disability services in the South in precolonial times often arose from charitable motivations related to indigenous religious or philanthropic concerns. In colonial eras, the development of disability services in the South reflected dominant development and thinking in the North. These developments often ran concurrently with traditional, long-established practices about which very little was written and even less was known by professionals in the North (Mba 1990). It is important to acknowledge that a community system existed long before colonial interventions and that the "community management" of disability ranged on a continuum of solutions from "eradication" at one end, to "idolisation" at the other (Mallory 1993). It is also, of course, important to acknowledge the impact that colonial influences had on the creation of disability services in the South.

In the post-colonial era, disability services were often built upon the activities of special schools, vocational training centres and other institutions. The special schools that had formerly been run by missions and other charitable foundations were either absorbed into national programmes or affiliated to them, with a view to providing educational opportunities for disabled children and, sometimes, young disabled adults. The schools tended to retain their impairment-specific bases (a carry-over from the past) and for 20 years or more have had leadership from special educators who, as young scholars in the 1960s and 1970s, were trained in more developed countries. The courses which these leaders followed were also impairment-based. Indeed, one of the authors recalls being involved with British Council courses for teachers of "the Blind", "the Deaf" and "the Mentally Handicapped" at Moray House College in Edinburgh during the 1970s. There, students were taught in almost watertight compartments, sealed off from each other as well as from similar courses that were run for Scottish students! A consequence of this exposure for the leadership in the South was the persistence and dominance of impairment-based special education in the South long after such exclusive practices had come to be seen as outdated in Britain. For example, the place of sign language in schools for deaf children and the use of deaf and signing teachers are still issues of current debate in many Southern countries, while they are accepted practice throughout the UK (UNESCO 1988).

It may be that the retention of special schools as a focus for disabled children is appropriate in a country with low school enrolment and where the opportunities for disabled children in an educational ghetto – rather than no education at all – outweigh the disadvantages of exclusion from their local community. This is a local decision. But such decisions must be made in the full understanding that alienation from one's community is a difficult burden to place on any child.

It is frequently the case that if schools remain impairment-based, local disabled people's organisations are also likely to be impairment-specific rather than cross-impairment, and that disabled people's organisations which represent people with physical impairments tend to dominate to the exclusion of others who find it harder to articulate their voice. Rehabilitation International, Disabled Peoples' International and other organisations have done much to address the issues of local advocacy from single impairment towards multidisability organisations.

The nature of disabled people's organisations can be influenced by the ethos and practice of the local special school, especially where former pupils become involved in the organisation. The disabled people's organisation and special school can also influence community perceptions and have an influential impact upon local CBR projects. It is often from such schools, centres or organisations that CBR activities develop as a form of outreach. Present-day CBR programmes remain small and the challenge remains about if and how they can be "scaled up" effectively to meet the needs of larger numbers and become part of national programmes.

NORTH-SOUTH TRANSFERS: THEORIES AND MODELS

Disabled activists and academics in the UK have led the world in the creation and development of theoretical frameworks with which to understand disability (Campbell & Oliver 1996, Davis 1996, Morris 1991, Oliver 1992, Swain *et al* 1993 for example). The theories and frameworks advocated (most notably, the "social model of disability" and "independent living") have had an important impact on the development of policy and practice in the UK, but as yet none of these academics has seriously addressed the issue of how their ideas relate to disability, services and disabled people in the South. Unfortunately, that gap has not yet been filled by disabled activists and academics of the South who have not yet explored theoretical bases for their (often very effective) advocacy work. The perhaps inevitable result is that Northern theories and models have been transferred to the South – sometimes by Northerners (e.g. educators, researchers, practitioners, activists, development planners, development funders), and sometimes by Southern professionals, practitioners, planners and activists.

A handful of Northern/Northern-trained academics and practitioners have opened the debate on the desirability of such transfers. Lang (1998) provides a challenging discussion of the limitations of Northern disability constructs for disabled people in the South. Mallory *et al* (1993) discuss the transfer of Northern ideas and ideals of "independence" to Southern contexts, where "independence" may be an empty concept given different socio-cultural constructs of person, family and society (see also Lang 1998, Miles 1996). In many countries of the South, inter-dependence rather than independence is the key value and in such a setting, rehabilitation for disabled people which is predicated on independence, is of questionable value (Miles 1996, Al Sherhery 1996).

It is vital that the transfer of Northern theories, definitions and models to Southern contexts does not go unchallenged, and that a critical approach to Northern theories is fostered amongst Southern students and professionals. To illustrate this further, and to show how this issue is tackled at CICH, the example of Community Based Rehabilitation is used.

Example: Community Based Rehabilitation and Northern Models of Disability

CBR programmes usually include all or some of the following activities: awareness raising, parents' and carers' groups, income generation, rehabilitation, referral networking for education, employment and/or health services. In addition, most people would agree that CBR is essentially about delivering services, based in the community, for and with disabled people. The number of variations on a CBR theme is numerous; so also are the definitions and classifications of CBR, and the criticisms that have been levelled at the concept.

Several of the criticisms of CBR have been informed by developments in disability theory, activism and service provision (see Coleridge 1993 for example); and/or are the outcome of international discussions about disability and development among professionals and organisations (Jaffer & Jaffer 1990, Mendis 1992, Rahaman 1997, Thorburn 1986, UN 1996). For instance, the following questions have been asked when assessing individual CBR programmes and the bigger concept of CBR as a model:

- Does CBR espouse a medical model or a social model of disability?
- Is CBR led by professionals or by a disabled people's organisation?
- Is CBR focused on impairment, disability, or handicap?
- Is CBR a disability programme located in a developing country, or a development programme with in-built disability awareness?

These questions and implicit criticisms reflect developments and thinking in the North, in particular the growth of disabled peoples' organisations, their campaign for rights to self-determination, and their challenges to dominant attitudes, policy and practice. But how useful are these questions when assessing the impact of a programme in the South?

At CICH, we suggest that attempts to classify CBR programmes according to dichotomies like "professional-led or user-led" and "medical model or social model" are often unhelpful, since they mask the complexity and diversity both of CBR programmes and also of Southern contexts and cultures. For example, we know from our experience that it is possible for organisations seated in a health base to adopt a social model approach to their CBR work, while there are also programmes which are led by organisations of disabled people and which have a strong technical and rehabilitative focus. This in itself suggests that a more flexible approach to defining, planning and evaluating CBR is required. With this in mind, the joint definition proposed by the ILO (International Labour Organization), UNICEF (United Nations Children's Fund) and WHO (World Health Organization) can be particularly useful:

> Community Based Rehabilitation is a strategy within community development for the rehabilitation, equalisation of opportunities and social integration of all people with disabilities. CBR is implemented through the combined efforts of disabled people themselves, their families and communities, and the appropriate health, education, vocational and social services (ILO, UNICEF, WHO 1994).

The above definition is not overly prescriptive; it leaves space for interpretation by programme planners, trainers and educators. This flexibility is important for several reasons. A flexible, open definition of CBR is an acknowledgement of the wide range of practice that currently exists in and between CBR programmes. Such diversity is a strength, not a weakness. Furthermore, a more open definition allows projects to locate themselves along a continuum of models and activities: some CBR projects have an exclusive technical and rehabilitative focus; others have an exclusive human rights focus; many more incorporate a range of elements, including both rehabilitation and advocacy.

Therefore, at CICH, we feel that best practice in CBR should: a) involve a range of objectives and methods; b) meet the specific and diverse needs of individuals and communities; c) suit the specific and diverse skills of local development workers, disabled people's groups, and disability professionals; and d) suit the socio-cultural norms of the particular locality and culture. The importance of cultural sensitivity in planning and delivering all disability-related provision is now widely accepted (Groce 1998, Rahaman 1997).

Further, when considering the respective strengths and weaknesses of different CBR programmes, we have found that it is more helpful to adopt a multi-level approach than merely to ask "is the programme led by professionals or led by local disabled people?". Helander (1992) and others within WHO and UNDP (United Nations Development Programme) identified three levels of CBR:

- grassroots workers who deliver services in the community;
- mid-level workers who organise and support the grassroots workers; and
- professionals to whom referrals can be made from the community, and from whom referrals are made to the community.

Some programmes which subscribe to this WHO model focus exclusively on mid-level workers and professionals, while overlooking the potential and involvement of those at the grassroots level. In contrast, there are other programmes that may be very strong on the active involvement of disabled people's organisations in planning and training at the grassroots, but do little in the way of training or support for the professionals on whom all community services will have to call at some time.

Finally, when considering the various approaches of different CBR programmes, we suggest that it is more helpful to adopt a "comprehensive model of disability" (Wyller 1997), than to argue for either a "medical model" or a "social model". A comprehensive model of disability communicates the importance of integrating both the social and medical approaches. This resonates well with the way in which the MSc in Community Disability Studies course at CICH has developed over the past few years.

Example: Community Based Rehabilitation and Northern Approaches to Research

It is generally accepted that the implementation of CBR programmes must be accompanied by rigorous evaluation and constant revision. Unfortunately, much research which purports to be CBR research is very limited and often merely describes practice. Where CBR research does move away from describing practice towards describing data, it tends to be very impairment-oriented. There is some published work (e.g. O'Toole (1991) and Thorburn *et al* 1992), which describes different approaches to service planning and demonstrates how practice is informed by evaluation and research. But such examples are few.

In CBR research, the key research questions include:

- What effect will this service have?
- What will it cost?
- Is it what disabled people and family members want?
- What will happen if the service is not provided?

At CICH, we suggest that these questions are best answered through research which embraces both quantitative and qualitative methodologies (see Pope & Mays 1995, and Mays & Pope 1995). Both types of data and method are needed to ensure an holistic exploration of relevant issues which is in line with a "comprehensive model" of disability. Regardless of method, research must be conducted with rigour and transparency, so that results can be verified and used to inform disability service planning. Also, good research practice entails practice similar to that of a good community development worker, who uses problem-solving approaches to enable community members to identify and prioritise problems, and find their own solutions, while the community worker does not impose predetermined values and beliefs upon community members.

Researchers of CBR issues in the South may wish to look to the North for different innovative methodologies. Among the many who can offer both ideological and practical help to researchers is Mike Oliver, who has written extensively about disability research methodologies in the North, especially emancipatory and participatory research (Oliver 1992). Involving disabled people with certain impairments in research can be very difficult. Here, it is helpful to turn to Parr, Byng and Gilpin's (1997) study of aphasia and disability, in which interviewers who themselves had residual dysphasic difficulties interviewed people with long-term dysphasia. This proved to be a very difficult methodological task, but one which revealed unique insights.

Here again, however, it is important to question (and encourage questioning of) the relevance of Northern methodologies to Southern contexts. Stone (1997) has explored the dilemma of how to use research methodologies developed by disabled research activists in the North when doing research outside the North (in China); and how to analyse findings within a social model of disability framework, when research participants appear to adhere to a different, more medical model of disability.

* * *

To summarise, universities of the North have a role as "conduits" to bring the rich disability literature that has developed in the North to the attention of Southern colleagues. Simultaneously, universities and professionals of the North must create spaces where different perceptions about disability and appropriate services can be shared, in the light of ideas and experiences from both North and South. In the 1990s, it is no longer sufficient or appropriate for Northern universities to prioritise the "transfer of knowledge" through courses designed for students from the South without supporting the development of critical reading and problem-solving skills among their students (Wirz 1998). After all, it is the students who will have to determine for themselves how much information is of value to their home situation, and how far (if at all) they intend to adopt and adapt Northern theories to Southern contexts.

NORTH-SOUTH TRANSFERS: PROFESSIONS AND PRACTICE

North-South transfers extend beyond the transfer of models and methodologies, reaching into the realms of professional practice and knowledge. Over the years, there has been growing recognition of the dilemmas that exist in disability-related work in countries of the South. Many of these dilemmas are linked to North-South transfers of professional training and practice.

For example, in both North and South, educational agendas have shifted from segregated, special education towards mainstream, inclusive education. But is this shift always and automatically appropriate? There may be places where school enrolment is low, and where special schools provide the only educational opportunity for disabled children. Does education in an educational ghetto and exclusion from one's own community outweigh the alternative prospect of no education at all? What is the appropriate view to take in the case of a deaf child where special education gives fluency in a language (signed or spoken) which is not used in his or her own community?

This "education dilemma" is discussed by Hartley (1995) together with other dilemmas relating to technical, social and contextual issues. Should hearing aids be provided when there are no facilities to maintain them? Should centralised services be encouraged when they result in children being brought into towns from rural areas and their own communities? Should centralised services be discouraged even though there may be no day-care or school facilities in the child's rural home community, and the child may spend much of the day locked inside whilst all other family members are out working? These are difficult decisions – hardly "choices" – which have to be made in full knowledge of the potential implications on an individual's life and life chances.

Dilemmas such as these are made yet more difficult by the pressures placed on professionals to adhere to "professional fashions". By this, we mean the way in which certain practices and approaches are promoted as the way forward in a given field. The recent emergence and promotion of "inclusive education" can be seen as one example of this. Already, many countries have signed up to the Salamanca Agreement (UNESCO 1994) in which inclusive education is promoted as the best approach in educational provision in both North and South. But is this appropriate to all countries and contexts, irrespective of other considerations? The experience of many local education authorities in Britain is that the move from special education to inclusive education is neither quick, nor easy, nor cheap. And yet, the model is being promoted worldwide, including contexts where there are few human or financial resources to support it. Isn't there a danger that the current fashion of inclusive education may be pushed and imposed on the South without appropriate, context-specific planning? If so, aren't we setting up professionals and communities to fail?

Another example of Northern fashions being transferred to Southern settings with little regard for context or culture lies with the increased status of Sign Language in the North. There are examples of expatriate rehabilitation volunteers (working on CBR programmes in the South) who have introduced an imported Sign Language to a locality (see Mba 1990 on Nigeria; Winterton 1993 on Nepal). Subsequently, local CBR programme workers have sought advice from Northern professionals on how to record the imported Sign Language so that it can be "taught" to local children, families and workers. At no point was any attempt made by the Northern or Northern/trained professionals to learn about indigenous sign languages from local deaf people, their friends and families!

The power of "professional fashions" is compounded by the often inappropriate nature of professional training provided by Northern universities to students from the South. Here, we consider the nature of professional training for therapists – mainly because therapists often play an integral part in CBR programmes.

Example: Professional training for therapists

The vast majority of professional training for therapists provided in Northern universities is, of course, conducted with Northern professionals in mind, or for those therapists in the South who will work predominantly in tertiary centres in their country. This is where the problems begin. In Britain, for example, most therapy services are rooted in the medical model of disability, which entails the following:

- disabled people are referred for assessment and then, depending on the outcome of assessment, are "treated" by professional therapists;
- services are offered FOR or TO disabled people, who are given the status of "patient" even when they are healthy individuals; and
- the focus for intervention and improvement is the "patient" – and the "patient" has a duty to respond positively to the therapy given.

The use of vocabulary like "patient" reflects the belief that it is the professional who knows what is best and who is the "expert". Since the early 1980s, disabled people have challenged the notion of "professional expertise" and have sought to redress the power imbalance between therapists and disabled people who use therapy services. The "social model of disability" has played a central role in this (Morris 1991, Swain *et al* 1993). Regrettably, despite a passing interest in shared responsibility and a nod in the direction of equality for disabled people, it is still largely the professionals who manage and arrange service delivery for disabled people in the UK and have access to the all-important resources.

Students in the South often attend courses where they are exposed to professional training and practice which may have been appropriate when the medical model reigned supreme in the North but now meets neither the needs of Northern nor Southern students. Therapists, whether they are from the North or the South, whether they spend 3/4 years training abroad or follow outdated training programmes in their own countries, are simply not being prepared for the huge changes which are taking place at grassroots level and the challenges of working with and for disabled people who use or require services. CBR in the South and community care and Direct Payments initiatives in the North make very different demands upon professional therapists compared to past notions of "professional practice" (Vasey 1996). For example, to be effective in a CBR setting, professional therapists have to:

- be prepared to "give up" their exclusive rights to knowledge about impairments to a cadre of workers without professional expertise;
- be able to work as trainers and also to support the grassroots CBR workers;
- develop referral patterns where more specialist input is required;
- continue to listen to disabled people and relate to disabling barriers rather than impairments as a basis for intervention; and
- be innovative in service planning in the face of severe resource constraints.

These are tasks for which young therapists are often ill prepared and as a consequence are often accused of lack of co-operation with CBR programmes. Newly-trained therapists in the South who experience difficulty in adapting their new (Northern) skills to community-based services are understandably inclined to turn to the relative safety of private practice (based in urban centres) rather than struggle on with community-based practice.

* * *

To summarise, if universities of the North support the move towards improving access to services for the vast majority of disabled people in the South (which is central to CBR), it surely follows that those universities should not continue to provide professional training for students from the South which concentrates upon the needs of a very small wealthy group of the population. Universities of the North act duplicitously if they profess to support inclusive services yet provide training which is more suitable for segregated settings. Finally, it is vital that the responsibility to provide information about the latest developments in thinking should be carefully balanced by an awareness of the dangers of imposing Northern "professional fashions" (models, ideologies, practices) without relating these to the economic, social, cultural and political context in question.

BENEFITS OF NORTH-SOUTH PARTNERSHIPS

The dangers and dilemmas noted, there are still a whole range of ways in which North-South partnerships can be beneficial to all concerned, both in training and in research. The following examples are drawn from our experience of partnerships at CICH.

Recently, CICH initiatives to relocate the Diploma for Trainers and Planners of CBR (taught in London for 15 years) to India and Uganda have afforded the opportunity for capacity-building and the development of strong North-South partnerships in training and teaching. The decision to relocate relates to a recognition that the different levels of service delivery and different activities in CBR require different approaches to training. The training of grassroots workers needs a contextual base and is best delivered locally by trainers who are aware of local needs, understand the local community and the wider society, and speak the local language. There is little place for outsiders in this level of training other than as supporters of trainers, or information providers (see Miles 1993 on Information Based Rehabilitation). Accordingly, CICH also supported the development of a Disability Resource Centre in Uganda as part of the relocation of the diploma course. This partnership is mutually beneficial. It enables Ugandan students to access all the information available at CICH in London; it also provides the opportunity for teachers, students and researchers based at CICH in London to access information generated in the South (e.g. on the impact of Ugandan low-cost aids).

Support has also been given to colleagues in South Africa who have taken the lead in the training of co-workers for an alternative form of service delivery through CBR (Aron 1991, Bortz 1996). From this base, trained therapists in South Africa have been inspired to become involved in training CBR workers as a way of improving access to therapy services for the whole population, rather than restricting their services to those who can access central, urban centres (Lorenzo 1994). Links with South Africa have served to highlight the unique situation which can be found there: the combination of professional and technical development together with sustained commitment provide the ingredients for innovative practices not found elsewhere (Tuomi 1994). Insights from this can inform professional training and also practice outside South Africa.

In the Philippines, all undergraduate therapy students at the University of Manila (in Occupational Therapy, Physiotherapy and Speech and Language Training) now undertake a long placement in a rural CBR programme, thus ensuring that all therapists have at least an understanding of other ways of working with disabled people (Magallona and Wirz 1994).

Meanwhile, research links with colleagues in Brazil have highlighted the very real difficulties that local professionals face in moving from a medical curative approach to community-based services. In turn, this has made Northern university-based trainers and teachers more aware of the importance of promoting service developments that meet the needs of service users and also the needs of local professionals.

It is the authors' view that universities of the North have much to offer and much to learn from working with students and colleagues in the South. For example, CICH can offer:

- teaching support to extend the range of skills of colleagues from the South, including problem-solving and active learning skills;
- good resources through libraries and increased access to the Internet;
- space to explore ideas which may not have immediate application, but which will build up an individual's body of knowledge (Baltutis 1995, Jennings 1997, Singleton 1996);
- student-centred course design, with flexible course assessment;
- opportunities to do independent research which is not unduly influenced by government or pressure from financial donors;
- peer support through university and student networks, including a forum to share perspectives and exchange information;
- networking opportunities to develop South-South as well as North-South contacts;

- an environment where their contribution is valued, and where the self-confidence that is essential for the success of research and service developments is nurtured.

In turn, Northern partners, like CICH, can gain:

- knowledge which can inform the development of community-based services in the North (e.g. awareness of the positive roles that family knowledge and strategies can play in supporting community-based services; understanding about the nature of "interdependence" in families and communities);
- a better understanding of the realities of the developing world, which can ensure that Northern training courses are appropriate to students from the South;
- a better understanding of the key questions for research in countries of the South;
- access to relevant research populations;
- access to local staff and colleagues in the South who can facilitate research; and
- opportunities for information exchange and international networking.

On this last point, it should not be forgotten that the concept of CBR promoted by the World Health Organization in the 1970s and 1980s – as a strategy to combat lack of resources and low coverage of existing services – contributed to changes in Northern countries where more community-based services were gradually introduced.

CONCLUSION

Student therapists from the South work hard to be awarded a scholarship to follow a degree course in North America, Europe or Australia. In addition, there are dynamic professional leaders in the South who work hard to establish and maintain professional training courses in their home country, often against great fiscal and medical opposition, and often influenced – for better and for worse – by Northern colleagues and courses. How might universities of the North best support these students and colleagues?

It is our contention that universities of the North have a role as facilitator in the context of strong partnerships with colleagues in the South. These partnerships can enable creative North-South links; they can also enable South-South links and, crucially, raise awareness among professional academics and practitioners in the North about service developments and contexts in the South. In turn, Northern universities can act as conduits for ideas, theories, practices and approaches from the North to the South – whilst always recognising that Northern ideas should be critically engaged with, not imposed or adopted without question. The flow of knowledge, learning and training between North and South can and should be two-way. At CICH, we reject the notion that the North has all the answers and all the best models. Indeed, the lessons learned from Southern partners are invaluable and have already influenced both teaching and research at CICH.

The challenge for Southern colleagues is to determine which lessons from the North are appropriate, and how. The challenge for universities of the North is to develop genuine partnerships and actively listen to and learn from colleagues from the South.

Finally, and in relation to CBR, the development of the concept of CBR appears to originate from observation of traditional good practice in the South. These observations were re-packaged by the World Health Organization, originally focusing on rehabilitation needs but – together with impact of contributions from disabled people themselves – the concept of CBR has since developed in diverse and dynamic ways. The process of implementing good CBR programmes must be accompanied by rigorous evaluations and constant revision to ensure appropriate development. It is the authors' view that universities of the North have a valuable role to play in nurturing the skills required to take such evaluation and revision into practice, and equip the promoters of CBR with the skills and confidence to promote best practice in partnership with disabled people. The inevitability of continued imbalance between North and South also reaffirms the need for Northerners who wish to work in countries of the South to have the opportunity to become as informed as possible, hoping to contribute to an improved track record in delivering CBR services.

REFERENCES

ARON, M. (1991), "Perspectives", *South African Journal of Communication Disorders* 38, p. 312.

BALTUTIS, D. (1995), "The Pledge of the Change Agent", unpublished MSc dissertation, Centre for International Child Health, University of London.

BORTZ M. (1996), "Training to Meet the Needs of the Communicatively Impaired Population in South Africa", *European Journal of Disorders of Communication* 31, pp. 465-75.

CAMPBELL, J. & OLIVER, M. (1996), *Disability Politics: understanding our past, changing our future*, London: Routledge.

CARPENTER (1994), "The Role of Institutions in CBR", in *Examples of Good Practice in Special Needs and CBR*, Paris: UNESCO.

CHAMBERS, R. (1997), *Whose Reality Counts: putting the first last*, London: Intermediate Technology Publications.

COLERIDGE, P. (1993), *Disability, Liberation, and Development*, Oxford: Oxfam.

DAVIS, K. (1996), "Disability & Legislation, Rights & Equality" in Hale, G. (ed), *Beyond Disability*, London: Sage.

GROCE, N. (1998), "Disability Issues in Local Culture and Beliefs: facing the issues", paper presented at the seminar on Cultural Values and Disability, Stressmann Institute, Bonn.

HARTLEY, S. (1995), "The history of Communication Therapy International", paper presented at the 1995 Annual Convention of International Affairs Association, American Speech Language Hearing Association, New Orleans, USA.

HELANDER, E. (1992), *Prejudice & Dignity: an introduction to CBR*, New York: UNDP.

ILO, UNICEF, WHO (1994), *Joint Declaration Position Paper on CBR*, Geneva: ILO.

JAFFER, R. & JAFFER, R. (1990), "The WHO-CBR Approach – Programme or Ideology: lessons from experience in Punjab, Pakistan" in Thorburn, M. & Marfo, K. (eds), *Practical Approaches to Childhood Disability in Developing Countries*, Newfoundland: Project SEREDEC.

JENNINGS, B. (1997), "The factors required for a successful partnership between Northern and local NGOs to ensure sustainability of a CBR project", unpublished MSc dissertation, Centre for International Child Health, University of London.

LANG, R. (1998), "A Critique of the Disability Movement", *Asia Pacific Disability Rehabilitation Journal* 9(1), pp. 4-8.

LORENZO, T. (1994), "The Identification of Continuing Education Needs for CBR Workers in Rural South Africa", *International Journal of Rehabilitation and Research* 17, pp. 241-51.

MAGALLONA, C. & WIRZ, S. (1994), "Transdisciplinary Approach: Is the Day of the Multitherapist with us already?", *Human Communication* 3(4), pp. 12-14.

MALLORY, B., NICHOLLS, R., CHARLTON J., & MARFO, K. (1993), Traditional & Changing Views of Disability in Developing Societies: causes, consequences, cautions, Monograph No. 53, Durham NH: World Rehabilitation Fund IEEIR.

MAYS, N. & POPE, C. (1995), "Rigour and Qualitative Research", *British Medical Journal* 311 (July), pp. 109-112.

MBA, P. (1990), "The influence of attitudes on the education of the deaf in developing countries", paper presented to the International Congress on Education of the Deaf, Rochester, NY, USA.

MENDIS, P. (1992), "Strengths & Weaknesses", paper presented at Seminar on CBR, Limura, Kenya.

MILES, M. (1993), "Service Development by Information-net Ideology", in Finkelflugel, H. (ed), *The Handicapped Community: the relation between primary health care and CBR*, Amsterdam: VU University Press.

MILES, S. (1996), "Engaging with the Disability Rights Movement: the experience of community-based rehabilitation in southern Africa", *Disability and Society* 11(4), pp. 501-517.

MORRIS, J. (1991), *Pride Against Prejudice*, London: The Women's Press.

OLIVER, M. (1992), "Changing the Social Relations of Research Production?", *Disability, Handicap & Society* 7(2), pp. 101-114.

O'TOOLE, B. (1991), "Community Involvement in Rehabilitation Programmes for Disabled Children – a Guyanese Experience", *Community Development Journal* 26, pp. 202-209.

PARR, S., BYNG, S. & GILPIN, S. (1997), *Talking About Aphasia*, Buckingham: Open University Press.

POPE, C. & MAYS, N. (1995), "Reaching the Parts Other Methods Cannot Reach: an introduction to qualitative methods in health and health service research", *British Medical Journal* 311, pp. 42-45.

RAHAMAN, F. (1997), *CBR in a Purdah Observing Province of Pakistan, Peshawar,* Pakistan: RCPD.

Al SHERHERY, S. (1995), "Social Model of Disability: A Strategy for Eastern Province of Saudi Arabia", unpublished MSc dissertation, Centre for International Child Health, University of London.

SINGLETON, T. (1997), "Diversity of Racism? Race issues in a voluntary organisation", unpublished MSc dissertation, Centre for International Child Health, University of London.

STONE, E. (1997), "From the Research Notes of a Foreign Devil: disability research in China", in Barnes, C. & Mercer, G. (eds), *Doing Disability Research*, Leeds: Disability Press.

SWAIN, J., FINKELSTEIN, V., FRENCH, S. & OLIVER, M. (eds) (1993), *Disabling Barriers, Enabling Societies*, London: Sage with the Open University Press.

THORBURN, M. (1986), "Early Intervention for Disabled Children in the Caribbean" in Marfo, K., Walker, S. & Charles, B. (eds), *Disabled Children in the Developing World*, New York: Praeger.

THORBURN, M., DESAI, P. & PAUL, T. (1992), "Service Needs of Children with Disabilities in Jamaica", *International Journal of Rehabilitation Research* 15, pp. 31-38.

TUOMI, S.K. (1994), "Speech and Language Pathology in South Africa: A profession in transition", *American Journal of Speech and Language Pathology: a journal of clinical practice*, Vol. 3 (2), May 1994.

UN (1996), *The Disability Dimension in Development Action: manual on inclusive planning,* Finland: The National Research and Development Centre for Welfare and Health.

UNESCO (1988), *Review of the Present Situation of Special Education*, New York: UNESCO.

UNESCO (1994), *Final Report of the World Conference on Special Needs: Access & Quality*, Salamanca, Spain, Paris: UNESCO.

VASEY, S. (1996), "The Experience of Care" in Hale, G. (ed), *Beyond Disability*, London: Sage.

WINTERTON, T. (1993), *Communicating with Children*, Katmandu: Redd Barna.

WIRZ, S. (1998), "The role of Northern universities in the training of CBR and other Community Disability Services", paper presented at the seminar on Cultural Values and Disability, Stressmann Institute, Bonn.

WYLLER, T. (1997), "Disability Models in Geriatrics: Comprehensive rather than Competing Models Should be Promoted", *Disability & Rehabilitation*, Vol. 19, pp. 480-483.

Evaluating Interventions

One of the most frustrating aspects of disability and development work is the lack of critical and careful evaluation of individual projects and programmes. In many ways, this is not surprising. First, project staff may not have the time, resources, energy or skills to do the kind of evaluation that would be most useful. Secondly, there is often a huge difference between "the kind of evaluation that would be most useful" and "the kind of evaluation that projects have to do to secure further funding". Thirdly, most development funders have yet to realise that a good evaluation requires extra and adequate resources.

There are many different views on what "good evaluation" looks like. For the most part, evaluation reports tend to be pithy, focused on those inputs and outputs that are basic but lend themselves to measurement. For example: how many workers were trained; how many people did they work with; how much did this cost, etc. If views and experiences from local disabled people and their families are included in the report, then this is often restricted to snapshots of success stories. All of this has a place in terms of completing formalities laid down by funders. But it doesn't tell the half of a project's story. What is needed is the kind and quality of information that will help other people and projects learn, so that wheels won't be reinvented, mistakes won't be repeated, and good practice and ideas can be replicated.

Questions should be asked about the process of a project; about the assumptions on which the project was based, and whether or not these had to be changed; about where the ideas and impetus came from; about how, and how well, disabled people were involved in different stages of the project; about what the project did and did not achieve; about how the project did or did not fit in with local culture, values and structures, and so on. All of this should be explored from the perspectives of all stakeholders, but especially seeking the views of the disabled children and disabled adults who were involved as agents or subjects.

The need to evaluate project interventions in their wider (cultural, social, structural) context, and with an eye on wider aims (like empowerment and attitudinal change) is vital. In this section of the book, the contributors strive to do just that. These are not "project evaluations" in the narrow sense of the term. Rather, they are papers that maximise the learning from specific interventions, and that use individual projects to deepen our understanding of issues around "doing disability and development" in the majority world.

OVERVIEW OF CONTRIBUTIONS

Translating Theory into Practice in a Different Cultural Context: A Bilingual Approach for Deaf Children in China

Alison Callaway's focus is an approach to educating deaf children that was developed in and for Britain, and later implemented in China (Callaway was involved in implementing and evaluating the project). Callaway situates the project in the wider context of Chinese parents' attitudes to their child's deafness, the status of sign language and of deaf people in China, and Chinese priorities in education. Callaway asks: "is transferring a foreign model to a different cultural context appropriate?"

Empowerment and CBR? Issues Raised by the South Indian Experience

Ray Lang's study begins with a useful discussion of the concept of Community Based Rehabilitation and the criticisms that have been levelled against it. CBR has become a buzzword in disability and development in the majority world. Lang's interest is how far CBR can enable disabled people's empowerment. He draws on the ideas of Paulo Freire, and preliminary findings from an evaluation of the Sourabha Project in India (its structures, strengths, weaknesses, and potential to enable empowerment).

Development, Cultural Values, and Disability: The Example of Afghanistan

Peter Coleridge looks at cultural values and a Community Based Rehabilitation programme in Afghanistan. What are "cultural values"? What happens when local culture is, or is seen as, an obstacle to the programme and to development aims? When outsider concepts like "discrimination" and "empowerment" are used? When local people are trained to be CBR workers and thereby agents of transferring outsider ideas and practices? These are some of the difficult questions explored in his paper.

DISCUSSION POINTS

- What lessons can be learned from these contributions about the rights and wrongs, risks and rewards, of transferring minority world ideas and practices to majority world settings?
- What works and what doesn't work? And why?
- What is required if project interventions are to be "empowering" or, rather, enable disabled people and the local community to empower themselves?
- How would you evaluate a community-based project? What methods and measures could you use to evaluate the process? What about the outcomes? How would you involve local disabled people in deciding what good outcomes are?
- How would you work in a context where local culture is an obstacle to the stated (and probably western) goals and process of a project?
- Should "changing attitudes" and "promoting equality" be objectives in disability and development projects? Even when promoting such goals means challenging the local culture, values and structures?
- How would you balance the need for a culturally appropriate project with views you might have on gender equality, children's rights, disabled people's rights, etc?
- Is it fair to put the responsibility for bringing about cultural and social change on local people as "agents" in a (probably outsider-funded) project?

CHAPTER 8

Translating Theory into Practice in a Different Cultural Context: A bilingual approach for deaf children in China

Alison Callaway

INTRODUCTION

In China, the last ten years have seen the beginnings of systematically organised, nationwide provision for preschool-age deaf children. The emphasis is on an aural/oral approach – providing hearing aids and speech training. While this is feasible for children with some residual hearing, it is not ideal for many children with profound hearing loss. As an experimental solution for this group, a "bilingual class" has been established in a nursery for deaf children in Nanjing. In practice, implementation of this bilingual class has been strongly influenced by its cultural context. Crucial factors are parents' attitudes to their child's deafness and its implications; and the status of deaf people and sign language in Chinese society.

This paper seeks to analyse the effects of these influences on the development of preschool deaf education in China; and to discuss key issues in terms of the different cultural perspectives and personnel involved: Western/Chinese, deaf/hearing. The paper begins with an outline of the principles and key issues of bilingual/bicultural education for deaf children as it is developing in the West, with reference to the educational and cultural context within which it has developed. The history of deaf education in China is then outlined, along with recent policies promoting auditory and speech training in preschool-age deaf children. The introduction and implementation of the bilingual class is then discussed, with feedback from English and Chinese deaf people. This is followed by a closer look at the attitudes and experiences of parents of deaf children in China, and of the status of sign language and deaf people, which emerge as key dimensions of the situation. Lastly, there is a discussion of possible directions of development of bilingual/bicultural approaches in the Chinese situation, with acknowledgement of the different viewpoints involved.

A few words about my own role seem necessary here. I have just completed a PhD thesis at the Centre for Deaf Studies at Bristol University on deaf children and their families in China; previously, I had taught at a medical college in China for several years and learnt Chinese. My proficiency in sign language is still only at a basic level: nevertheless, it has enabled me to communicate directly with deaf people in China on a few occasions – the attempt to do this (and to try and take this further) seems important. The Centre for Deaf Studies at Bristol University in the UK, where I am based, has carried out many research projects involving sign language and the deaf community, as well as initiating a bilingual/bicultural programme for deaf children in the Avon area; close research and working relationships between hearing and deaf personnel are of necessity central to these projects, and it seems important to promote these kinds of relationships in research and development projects abroad.

The project on which this paper is based is a small but innovative project for deaf children currently being developed by the Amity Foundation in China in cooperation with the Centre for Deaf Studies. The project adopts a bilingual/bicultural approach – a relatively new development in deaf education, based on a model of deafness representing cultural difference rather than medical deficit. For information, the Amity Foundation is a Chinese Christian non-governmental organisation based in Nanjing. It has introduced a range of small-scale, innovative social welfare programmes, mainly in rural poverty alleviation. Funding is obtained from church organisations in Europe and the United States, but there is no proselytising component to Amity's social welfare programmes. All staff at the Nanjing office are mainland Chinese.

BACKGROUND: UK

The development of sign bilingualism in the education of deaf children in the UK was encouraged by a number of different facilitating circumstances. A seminal event was the publication of Conrad's investigation into the educational achievements of deaf school-leavers in England and Wales (Conrad 1979), which found that after up to 12 years of education using an aural/oral approach, the majority of deaf school-leavers had poor speech and an average reading age of only nine years. Other researchers, including Gregory (1976), who interviewed the mothers of 122 preschool-age deaf children, pointed out the drawbacks of focusing exclusively on oral methodology and ignoring the possibilities of using sign language as a medium for developing communication and learning. At about the same time, specialists in linguistics in the United States and the UK were discovering the structure and properties of indigenous sign language. The hitherto invisible lives of deaf people, their culture and community, were also investigated. In the 1980s several researchers undertook detailed studies of the language acquisition, in sign, of deaf babies with deaf mothers: it became clear that acquisition of sign language went through similar stages to the acquisition of spoken language, and occurred at roughly the same time in terms of children's development.

With the recognition of sign language as a language in its own right, deaf people using sign language amongst themselves could be characterised as a separate linguistic group. This has been taken further to view deaf people as a distinct cultural entity on the basis of their identification with the deaf community, and common experiences in education and other spheres of life – often alienating or diminishing experiences in a hearing society that discriminates against them. In a radical presentation of the cultural and medical models of deafness, viewed respectively from deaf and hearing perspectives, Lane (1992) draws a parallel between the oppression of deaf people in hearing society, and the oppression and exploitation of African peoples by colonialist regimes.

In the UK, the cultural model of deafness has begun to influence educational policy; this process has been encouraged in a climate where educational provision is explicitly accommodating itself to the requirements of children from a variety of ethnic backgrounds growing up in a multicultural society. The guidelines for service managers issued by the National Deaf Children's Society are a good example of this trend. The guidelines propose that delivery of services should be viewed as a continuum, with the cultural ("difference") model at one end, and the medical ("deficit") model at the other; in practice, the two should not be regarded as mutually exclusive, and choices should be made with regard to the circumstances of individual deaf children and their families (NDCS 1992).

These, then, are the circumstances in which sign bilingualism has developed in certain areas in the UK. It is based on a particular set of values concerning deafness, the place of deaf people in society, and the nature of education. A full description of the bilingual/bicultural approach in terms of philosophy, policy and practice has been outlined in an article by Pickersgill (1997), on which the following account draws.

The **philosophy** of sign bilingualism originates in a view of deaf people as a linguistic and cultural minority within a hearing society using spoken language. Linguistic and cultural pluralism within a given society is regarded as a positive and valuable development. The tenets of sign bilingualism are congruent with a social model of disability which locates disablement in the societal response to impairment – and which predicates that empowerment of disabled people can occur when societal responses are altered in appropriate ways. For sign bilingualism, the focus of action is primarily in the education of deaf children.

Implementing a **policy** of sign bilingualism requires specific initiatives in the use of languages, in the organisation of staff, and in the involvement of parents. With regard to language, the fundamental belief is that British Sign Language is a language in its own right, equal in status to spoken English, and that it can be used in education. The aim is for children to acquire both BSL and English to high levels of proficiency. The initial emphasis is on the natural acquisition of sign language in the preschool period (the critical period for language acquisition) for use in day-to-day communication, and then building on this foundation by learning English as a second language. Children's progress in sign language is expected to be age-appropriate, in other words equivalent to hearing children's mastery of spoken English at the same age. The two languages, BSL and English, should be kept separate and used in separate situations. When English is being used/studied, Manually Coded English may usefully be used – but the exact role MCE has to play in implementing sign bilingualism is not yet clear.[1] A final feature of language use entails assessing individual children's progress and language preferences so that choices for their future provision and nature and level of communication support match the individual need.

A policy of sign bilingualism requires the involvement of deaf people. They should be involved as consultants in early intervention programmes, as classroom assistants providing language and role models in schools for the deaf, and as qualified teachers of sign language classes. More deaf people should be able to qualify as teachers of the deaf. Status, levels of pay and opportunities for training should compare favourably with those of hearing colleagues. Hearing teachers of the deaf need to have high standards of BSL in order to implement bilingualism effectively. Hearing parents of deaf children should be able to develop contacts with deaf people, and learn sign language. The aim is for parents to improve the level of sign communication at home.

The **practice** of sign bilingualism should comprise initial emphasis on a BSL-dominant approach, moving gradually towards an English-dominated approach by the time the child is in secondary school. Assessment of the effectiveness of a deaf child's education should include not only assessment of academic achievement, but also of self-esteem, of the child's sense of identity, and of communication/social skills.

The bilingual/bicultural approach to deaf education is still developing in the UK: only recently has a working model been clearly and fully described (Pickersgill 1997, Pickersgill and Gregory 1998). The model, as it has been developed so far, reflects the complexity of implementing a bilingual approach where the two languages concerned are in two different modalities. A number of difficulties have been identified: for example, parents experience difficulties and lack confidence in learning and using signs to communicate with their children (Young 1995). Within the school framework, it is difficult deciding how to keep the two languages separate, and choosing the nature and level of communication requires flexibility and sensitivity on the part of teachers to individual children. Clearly this requires constant resourcefulness on the part of teachers. There are a number of areas where policy and practice are problematic and require further definition. Further, the effective implementation of sign bilingualism undoubtedly requires substantial resources to fund all aspects of intervention and the educational programmes outlined above.

BACKGROUND: THE HISTORY OF DEAF EDUCATION IN CHINA

The first deaf school in China was started in Dengzhou, Shandong province in 1887 by Mrs Annetta Mills, the wife of an American missionary. Mrs Mills' school exerted a strong influence on deaf education in China in the first half of this century, serving as a model for other deaf schools. By 1949 there were over thirty schools for the deaf in China.

The new Communist government which took power in 1949 instigated sweeping educational reforms. Deaf schools which already existed were brought under state ownership, and each region was required to provide schools for disabled children in their area. New schools for the deaf were set up, typically in the provincial capitals or other large cities, establishing a network of schools under central control. Curricula were designed and specially written textbooks issued from Beijing (Piao 1987). Since 1949 there has been a steady increase in the number of deaf schools: there are now 980 schools for deaf and blind children in China, accommodating over 90,000 children (China Statistical Yearbook 1997; statistics for schools for the deaf and schools for the blind are presented in one category: however, schools for the blind represent only about 5% of the total figure). The vast majority of deaf children living in or near urban areas now have access to education in deaf schools. In addition, many deaf children, especially in rural areas where there are no special educational facilities, attend local mainstream schools even though they may derive little benefit from the lessons. The age for starting mainstream school in China is seven; for large urban deaf schools, the starting age is between seven and nine years of age generally speaking; however, children in the countryside may not start deaf school until they are ten or eleven or even in their teens. Until recently there has been no preschool provision for deaf children in China: the implications of this are very significant, since the critical period for language acquisition is in the early preschool years.

The aim of teaching throughout the nationwide system of deaf schools has been for children to acquire speech: but because of the severe shortage of hearing aids and other assistive technology such as speech trainers, and because children start their language learning relatively late, it has not been feasible for deaf schools to adopt a comprehensive oral policy, although there are a few deaf schools in cities such as Beijing and Shanghai which have done so. In order to teach the curriculum, a policy of using Sign Supported Chinese has been adopted.[2]

In order to teach effectively using Sign Supported Chinese, it was perceived that there had to be some standardisation of the signs in current use by deaf people all over China: these varied from area to area. A Sign Language Reform Committee was convened in 1958 to collect signs, decide on standardised versions, and issue these for use in deaf education. Deaf school teachers and members of the Chinese Deaf Association contributed to the process. After interruption of work during the Cultural Revolution, the Committee resumed and produced a series of dictionaries to support dissemination of standardised signs. The resultant body of sign vocabulary is called "Chinese Sign Language" (*Zhongguo shouyu*) or "standardised sign language" (*guifan shouyu*).

From 1988 a new state-instigated campaign got under way in deaf education. As part of a range of initiatives spearheaded mainly by Deng Pufang (the disabled son of the Chinese Premier) and the organisation he heads (China Disabled People's Federation), the 1988-1993 Workplan for Disabled People made speech training for deaf children a priority. This initiative has been focused on the preschool age-group, and the special training has been carried out through a network of rehabilitation facilities based mainly in cities. The model or models of rehabilitation of deaf children through auditory and speech training have been derived from several sources outside mainland China, not least from well-developed models in Hong Kong, and reflect a drive for "normalisation" of the deaf child chiefly through acquisition of speech, though other aspects such as healthy psychological development are also stressed. The associated technology – equipment for diagnosing deafness, and hearing aid technology – has also of necessity been imported. The teaching methodology has been developed to match Chinese educational aims and, like the curricula and teaching content of the deaf schools, is centrally defined and directed. The China Research and Rehabilitation Centre for Deaf Children in Beijing is the model for rehabilitation centres throughout China, and is constantly seeking to improve policy and practice in teaching methodology as well as prevention and therapy for treatable causes of deafness. Their quarterly publication, "Rehabilitation of Deaf Children in China" (*Zhongguo Long'er Kangfu*), publicises new developments and discusses key issues. Initially debate was focused on promoting early intervention; then on the importance of involving parents as teachers of their deaf children; the latest development is debate on how to integrate children who have attended preschool rehabilitation centres into mainstream schooling.

The characteristics of the base population of preschool-age deaf children have to be taken into account when considering provision. Large numbers of deaf children in China have acquired hearing loss due to disease or the effect of ototoxic antibiotics: they may have acquired some language before becoming deaf, and in many cases have significant levels of residual hearing. Thus early intervention with speech training is likely to enable a proportion of deaf children to acquire speech and language so they can be educated in mainstream schools. However, for those children who are congenitally deaf, and who have little or no useful residual hearing, such methods are unlikely to provide adequate early access to language. There is little in the way of alternative preschool provision for profoundly deaf children in China at present. This is the context in which the bilingual project described below was set up.

IMPLEMENTATION OF BILINGUAL/BICULTURAL PROJECT IN CHINA

Following a series of contacts between Bristol and Nanjing, a "bilingual experimental class" was established by the Amity Foundation in March 1996 within a preschool rehabilitation centre for deaf children which Amity had set up in 1991. Of the sixteen children in the centre, nine were very severely or profoundly deaf, and these children formed the first experimental class. Seven of these children were six years old; two were four years old. Every school day they would have a 40-minute storytelling session, in sign language, with a deaf teacher, a woman with many years teaching experience in Nanjing Deaf School. For the remainder of the school day, this group of children followed the regular rehabilitation centre curriculum, focusing on auditory and speech training as well as other activities such as physical exercise and art.

To support the aim of introducing sign language to deaf children and their families, a sign language class, taught by a hearing teacher from Nanjing Deaf

School, was started on Saturday afternoons: this class was expressly for parents of children in the experimental class, but was also advertised in the city newspaper as open to anyone interested in learning sign language. Most of those who enrolled in the sign language class were mothers of deaf children; there were also a few others, including an 80-year-old man, who thought it would be interesting to learn sign language.

The setting up of the bilingual class, the funding of the two teachers, and incidental arrangements, were all implemented and paid for by Amity. The amounts of funding involved were very modest – for example, a payment of £30 per month for the teacher of the class. Implementation depended on close co-operation between Amity personnel and key staff at Nanjing Deaf School who supported the concept of introducing sign language to deaf children at an earlier age, in order to improve their academic performance when they reached deaf school.

In May 1996, three months after the bilingual class had started, I visited Nanjing to assess the project and discuss its development with Amity: regular contact with personnel from the Centre for Deaf Studies in Bristol had been part of the original project proposal. Subsequently I wrote a brief report which was sent to Amity and Bristol as part of an ongoing framework of assessment, feedback and exchange of information. The teacher of the experimental class agreed to have one of her classes video'd, and the video was taken back to Bristol for deaf colleagues there to view and provide their suggestions, queries and comments. These were relayed back to the deaf teacher in China, by letter, for her to respond to: this particular interchange, between deaf teachers in China and the UK, was especially illuminating and raised a number of key issues. The main points from my 1996 report, and those brought out in the exchange of views between deaf counterparts in China and the UK, are given below.

KEY FINDINGS

Observation of the experimental class showed that the deaf teacher had excellent rapport with the nine children in her class, who were attentive and interested throughout the session. Her basic lesson plan was to tell a simple story, making extensive use of illustrations on the blackboard, to provide the children with new vocabulary and ideas through the use of sign. She used a variety of activities, including role-play and games with flash-cards, to reinforce learning of signs and written characters. It was evident that a key part of each lesson, often following the storytelling, was devoted to learning characters, phrases and sentences in written Chinese, and that at these points signs were used in the order of written Chinese to support this goal. There were several examples of the children being required to learn signs which would be redundant in living sign language.

Deaf teachers in the UK viewing the video of the class in China were generally enthusiastic, noting in particular the teacher's good relationship with the children and the great value this would have for their feelings of confidence and self-esteem. They also commented on her imaginative and artistic illustrations which they felt gave strong visual interest and support to her teaching. However, they made several more critical points. They noted the high proportion of mime in the storytelling in relation to evolved sign language; but agreed that this matched the children's lack of competence in sign at that stage and was probably appropriate to their current level. They were concerned that the teacher stood up and moved about in front of the blackboard rather than sitting down in front of the children at their level. (The Chinese teacher responded to this comment by saying that it was conventional for Chinese teachers to stand in front of their class.) The English teachers were particularly concerned at the mixing of written language with signing stories – they felt it would have been much better to exclude written language until the children were communicating well in sign and had a good foundation in sign language. This is a core observation and is returned to below.

What about parents' involvement in their children's acquisition of sign language? It transpired that although several parents may have started the sign language classes, only one parent of a child in the experimental class was still attending after three months. Observation of the sign language class showed that the class was very formal, with emphasis on the teacher demonstrating individual signs so the class could memorise them, rather than on developing competence in using sign language for communication purposes at home. This contributed to the overall impression that for the deaf children concerned, sign language and association with deaf people was limited to the daily session with their deaf teacher, and was not supported or extended by involvement of other family members. There was one exception: there appeared to be a significant change in the family of the deaf girl who had deaf parents: following the introduction of the experimental class, the relationship between the deaf girl and her mother became much closer and happier, with the mother helping her daughter read books by signing the characters with her. Previously the hearing grandmother, who was illiterate, had borne the responsibility for her granddaughter's education, with the deaf parents excluded and her mother feeling depressed that her daughter might follow her example and have to go to deaf school.

The apparent lack of involvement of hearing parents in an educational approach using sign requires closer examination. There is also a need for caution, since this is a difficult area to research. For example, parents are unlikely to say outright that they do not believe in the class, or object to a deaf teacher. More can be learnt from their behaviour, in this case lack of engagement with the programme. It should also be pointed out that with both parents working full-time, it is hard for them to find time for additional activities. With these caveats in mind, an account of parents' attitudes and views on the implications of their child's deafness is provided, based on the writer's fieldwork interviews with parents of preschool-age deaf children in China in 1994 and 1996, as well as a range of documentary sources (Callaway 1997).

PARENTS' ATTITUDES TO THEIR CHILD'S DEAFNESS

A number of professionals in the United States and the UK involved in counselling parents of deaf children have described the severe emotional reactions to the diagnosis of deafness in their child, and stressed the importance of their resolution if parents are to play a positive role in their child's development. Chinese professionals also note the traumatic impact of the diagnosis of deafness on Chinese parents, and point out that this is exacerbated by the one-child family planning regulations which produce a situation in which parents put all their hopes and expectations on their one child: diagnosis of disability in these circumstances is shattering. Unwillingness to accept their child is deaf or to consider the implications of deafness lead Chinese parents to take their child to one doctor after another, first to repeat the hearing tests in the hope that the initial diagnosis was mistaken, and then to search for a cure for deafness. With the plethora of treatments afforded by Chinese traditional practitioners (various forms of acupuncture, *qigong*, herbal medicine, etc.), there are an infinite number of treatments to try. The majority of Chinese parents expend enormous amounts of time, energy and money trying to find a cure; the effort expended in this direction detracts from efforts parents could have been making to habilitate their child (Callaway 1996).

Interviews with parents and grandparents (conducted on a one-to-one basis in their homes) showed that parents had no counselling and little guidance following diagnosis: there is no organised network of referral, and parents had to decide their own course of action. There was no well-planned provision of information, and parents generally had little contact with deaf people or knowledge of the implications of deafness. Enrolment of their child in a rehabilitation centre, when he or she was anywhere between three and seven years of age, was the crucial stage at which hearing aid use could be introduced, and systematic speech training with parental involvement could begin. Parents met teachers regularly to discuss their children, and also had meetings with other parents which enabled mutual support and exchange of useful information – including new cures for deafness as well as different educational strategies.

In interviews, parents were also asked about their views towards using sign language with their children: parents generally expressed negative views about the use of sign; parents who had to use gestures with their children to communicate because they were profoundly deaf emphasised the importance of their child learning to read and write so they could communicate through writing.

When parents enrolled their children in a preschool rehabilitation centre, their hopes were that after two or three years' speech training, their child would have enough speech to be able to attend mainstream primary school. By the time children were seven (the age when children start primary school in China, at least in urban areas), it was usually clear to teachers and parents whether the child would go to deaf school or to mainstream schooling. Severe hearing loss correlated closely with enrolment in deaf school. Of 14 children attending the centre in 1994, six went on to mainstream schooling, of whom two were considered by teachers to be unlikely to cope in that setting; one girl, whose parents lived in the countryside, dropped out of schooling altogether; and the remaining seven children went on to segregated schooling. Once placements are made it is very difficult to transfer from segregated to integrated schooling or vice versa. Thus the route taken at age seven has great significance for the child's future, and parents perceive their child has lost their chance to become a "normal" person if they have to go to deaf school. While children in deaf school learn sign language rapidly, parents tend not to learn sign, so they cannot easily support their children's education or even communicate well with them at home. More insidious are parents' persistent feelings of grief and rejection of the child's deafness.

In view of the fact that the use of sign language is a key issue in communication at home amongst families with deaf children, and in the education of children in deaf schools in China, it seems important to provide an account of the status of sign language in China. This is closely related to the status of deaf people in Chinese society, which is also considered below.

STATUS OF SIGN LANGUAGE IN CHINA

As outlined in the previous section on deaf schooling in China, a sustained and concerted effort has been made to introduce a standardised system of signs for use in deaf schools. In other words, children in deaf schools achieve literacy and obtain access to the range of curricular subjects because their teachers support the Chinese spoken/written material with signs – in the order of, and using the grammatical construction, of spoken/written Chinese, not that of indigenous sign language.

Chinese educationalists and teachers in deaf schools recognise that deaf people, and deaf children outside the classroom, often use a different order of signs to communicate than that of the spoken language:

> When Chinese deaf people use their hand shapes to communicate there are usually two ways to express their meaning. One way is to use their hand shapes following the order of the oral language. They usually use this way when they talk with normal [*sic*] people or in formal situations. The other way is to use the hand shapes without following the order of the spoken language. This way is often used among the deaf people or between them and normal [*sic*] people knowing the sign language. Those deaf people with no education or the ones who do not know Hanyu usually use this way too ... Obviously the order of words is extremely important. The deaf people will often make grammatical mistakes in their written language after they get used to the sign language (Piao 1984).

This passage raises a couple of key points about the status of indigenous sign language. It is associated with lack of education – not surprisingly, since sustained exposure to standardised sign language occurs only in the domain of segregated education in Chinese schools for the deaf. And the last sentence reiterates a belief that is voiced time and again – that the use of indigenous sign language disorganises and interferes with the comprehension and production of written Chinese. The solution is held to lie in reinforcing the use of standardised sign language and discouraging the use of indigenous sign language, until such time as high levels of education amongst deaf people will eradicate indigenous forms. In fact, the real problem for deaf children in China (and other countries) is that they have not had appropriate or adequate access to language, whether spoken or sign, in their early years, and without this they will have great difficulty mastering the use of language at a later stage. The bilingual approach is based on the theory that if deaf children learn indigenous sign language early, through a process of natural acquisition, they have a basic linguistic foundation on which they can learn a second language – the spoken/written language of their country – *as a separate language*.

Indigenous sign language in China is not only seen to be inimical to effective education, but also limited and inferior in relation to spoken language. Professor Piao Yongxin, China's acknowledged authority in special education, argues that sign language is inferior because its use is limited to deaf people and a few others; its vocabulary and range of expression is limited; abstract concepts cannot be expressed; and meanings of various signs are not exact (Piao 1992). He also states the widely-held belief that the use of (indigenous) sign language by deaf people detracts from their competence in using the written language, and from success in the educational system.

It should be noted that, while the whole process of standardising signs to achieve consistency and uniformity in use of language can be viewed as an appropriation by Chinese (hearing) educationalists of deaf people's language, it also constitutes a recognition and legitimisation of the role of sign language, particularly in education. The "reform" by committee of sign language parallels other mass reforms in language use in mainland China – the introduction of *putonghua*, the northern Chinese dialect, as China's official language; and the ongoing reform of the written language.

THE STATUS OF DEAF PEOPLE IN CHINA

As in other countries, deaf people in China are defined officially as a category of disabled people. The Chinese government has made great efforts to provide education and employment, largely through segregated facilities, for deaf people. Their rights and interests are protected through the 1990 Law for Disabled Persons, which states that disabled people have the right to full participation in their society. Although the pressure of population and severe lack of resources in China limit provision for deaf children and deaf adults, the 1990 Law represents a declaration of basic policy aims.

Deaf people in China are represented by the Chinese Deaf Association, which defines its membership in medical terms: all individuals with a hearing loss of over 40 dB are automatically members. (By contrast, membership of the deaf community in Britain, and such representative organisations as the British Deaf Association, is a matter of individual choice and reflects individual preference for the use of sign language, identity as a deaf person, and affiliation with the deaf community.) The Chinese Deaf Association has branches throughout China, and works closely with the government to implement government policy for deaf people – a current priority is providing food and clothing for deaf people in poverty-stricken areas in rural and remote parts of China (Callaway 1998). There do not appear to be the societal mechanisms for an organisation representing the interests of deaf people to adopt an independent stance, or voice any criticism or opposition to government policy in education or other areas.

As in many Western countries, deaf teachers in Chinese deaf schools have been phased out as requirements for increased levels of qualifications have made themselves felt, unmatched by complementary measures to give deaf people access to mainstream training courses. Changchun University in northern China runs courses for disabled students, including fine arts for deaf students, so many deaf schools have deaf art teachers. Deaf people may also teach vocational subjects such as sewing, or may be in administrative posts in deaf schools. But the general trend is for the few deaf teachers who have been in teaching positions to be replaced by hearing staff when they retire.

There is evidence that deaf people in China who have been or are teachers feel strongly that deaf people have particular qualities which make them especially effective as teachers of deaf children. Liu Zhenxing, a deaf man who is one of the few deaf people in China to have completed a teacher training course, states in a newsletter for parents of deaf children that deaf teachers provide deaf children with a positive example of an academically and professionally successful deaf person: this kind of encouragement prevents the development in deaf children of psychological problems such as low self-esteem and lack of confidence (Liu 1996).

VALUES AND PRIORITIES

It should be evident from the account given above that the implementation of bilingual/bicultural concepts in a programme for deaf children in China has been influenced by a different set of values and priorities than in the UK. A closer look at these may indicate the direction of development of sign bilingualism in China.

Deaf teachers in Bristol and deaf teachers in Nanjing believed that deaf teachers were very important for the successful education of deaf children. The UK teachers stressed early use of sign language at home, and the use of sign language for communication with other deaf children and deaf adults. The Chinese deaf teachers consulted put much more emphasis on the importance of deaf children succeeding in the educational system: since this meant achieving knowledge of Chinese, their emphasis was on the value of sign as support for learning to read and write Chinese, from an early age. The use of sign language for communication, informal conversation, exchange of ideas or play seemed far less significant to them.

For hearing teachers in the Chinese deaf school system, the main priority is seen as improving educational standards and increasing the number of deaf children who can graduate at high school level. To achieve this, it is felt necessary for children to start learning at a younger age, and to learn standardised Chinese Sign Language in order, so the reasoning goes, that they might learn Chinese better. Since the implementation of the programme discussed here depended on the support of hearing senior teachers in the deaf school, it is likely that this view will prevail. (If deaf children are brought together at a younger age, they will of course sign amongst themselves and develop their own ways of signing which will depart from standardised forms – natural signing cannot be suppressed.)

IS TRANSFERRING A FOREIGN MODEL TO CHINA APPROPRIATE?

It seems important to address the general issue as to whether it is appropriate to introduce a model for deaf education derived from experience in different cultural situations into the Chinese context. The alternative would be adoption of models developed wholly in China.

In practice, over the last ten years China has been actively encouraging other countries with more evolved special educational provision to provide information, expertise and relevant technology so that China can develop its own special educational services. In other words, there has been a strong initiative from Chinese professionals themselves to seek advice and assistance in this area. For example, the national model for preschool rehabilitation of deaf children, based on an aural/oral approach, developed with extensive input from abroad. A typical procedure is for new approaches or new technology to be acquired from other countries, then adapted by Chinese professionals to suit Chinese institutions, established practices and priorities. Thus, unless a particular approach is introduced under the aegis of a foreign NGO (non-governmental organisation) and is kept largely under the NGO's immediate control, it is characteristic for new practices to be adapted and reformulated by Chinese agents for use in Chinese settings. In this sense, it is unlikely an imported model could be imposed inappropriately since control over implementation at different levels is in Chinese hands. In educational settings, "experimental classes" are accepted ways of trying out a new approach and seeing which elements may need adapting.

In the particular case of the project described in this paper, the involvement of a Chinese NGO – the Amity Foundation – has been crucial. The Chinese NGO staff are familiar with the local situation and the network of professionals involved. They can therefore negotiate steps of implementation more diplomatically and more effectively than Western professionals who do not have the support of well-placed and expert Chinese counterparts. In the context of this jointly managed project, the Amity Foundation are in the position of being able to modify elements of the project they consider unrealistic or inappropriate, or emphasise aspects they consider particularly important, thereby introducing an effective filter or buffer to the introduction of outside concepts or practices. In fact, in this project the Chinese NGO has generally been keen not to dilute or modify the original concepts, which however may yet alter considerably in the process of implementation.

The project discussed in this paper had three basic aims – to affirm the status of deaf people and indigenous sign language; to build a positive sense of deaf-identity in deaf children and enhance their self-esteem; and to improve their access to language and learning. The first two aims are strongly emphasised in UK bilingual programmes. However in China, it seems likely that due to the difficulty of challenging entrenched prejudice against deafness (also present in other countries), these first two aims can only be tackled gradually, while on the other hand the third aim will have particular appeal for teachers trying to raise standards of academic attainment, and parents who want their children to succeed at school. Given the enormous value attached to education in Chinese culture, and the priority given to expanding educational provision in government policies, it may well be appropriate to focus on the third aim in making the project appealing and acceptable to those involved. In other words, how the bilingual programme is presented to parents and teachers and the manner in which it is implemented is significant, and presentation and implementation need to be closely matched and responsive to the concerns of those involved.

PROJECT UPDATE & FUTURE DIRECTIONS

Since the first draft of this paper was written, further steps have been taken to bring the principles and practice of a bilingual/bicultural approach to the attention of Chinese professionals. In March 1998, a three-day training session was held in Nanjing for teachers and administrators from 24 deaf schools in Jiangsu province. At the meeting, particular emphasis was placed on the detailed practical steps that need to be taken within a given school to implement a bilingual approach effectively. This included detailed discussion of management structures within schools, so deaf staff are on a par with hearing staff and so there are explicit mechanisms in place to ensure good practice. There was also specific and detailed discussion of the use of sign language in children's learning, with examples of vocabulary lists for each age level and of schemes to assess individual children's progress in reading and writing. This kind of specific treatment of concerns relevant to teachers seems to be a necessary and practical way of motivating teachers and administrators to consider change in their particular schools.

In addition to supporting implementation of sign bilingualism in the deaf school system, a research agenda is also proposed. Based in the Linguistics Department at Nanjing Normal University, sign language research is planned which will involve deaf people as research partners. The aim is to promote research into the characteristics of indigenous sign language used by deaf people amongst themselves, and thus to strengthen the possibility of its official recognition as a true language. Research is also required to develop appropriate assessment measures for use in schools so that aspects of learning using a bilingual approach can be properly evaluated.

A major area that has yet to be given more attention is the involvement of parents. Whichever educational approach is used, work with parents is crucial to support good communication at home, and to promote effective co-ordination with learning in school.

In all these areas it is appreciated that challenges will arise just as they do in the UK context. It seems feasible to suggest that solutions can be found in the experience of Western professionals which may be useful in China – provided they are implemented with sensitive regard to the specific characteristics of the Chinese context. If the planned steps for research and for implementation in schools can be carried out effectively, then valuable and constructive changes for the adults and especially the children concerned should ensue.

CONCLUSION

In conclusion, it is to be hoped that more deaf people in China will be able to become involved in the education of deaf children – in preschool, deaf school and mainstream settings. If deaf children are able to have good access to sign language in their early years, and if the importance of acquiring a good foundation in sign language as a language of daily communication is recognised, then deaf children are likely to be far more successful in school when they start to learn to read and write. Perhaps most important of all, parents will acquire more positive images of deafness and deaf people so they will be more likely to accept their child's difference as well as maintain their expectations that their child will succeed academically and have a positive role in their society.

END-NOTES

[1] In Manually Coded English, signs from British Sign Language together with finger spelling are used in the word order of spoken English. In educational settings MCE can be used to facilitate access to English text.

[2] Sign Supported Chinese (English terminology, by analogy with Sign Supported English) is a communication system whereby signs taken from Chinese sign language together with fingerspelling are used in the order of spoken Chinese to supplement spoken words.

REFERENCES

CALLAWAY, A. (1996), "Chinese Parents Search for a Cure for Deafness", TALK 159, pp.15-16.

CALLAWAY, A. (1997), *Deaf Children and Their Families in China*, unpublished PhD dissertation, University of Bristol.

CALLAWAY, A. (1998), "Chinese Government Gives Positive Lead", *British Deaf News* February issue, p.9.

CHINA STATISTICAL YEARBOOK (1997), Beijing: China Statistical Publishing House.

CONRAD, R. (1979), *The Deaf School Child*, London: Harper Row.

GREGORY, S. (1976), *The Deaf Child and his Family*, London: George Allen & Unwin.

LANE, H. (1992), *The Mask of Benevolence: Disabling the Deaf Community*, New York: Knopf.

LIU ZHENXING (1996), "Qian tan longren canyu longxiao jiaoyu" ("Notes on the Participation of Deaf People in Deaf Education"), *Long'er jiating kangfu xinxi (Rehabilitation News for Families With Deaf Children)*, a newsletter for parents of deaf children in Nanjing.

NATIONAL DEAF CHILDREN'S SOCIETY (1992), *Deaf Children, the Children Act and Care in the Community: Guidance for service managers in social services, education and health*, London: NDCS.

PIAO YONGXIN (1984), "The Deaf and Sign Language in China", paper presented at the International Sign Language Workshop, University of Bristol.

PIAO YONGXIN (1987), "China, People's Republic of", entry in Van Cleve, J. (ed), *Gallaudet Encyclopedia of Deaf People and Deafness*, McGraw-Hill.

PIAO YONGXIN (principal ed) (1992), *Zhongguo shouyu: jiaoxue fudao (Chinese Sign Language: A Study Guide)*, Beijing: Huaxia chubanshe.

PICKERSGILL, M. (1997), "Towards a Model of Bilingual Education for Deaf Children", *Deafness and Education (JBATOD)* 21(3), pp. 10-19.

PICKERSGILL, M. and GREGORY, S. (1998), *Sign Bilingualism*, Wembley, Middlesex: LASER.

YOUNG, A. (1995), *Family Adjustment to a Deaf Child in a Bilingual Framework*, unpublished PhD thesis, University of Bristol.

CHAPTER 9

Empowerment and CBR? Issues raised by the South Indian experience

Raymond Lang

INTRODUCTION

Community-Based Rehabilitation (CBR) and empowerment are critical issues in contemporary discourse within both development studies and disability studies. These issues have long been fraught with controversy, yet there remains little understanding of how CBR and empowerment interrelate, not only within programmes but also in a normative sense. There is even less understanding of what the outcomes would be were Non-governmental Organisations (NGOs), governments and the international development community to make empowerment a central tenet of practice in disability provision in developing countries.

In the first part of this paper, and by way of background, I review the main definitions and criticisms of CBR (CBR may have gained common currency in developing countries and international development agencies, but it is not a term that is frequently used in the industrialised countries of the North). Secondly, I examine the critical dimensions of the relationship between CBR and empowerment. Can CBR be empowering? Thirdly, I draw on some lessons learned from a CBR programme near Bangalore in South India. The case-study is based on data gathered as part of my doctoral research. It must be emphasised that this paper offers a preliminary and tentative analysis only, since my research is still in process. Even so, I believe that some interesting observations can be made that will help to move the empowerment/CBR debate forward.

COMMUNITY-BASED REHABILITATION: WHY?

The past two decades have witnessed the emergence and development of Community-Based Rehabilitation (CBR) as a strategy for disability-related service provision in countries of the developing world. The prime objective is to improve the quality of life of the majority of the world's disabled people: those who live in absolute and relative poverty in urban and, especially, rural areas in developing countries. In effect, CBR was born out of a recognition that unless there was a substantial change in disability service provision in Asia, Africa and Latin America, the vast majority of disabled people would never benefit from any services whatsoever.

The services which did exist tended to emulate western models of health-care provision: rehabilitation professionals, working in institutions with state-of-the-art medical technology. Services, as in the west, were rooted in a medical model of disability, prioritising diagnosis and therapy interventions. In addition, there was a fundamental mismatch in the allocation of human and financial resources devoted to disability service provision: most people lived in rural areas, yet the vast majority of services were located in large cities, for the benefit of the urban élites. Meanwhile, demand for services was rising.

CBR was held up as the best way forward. CBR would expand disability service provision through establishing working partnerships between local communities, disabled people and their families, governments and rehabilitation professionals. Such partnerships would use local (mostly human) resources to provide basic rehabilitation to a larger number of people than had ever been possible. It was felt to be better to provide basic rehabilitation to the many, than to provide high-tech services to the few.

DEFINITIONS OF CBR

As with many other fields within development work, there is a high degree of definitional controversy and lack of clarity as to what CBR *actually is*. As Wolffers and Finkenflügel have argued (1993), this may be explained by power conflicts between different interest groups, fostered by competition for financial resources from donor agencies. In order to give a flavour of the range of definitions that exist, a few examples are listed below.

> The goal of CBR is to demystify rehabilitation and to give responsibility back to the individual, the family and the community. It draws on existing organisations and infrastructure for the provision of services, by recruiting and training local supervisors from the community. .... Simple rehabilitation techniques are delegated to auxiliaries and volunteers .... CBR attempts to involve the community in the planning, implementation and evaluation of the programme. ... The intention is that rehabilitation is perceived as an integral part of the community's own development efforts. Only when a community takes responsibility for the integration of its disabled people can the process be truly called community-based rehabilitation (O'Toole & Maison-Halls 1994, p. 25).
>
> Community-based rehabilitation (CBR) is a response, in both developed and developing countries, to the need for adequate and appropriate rehabilitation services, to be available to a greater proportion of the disabled population. It aims to rehabilitate and train disabled individuals, as well as to find ways to integrate them into the communities. In CBR, the disabled person, the family, the community, and health professionals collaborate to provide services in a non-institutionalised setting, and in an environment or community where services for disabled persons are seriously limited or totally absent. Its essential feature is its focus on partnership and community participation (Peat 1991).
>
> Community-based rehabilitation (CBR) is a strategy for enhancing the quality of life of disabled people by improving service delivery, by providing more equitable opportunities and by promoting and protecting their human rights [...] It calls for the full and co-ordinated involvement of society: community, intermediate and national. It seeks the integration for the interventions of all relevant sectors – educational, health, legislative, social and vocational – and aims at the full representation and empowerment of disabled people. It also aims at promoting such interventions in the general

> systems of society, as well as adaptations of the physical and psychological environment that will facilitate the social integration and self-actualisation of disabled people (Helander 1993, p. 8).
>
> CBR is a process to bring about a transformation in the community (change in attitude, knowledge and skills), to enable community members to have a better understanding of disability services (medical, preventive, psychological, economic, socio-cultural, educational, etc.) and to improve the quality of life of persons with disability (Spastics Society of Tamil Nadu 1993, p. 7).
>
> Community-Based Rehabilitation is a strategy within community development for the rehabilitation, equalisation of opportunities and social integration of all people with disabilities. CBR is implemented through the combined efforts of disabled people themselves, their families and the appropriate health, education, vocational and social services (ILO, UNESCO & WHO 1994, p. 1).

As much as the emergence and development of CBR has been characterised by competing definitions, it has also been characterised by strong criticism.

CRITIQUES OF THE CBR CONCEPT

During the last 20 years, the majority of countries in the developing world have established CBR programmes, sometimes using the WHO approach, sometimes developing other versions of CBR. Many with experience of trying to "do" CBR at the grassroots, along with academics and other practitioners, have questioned its philosophy and efficacy. Some of the main criticisms are set out below.

• CBR hasn't really involved disabled people and local communities

All the definitions cited above highlight the critical role of the local community, including local disabled people, in CBR. Yet it has to be admitted that many CBR projects have in fact been managed and directed with few real inputs from the community and disabled people. Instead, the pre-existing medical approach has been adapted and applied within community settings. While the rhetoric of CBR promotes community decision-making and a "bottom-up" approach, the reality of CBR is often (although not always) "top-down": rehabilitation professionals are still the decision-makers. In these cases, participation is seen as a long-term goal rather than a prerequisite for disability service provision.

- **CBR tends to be medical and technical, not social and political**

Another key element in many visions of CBR is the understanding that disability is essentially a human rights issue. Yet CBR programmes based on the WHO model (and variations on the same theme) have generally advocated a medical, technocratic approach, and have completely excluded the social and political dimensions of disability. As Wolffers and Finkenflügel argue:

> One could summarise the WHO-CBR as dispersing basic rehabilitation techniques to communities and people with disabilities. The model is very much based on improvement of functions such as walking, cooking etc. The rehabilitation worker plans the training and the community facilitates and carries it out. ... Some professionals understand CBR as an outreach system in which they leave their institutions and come near to the community. They have not understood, or have not agreed, that the community's participation and decision-taking are at the heart of the concept (Wolffers & Finkenflügel 1993, pp.7, 9).

Or, in Susie Miles's words:

> CBR has been packaged and marketed from a western individualistic perspective and there tends to be a strong focus on correcting or minimising the impairments of individual disabled people. Focusing exclusively upon rehabilitation needs of individuals is likely to be counter-productive unless the informal support networks and the basic needs of the whole community are recognised and addressed (Miles 1996, p. 503).

The dominance of a medical focus has been compounded by the WHO's promotion of its training manual, which stressed the technical aspects of delivering rehabilitation (Helander *et al* 1989). If the manual is used uncritically, local services may develop in a way which ignores the surrounding social, economic and political contexts.

Fortunately, this narrow medical focus is starting to change, and more programmes now encompass employment, education and human rights as well. Even WHO has widened its perspective (ILO, UNESCO, WHO 1993).

- **CBR depends on a simplistic notion of "community"**

CBR advocates have been criticised for an apparent assumption that local communities are benevolent, homogeneous, willing to get involved in meeting the needs of some of the most marginalised members of their community, and have adequate resources to do so. But in many communities in developing countries, people struggle for survival. In addition, negative social attitudes to impairment can act against effective community participation:

> The difficulty with the classic CBR approach is that it assumes a rather bland view of community action in which the entire community – family, neighbours, health service, social workers, local authorities, employers, etc. – all play their part in recognising the needs of disabled people (Coleridge 1993).

- **CBR doesn't leave room for appropriate institutional services**

Another criticism of CBR is the stark dichotomy that has been drawn between institutional and community-based services. Miles has highlighted some of the positive aspects of rehabilitation located in day-care centres, such as the visibility of the rehabilitation process and the need for respite care for family members (M. Miles 1985).

- **CBR is not a cheap option**

Finally, several commentators have questioned the sustainability of CBR. CBR was conceived as a low-cost strategy, but many have found it to be high-cost. Good services (incorporating good follow-up and the necessary infrastructure in staff and transport) make considerable demands on resources (Finkenflügel 1993). An International Labour Organization review of 10 years experience in CBR revealed that the ILO could not name one programme that had been fully sustainable after external funding had been withdrawn (Momm & König 1989).

CAN CBR BECOME A TOOL FOR EMPOWERMENT?

Notwithstanding the criticisms described above, it is my contention that CBR *has the potential* to be an important instrument and catalyst for real social change ... change that gives rise to a new "social consciousness" in the community, and that ensures that disabled people attain full citizenship.

> Too often the tacit objective of rehabilitation – especially when approached from the top down – is to normalise disabled persons into the existing and discriminatory society. By contrast, the goal of the alternative, bottom-up approach is to empower disabled persons to join into an organised struggle of all disadvantaged and marginalised groups, to change our present society into one that is fairer, more truly democratic and more accepting of human differences (Werner 1995, pp. 24-25).

If this is to happen, there must be a quantum shift in how CBR is perceived and, crucially, in the roles of all professionals involved.

David Werner, a disabled activist who has spearheaded the establishment of community-based disability services that are run and managed by disabled people in Mexico, has outlined several key factors which can help make empowerment a reality in CBR (Werner 1995, pp. 26-27):

- CBR should be "based, planned, and managed within the community itself";
- CBR requires setting the "skills pyramid...on its side so that disabled persons and family members become front-line workers ... mid-level rehabilitation workers become facilitators and back-up persons rather than 'supervisors' ... rehabilitation professionals are on tap but not on top";
- Rehabilitation (and other) professionals need to "involve their disabled partners ... in defining and resolving their needs"; and "encourage their participation and leadership in the planning, administration, delivery and evaluation of rehabilitation services" (Werner 1995, pp. 26-27).

CBR should be redefined to encompass "community development". CBR workers and health-care professionals should become enablers and facilitators – facilitating effective community participation by disabled people, their families and others. They should engage in genuine dialogue with disabled people and the community, to establish what their needs and aspirations are, and to support disabled people in the achievement of their aims. This way of working would have revolutionary implications for the structure and management of community disability services throughout the developing world, because it would completely transform the notion of "professionalism" within health-care management.

Historically, the culture of professionalism (especially in medical fields) has been based upon the acquisition and application of "expert knowledge" gained through formal training. This model places a high premium upon solving problems through the correct application of pre-determined rules governed by the scientific method. Such a model leaves little room for alternative methods of achieving specified aims; and seldom recognises that selection of solutions is socially determined. All of this reinforces hierarchical forms of decision-making and acts against the effective involvement of disabled people and their families in programmes such as CBR. Yet, as has already been stated several times, effective community participation (and thereby the empowerment of disabled people) will only be realised when disabled people become aware of their abilities to achieve within the social contexts of their local communities. The next question is: how? How can professionals promote empowerment within CBR?

CBR & EMPOWERMENT: LEARNING FROM PAULO FREIRE

Practitioners within CBR programmes, wishing to pursue policy and practice that genuinely empower disabled people may benefit from considering the work of the Brazilian educationist, Paulo Freire (see Freire 1970).

Freire maintained that social transformation and the liberation of oppressed, marginalised groups in any society can only be realised when such groups come together to reflect on their situation (past and present) and collectively plan for change. This process can take place irrespective of the degree of oppression experienced, as long as an effective learning environment exists.

What makes an effective learning environment? The answer is "praxis". Here, it is helpful to distinguish between *practice* and *praxis*. Practice is about what people do. Praxis is the dynamic interaction between theory and practice, between knowledge and action, between reflection and doing. And reflection is as vital as action:

> Only by starting with the issues on which the community have strong feelings – hope, fear, worry, anger, joy, sorrow – and bringing these to the surface, will we break through the deadening sense of apathy and powerlessness which paralyses the poor [and disabled people] in many places (Hope & Timmell 1993, p. 17).

There are two prerequisites for grassroots social transformation. First, liberation (empowerment) can only be achieved through a collective (group) process, since: "Liberation is a social act" (Freire & Shor 1987, p. 109). It requires collective understanding of shared interests and the collective identification of a strategy for social change, realised through collective means. Furthermore, empowerment cannot be *given* to an oppressed group.

Secondly, the role of the facilitator (be s/he a disability activist, a rehabilitation professional, a CBR worker, a grassroots development worker, a social researcher, etc.) is radically different from other professional roles. The facilitator (Freire uses the terms "revolutionary educator" or "teacher-student") is a co-learner:

> In problem-posing education, people develop their power to perceive critically the way they exist in the world with which and in which they find themselves; they come to see the world not as a static reality, but as a reality in process, in transformation ... Hence, the teacher-student and the student-teachers reflect simultaneously on themselves and then on themselves and the world without dichotomizing the reflection from action, and thus establish an authentic form of thought and action (Freire 1970, p. 64).

In CBR terms, disabled people, the local community and CBR professionals would interact with each other. Through this interaction, the potential of disabled people becomes more fully recognised by themselves and their community. Thereby disabled people are enabled to empower themselves, secure their human rights, and make the decisions that directly affect their lives.

In current CBR practice, there are already some examples of this process underway. One important mechanism is the promotion of genuine partnerships between CBR programmes and disabled people's organisations. This strategy has been used in southern Africa by Save the Children (UK).

Susie Miles (1996) has described how, when disabled adults and parents have been centrally involved in the design and development of CBR, the programme priorities have shifted from medical rehabilitation to education, employment and poverty alleviation. Thereby, CBR programmes have become more consumer-focused, while disability has become recognised as a development issue, not a medical or technical individual problem. Miles goes on to make the powerful argument that:'

> community-based rehabilitation is in danger of repeating the mistakes of institutional-based rehabilitation (IBR) if it does not enter into genuine consultation with disabled people's organisations (Miles 1996, p. 501).

Changing the process and management of CBR programmes along the lines suggested by David Werner, Paulo Freire and Susie Miles – which are clearly in keeping with a social model of disability (Oliver 1990) – could potentially improve the quality, and equality, of life of disabled people in developing countries significantly. Such changes would also entail the redefinition of indicators of "good CBR" from an empowerment perspective:

> The long-term value of any rehabilitation or development effort must be evaluated in terms of how much it empowers marginalised groups and moves us towards fairer, more fully democratic structures (Werner 1995, pp. 24-25).

A CASE STUDY FROM INDIA: SOURABHA CBR PROJECT, KANAKPURA

The previous section proposed a process for change for CBR's future development. But how feasible is that process in terms of its operationalisation?

One of the CBR projects I have linked with in the course of my fieldwork has been attempting to undertake that crucial transition from a service-providing organisation dominated by a medical approach, to an organisation which acts as facilitator first, provider second. In this section, then, I outline the progress that has been made to date, indicating where there appear to be difficulties. Again, it must be emphasised that data analysis is still in its early stages.

BACKGROUND TO THE SOURABHA CBR PROJECT

The Sourabha CBR Project is managed and run by the Shree Ramana Maharishi Academy for the Blind in Bangalore. "Sourabha" is derived from the ancient Sanskrit word for "fragrance", since fragrance brings pleasure to all without discrimination. The project is located in Kanakpura, a medium-sized town some 54 kilometres south of Bangalore, in the largest taluk (or district) in the State of Karnataka. At the end of 1997, the project was providing services to approximately 1,700 disabled people in 147 villages (total population of 154,000).

The project started in July 1990 with funding from ActionAid (India) for 10 years. Initially, emphasis was placed upon providing services in the areas of health and medical rehabilitation, nutrition and awareness raising. However, two years after the project first started, education, vocational training and income generation programmes were also added.

In 1993, the Disability Division of ActionAid (India) conducted a mid-term evaluation. The findings showed that services were mostly provided in a very "top-down" manner. Rehabilitation professionals provided services that they thought met the needs of disabled people, without consulting local people themselves. As a result, local people were recipients not participants and contributors in the programmes (AAIDD 1997). In the light of these criticisms, and spurred on by prospect of complete financial withdrawal by ActionAid (India) in 2002, the project managers worked with ActionAid (India) to re-draft the programme priorities and devise a strategy that would work towards project management and implementation by disabled people and the local community, supported by a much reduced team equipped to provide technical assistance.

The emphasis of the project shifted from being exclusively concerned with service provision to prioritising community development. It was hoped that these organisational changes would transform the role of disabled people from being passive recipients of services to "active stakeholders in most of its programmes" (AAIDD 1997, p. 9), as the revised aims and objectives illustrate.

Revised Aim

To empower persons with disabilities, enhance their quality of life, and integrate them into the societal mainstream.

Revised Objectives

> To provide comprehensive medical, education and vocational rehabilitation services to 950 persons with a disability in the age group 0–50 years in 147 villages covering a radius of 40 kilometres, from the project office in Kanakapura.
>
> To sustain CBR programmes in 5 hoblies in Kanakpura District by 2002 A.D. through formation and strengthening of local groups, providing training and sensitisation to local groups in disability rehabilitation, management and networking.
>
> To generate income through income generation activities and raise funds from local and external sources for sustainability of CBR programmes in the community (AAIDD 1997, p. 7)

The aim of the project is "to empower persons with disabilities". This, however, is not possible from a Freirean perspective nor according to many disabled people and their organisations (see Campbell & Oliver 1996), on the basis that people can only empower themselves.

Sourabha's management team, in collaboration with ActionAid (India) and after an extended three-year period of consultation with the community, have now established a three-tiered hierarchy of self-supporting groups, predominantly made up of disabled people and their families, who will ultimately run the CBR project. These groups are: the Amarjyothi Disabled Persons' Association, the Hobli Rehabilitation Committees, and the Self-Help Groups (these are detailed below). A community organisation sector has also been established to spearhead this initiative. In addition to the three groups described above, the Sourabha management team has been making concerted efforts to make links within the local community. For example, representations have been made to the Lions and Rotary Clubs in Kanakpura, to local government departments and local youth clubs.

Amarjyothi Disabled Persons' Association (ADPA) is charged with overall responsibility and project management (including planning, monitoring, resource mobilisation, networking and evaluation). It is envisaged that this group will ultimately take over the role currently played by the management team of Sourabha. ADPA also acts as a pressure group at the taluk (district) level, to influence policy on disability and rehabilitation services. ADPA's membership is elected by the Hobli Rehabilitation Committees and the Self-Help Groups.

There are five Hobli Rehabilitation Committees (HRCs) – a "hobli" is a group of villages. The HRCs are envisaged to comprise an informal group of key players/resource persons within the community who can develop the local CBR project. HRC members might be elected representatives of local panchayats (local councils), the medical officer of the local primary health-care centre, the headteacher of the local school, village leaders, and members of the Self Help Groups. HRCs co-ordinate the activities of the CBR programme, thereby taking on the responsibilities currently performed by Sourabha's CBR Sector Co-ordinators (e.g. networking, resource mobilisation, prevention and awareness programmes, supporting ADPA and the Self-Help Groups).

It is also planned to set up a Self-Help Group for every cluster of 20 villages involved in the CBR project. Ten groups have been established so far. The group are conceived as the first step in preparing disabled people to become actively involved in the management and running of the CBR programme, with the objective of securing long-term sustainability at the grassroots. Ideally, the groups will be entirely made up of local disabled people, but in cases where the disabled person is a child, or where disability is severe, then a family member may represent the interests of that individual. The Self-Help Groups will identify the rehabilitation and other needs of disabled people living within their vicinity, taking on the role previously done by the CBR worker. Each group democratically elects four office bearers (President, Secretary, Treasurer and Convener) who are then appointed as representatives on ADPA and the Tuluk Rehabilitation Committees. Each member of the Self-Help Group pays a monthly subscription fee, which is then put into a revolving loan-fund for rehabilitation. Loans are repaid on an agreed basis with a 1-3% monthly interest rate.

Financial resources have been injected by ActionAid (India) to sustain the Self-Help Groups during the initial start up phase. However, it is envisaged that the entire structure will be self-sustained by 2002, when ActionAid (India) and the Sourabha management plan to withdraw. Even after withdrawal, it is expected that a small technical team will remain to give expert advice ("on tap, not on top") and support to ADPA to maintain the quality of services provided. The staff and running costs will, it is hoped, be met from the profits of income generation programmes.

SOURABHA: EMERGING ISSUES

In 1997 (March/April, and again in November), I conducted interviews with the officers of the Sourabha project teams as well as disabled people involved in the programme (some as staff, some as beneficiaries also). What follows is based on preliminary analysis of these interviews and personal observations. Most of the interviews took place approximately one year after the introduction of the new structure.

One intuitively feels uneasy when CBR programme managers suddenly start making pronouncements about the active involvement of disabled people in managing and running a project. One is left with the suspicion that the real driving force behind the Sourabha project's structural reorganisation is the need to ensure financial sustainability after 2002, when ActionAid (India) withdraws its financial support. Even if this is not so, it is important to question the many assumptions that underpin the planned involvement of disabled people.

Sourabha's revised plan assumes that, given the correct dosage of training from Sourabha staff, local disabled people will have the skills, capacity and inclination to manage and implement the CBR programme. Yet interviews revealed that many disabled adults had experienced a high degree of negative social attitudes from other community members, and so had very low expectations of their own capabilities. Many local disabled people expressed resignation to their own "fate" and that their needs would always be met through charity. Evidence also suggests that even the training provided to those disabled people in Self-Help Groups has been handled in a very "top-down" manner. Sourabha's Community Sector Co-ordinator, who is blind, stated in an interview that skills training involves himself telling trainees what their needs and priorities should be.

Other worrying signs emerged from focus-group interviews with Self-Help Groups. Even though these groups had been established for over one year, meeting fortnightly, disabled people were still unclear as to their role. It became clear that these groups mostly discussed how to get their own disability pensions and allowances. There was little comprehension of how they might develop into the front-line CBR workers envisaged by the Sourabha management team. This was the case despite the fact that existing CBR workers attended every meeting.

A further area for concern is Sourabha's apparently over-optimistic view of the role that can be played by the community – especially local government officials – in providing community-based disability services. Indeed, one of the strongest messages to come out of focus-group interviews with disabled people was that corruption was rife among officials in the local panchayats. Instances were cited where disabled people had to bribe officials to receive their disability pension or allowance.

The Sourabha CBR programme is evidence that the operationalisation of empowerment in CBR is fraught with difficulties. This is perhaps to be expected. Several writers (Long & Long 1992, Hammersley 1995) have questioned how far the translation of theory into practice is possible in relation to social and economic policy. Also, the process of change is inherently political and will have a differential impact on different "stakeholders" who have different interests and agendas.

Recognising the politics of CBR is vital. For example, claims may be made about the advantages of a project which solely serve to buttress the position of a particular stakeholder. Is the clamour for grassroots involvement of disabled people in CBR always an accurate reflection of grassroots demands? Or might it sometimes be led by those, such as local officials and NGOs, who seek to pass the financial buck to local people in the name of long-term sustainability?

In summary, it seems that Sourabha has restructured the project in name only, and based the restructuring on an ill-conceived and limited understanding of the processes of social change and empowerment, and the nature of genuine partnership and involvement. There are few signs that the consultation process initiated by Sourabha has been effective in ascertaining the needs, aspirations of disabled people within the community. There is little evidence that local disabled people have felt supported to empower themselves (or even see self-empowerment as an objective) through the CBR programme.

ADDITIONAL BARRIERS TO EMPOWERMENT THROUGH CBR

Within the wider context of India, other barriers can also be identified which work against the genuine involvement of local disabled people and their organisations in development projects like the Sourabha CBR programme.

First, legislation has been passed by the Government of India which has been criticised by some local NGOs as stultifying a developmental approach to disability and rehabilitation. The Rehabilitation Council of India Act (1992) established a statutory body, the Rehabilitation Council of India (RCI), to monitor the training and activities of those working in the field. So, all rehabilitation training courses now have to be certified by the RCI. Yet this goes against the principle of building and using local (rather than outside and expert) resources. The Act also discourages a holistic approach and a focus on basic rehabilitation carried out by family members or workers without formal medical expertise. In setting the agenda for rehabilitation services, the Act works against disabled people defining their own needs. Instead, it promotes the continuation of medically-orientated rehabilitation services which exclude disabled people from decision-making and stifle local community initiative.

Secondly, until recently there has been no cross-disability organisation of disabled people in India. Disabled Peoples' International have now established an Indian chapter, but this is still in an embryonic stage of development. Historically, organisations of disabled people have existed, but these have been for single-disability groups, such as blind people, and deaf people. The Asia-Pacific Regional Seminar of Disabled Peoples' International, held in New Delhi in January 1997, advocated that all CBR programmes should be managed by disabled people. However, in the short to medium-term, this is unlikely to happen ... unless and until the capacity of the disability movement in India is strengthened. This clearly highlights the need for local and international NGOs and donor agencies to fund the development of organisations of disabled people (Miles 1996).

Finally, evidence gathered from interviews for this research indicate that many disabled people within South India have been so disempowered and socially excluded that it will take a very long time indeed, perhaps another generation, for significant numbers of disabled people to acquire the skills and confidence to become competent managers of CBR programmes. Where disabled people have these skills, there is no guarantee that they will want to get involved in CBR. Interestingly, ActionAid (India) has also voiced concern about making "unrealistic expectations" of disabled people, their families and communities (AAIDD 1997, p. 8).

For the time being, then, the best strategy might well lie in the establishment of more linkages and partnerships between fledgling disabled people's organisations and CBR programmes.

CONCLUSION

This paper has suggested that CBR programmes, within India and within the broader international context, should look to the principles of social transformation set out by Paulo Freire. It has been argued that CBR needs to be conceived as an interactive (dialectical) process, whereby disabled people become aware of what they can achieve, the local community becomes confident in supporting disabled people's self-empowerment, and professionals become aware of the way in which their knowledge can best be used to support social transformation (on tap, not on top). There is much that can be learnt, and will need to be learnt, if CBR is ever to become an instrument and catalyst for social change and disabled people's self-empowerment. The role of disabled people and their organisations is central to this process, and therefore it has also argued that aid and development agencies could do much more in terms of supporting the development of these organisations; and that disability needs to be seen as a development issue – social and political, not just medical and technical.

These arguments have been made with reference to the Sourabha CBR project in South India and to existing literature on CBR, empowerment and disabled people's organisations in developing countries. The experience of Sourabha, especially the views of local disabled people, have highlighted several difficult questions relevant to implementing CBR which aims to empower. For example:

- Given that able-bodied professionals have "expertise" and "knowledge", based on several years training, is it realistic to expect them to adopt the role of a facilitator, as outlined in this paper? To be on tap, not on top?
- Given the politics that underpin development projects, and the social position of most disabled people in countries like India, is it realistic to expect local disabled people to assume managerial responsibility for delivering community-based services?
- Given that relative paucity of grassroots and national disabled people's organisations in developing countries, and the constraints they operate under, which disabled people should service planners and development workers consult with, when there is a genuine desire to meet the needs and aspirations of disabled people?

Clearly, there is a need for more research and more reflection on the potential for empowerment within CBR development programmes.

REFERENCES

AAIDD [ACTIONAID (INDIA) DISABILITY DIVISION] (1997), "Perspective Document (1998 – 2000), Sourabha CBR Project of Shree Ramana Maharishi Academy for the Blind", Bangalore: ActionAid (India).

CAMPBELL, J. & OLIVER, M. (1996), *Disability Politics: Understanding our Past, Changing our Future*, London: Routledge.

COLERIDGE, P. (1993), *Disability, Liberation and Development*, Oxford: Oxfam.

FINKENFLÜGEL, H. (ed) (1993), *The Handicapped Community*, Amsterdam: VU University Press.

FREIRE, P. (1970), *Pedagogy of the Oppressed*, London: Penguin Books.

FREIRE, P. & SHOR, I. (1987), *A Pedagogy of Liberation: Dialogues in Transforming Education*, Basingstoke: MacMillan.

HAMMERSLEY, E. (1995), *The Politics of Social Research*, London: Sage.

HELANDER, E. (1993), *Prejudice and Dignity – An Introduction to Community-Based Rehabilitation*, New York: United Nations Development Programme.

HELENDER, E., MENDIS, P., NELSON, G. & GOERDT, A. (1989), *Training in the Community for People with Disabilities*, Geneva: World Health Organization.

HOPE, A. & TIMMELL, S. (1993), *Training for Transformation: A Handbook for Community Workers*, (3 vols), Gweu, Zimbabwe: Mambo Press.

ILO, UNESCO, WHO (1994), *Community-Based Rehabilitation for and with People with Disabilities: Joint Position Paper*, Geneva: United Nations.

LONG, N. & LONG, A. (1992), *The Battlefields of Knowledge*, London: Routledge.

MILES M. (1985), *Where There is no Rehabilitation Plan*, Peshawar: Mental Health Centre.

MILES, S. (1996), "Engaging with the Disability Rights Movement: The Experience of Community-Based Rehabilitation in Southern Africa", *Disability & Society* 11(4), pp. 501-517.

MOMM, W. & KÖNIG, A. (1989), "ILO conceptual Paper on CBR", paper submitted to the sixth Inter-Agency Meeting of the United Nations Decade of Disabled Persons, Vienna, Austria, 5th-7th December, 1989.

OLIVER, M. (1990), *The Politics of Disablement*, Basingstoke: Macmillan.

O'TOOLE, B. & MAISON-HALLS, G. (1994), "Community-Based Rehabilitation and Development: Disabled Children in Guyana", *Development in Practice* 4 (1), pp. 23-34.

PEAT, M. (1991), "Community-Based Rehabilitation – Development and Structure: Part 1", *Clinical Rehabilitation* 5, pp. 161-166.

SPASTICS SOCIETY OF TAMIL NADU (1993), *Report of the Southern Region Seminar on Community-Based Rehabilitation*, 2-3 September, SPSTN, Madras.

WERNER, D. (1995), "Strengthening the Role of Disabled People in Community-Based Rehabilitation Programmes", *in* O'Toole, B. & McConkey, R. (eds), *Innovations in Developing Countries for People with Disabilities*, Chorley: Lisieux Hall Publications.

WOLFFERS, I. and FINKENFLÜGEL, H. (1993), "PHC and CBR: Concepts for Empowerment", *in* Finkenflügel, H. (ed), *The Handicapped Community*, Amsterdam: VU University Press.

CHAPTER 10

Development, Cultural Values and Disability: The example of Afghanistan

Peter Coleridge

"I see humanity as a family that has hardly met" (Theodore Zeldin)

INTRODUCTION

Afghanistan is suffering from nearly two decades of war. Even before the war it did not score high on indicators of social development. Now it occupies a spot almost at the bottom of the global league table. The primary factor affecting any attempt to do sustainable development work in Afghanistan is the war. However, to many development professionals working for the United Nations and foreign NGOs (non-governmental organisations), cultural factors also appear to present obstacles to development. These factors are a mixture of values that derive from culture, ethnicity, and religion, and tend to be lumped together as "cultural values". While foreign agencies agree in theory that "the core concern of sustainability is that the initiative be soundly rooted in the context and the consciousness of the environment in which it operates" (Tamas 1996), and therefore that "local culture" should be respected, in practice they often find that local cultural values in Afghanistan conflict with their own values, and indeed their own ethics. Dialogue to establish a common understanding is often abbreviated or absent. Often, the discussion about cultural values is regarded as too sensitive to even embark on. The result is that "development" remains largely an activity initiated and controlled by foreigners. Local people do not initiate, let alone control, such "development". This paper assumes a view of development that is about much more than material benefits. Development, as conceived here, is the sum of people's own aspirations, efforts, and learning towards bettering themselves materially, socially, intellectually, and spiritually. The paper draws on lessons learned in a large Community Based Rehabilitation (CBR) programme in Afghanistan run under the auspices of UNDP/UNOPS, and implemented by local NGOs. The extent to which the programme is relevant to local values is considered. In addition, it is argued that CBR (and, by implication, other) programmes can engage communities in a dialogue that seeks understanding with local values; and that the understanding engendered by such dialogue can in turn lead to a sustainable development process that goes beyond the field of disability.

'DOING DEVELOPMENT' IN AFGHANISTAN

Among the many challenges that face development agencies currently attempting to undertake sustainable development in Afghanistan, one could list the following:

- Afghanistan presents the classic profile of a war-torn country. The most essential requirements for sustainable development, such as stable communities, shared long-term aspirations, basic health and education services, and legitimate external trade, hardly exist. These factors are not to do with culture, but with the war. But the war has its roots in a conflict in which "values" (whether cultural, ethnic, or religious) have played an important part.
- Donor governments are reluctant to fund long-term development programmes on the grounds that it is an emergency situation and there is no government in control of the whole country. Funding is mostly short-

term, usually for two years or less; this inevitably means that project planning is forced to fit into short timescales.

- It is recognised that development efforts can play a role in either hastening the arrival of peace or (inadvertently) fuelling the conflict. Yet there is a general lack of understanding, among both donors and programme planners, that changing perceptions in a way that could lead to peace will take time, especially in a country like Afghanistan which is characterised by traditional cultural values and ethnic divisions. Programmes which change their focus every two years are unlikely to have the desired impact.

- Afghan NGOs exist, but they are not "grassroot" NGOs in the standard sense of that term. The open expression of opinion is not possible in all parts of Afghanistan. Accordingly, local NGOs have emerged in response to the availability of foreign funds, rather than as indigenous movements for development and social justice. Hence Afghan NGOs (as well as foreign agencies) tend to "do development projects" rather than engage in a development process based on local constituencies and a broader vision of social change.

- Most importantly, many "programmes do not know how to define the knowledge people have acquired through generations of survival in often inhospitable conditions and incorporate this information in the conceptualization and design of development initiatives" (Tamas 1996).

The general picture of development work in Afghanistan is of a series of top-down programmes that recognise, on paper, the importance of consulting local people but, in practice, generally fail to do this in a way that goes beyond discussing "shopping lists" of local needs. Fortunately, there are some exceptions (notably the Habitat programme in Mazar, which has fostered the creation of women's community fora; these fora can be described as "grassroot" in the sense that they are true community fora in which the members set the agenda for development).

All of these challenges boil down to one overriding quest: how to engage in a dialogue directed at building a common understanding between development workers and beneficiaries. This requires an approach to programme design, implementation and evaluation which values *process* as much as *product*.

The process of building common understanding requires much longer timescales than are currently accepted by donors and development agencies in Afghanistan. The process is as complex as it is time-consuming; it defies neat solutions and raises difficult questions. For example, how does a development agency get close to local people without playing into the hands of local power politics? With whom does it engage in dialogue about social development (which is of equal concern to men and women) when communities are typically represented only by the most powerful men?

A promising way forward lies in the use of field workers who see themselves as social animators, not just technicians; as people who raise questions and encourage thoughtful answers, rather than just deliver a service. Clearly, this will have implications for training: there is more to training social animators than technicians. But the benefits can be significant. One programme which has the potential to function like this is CBR, since a core feature in most CBR programmes is the use of cadres (teams) of field workers who engage on a daily basis with communities at family and village levels. Experience from a CBR programme in Afghanistan highlights the potential for taking this forward.

A LARGE CBR PROGRAMME IN AFGHANISTAN

In Afghanistan, local surveys indicate that probably about 3% of the population of 20 million is disabled. This gives a figure of about 700,000 people. War injuries (mainly from mines) and polio account for about half this number. The other half is composed of people with mental retardation, cerebral palsy, leprosy, deafness, blindness, and multiple impairments. As with all disability statistics one must distinguish between *incidence* (the number who are born or made disabled) and *prevalence* (the number who survive). 3% is an estimate of the prevalence. It would be almost impossible to measure the figure for incidence in the present circumstances.

Services for disabled people in Afghanistan have tended to focus on the provision of orthopaedic aids and physiotherapy. This is because the appalling conditions in most hospitals mean that a limb damaged by a mine explosion will be amputated rather than saved, so amputees are the most visible manifestation of disability in the country. One foreign NGO is working with deaf people and two others with blind people, but that is as far as specialised services go.

It is in this context that the Comprehensive Disabled Afghans' Programme (CDAP) was set up by UNDP and UNOPS in 1995. CDAP has developed into a national CBR programme which operates in thirteen provinces of the country, and employs some four hundred paid staff and several hundred volunteers. CDAP serves about 27,000 disabled people annually. All the staff are Afghan with the exception of one expatriate programme manager.

The key agents in the field are Mid-Level Rehabilitation Workers (MLRWs), male and female. They each cover a population of between 15-30,000. Their role is to: activate local CBR committees and disabled people's organisations; recruit volunteers; identify disabled people in their area through a local survey; and arrange appropriate services for each disabled person. For example, disabled children need to be integrated into schools, including *madrasas* (Quranic schools); disabled adults need training in employment skills and loans to set up small businesses; families need to be enabled to help their disabled child to develop – this may involve referral to a physiotherapy centre, or a prosthesis or orthosis from an orthopaedic workshop. The MLRWs arrange what is needed by mobilising local resources and, where necessary, by making referrals to appropriate services.

MLRWs are given a general training of five months spread over a year in topics such as community development, psychology, child development, teaching and learning, and CBR principles, as well as how to work with people who have specific impairments. MLRWs are supported in their work by a smaller group of specialists: physiotherapists, orthopaedic technicians, employment support specialists, special education resource persons, CBR supervisors, trainers, and a resource centre. The total number of paid staff in one project area may reach 90, half of whom are MLRWs. MLRWs are expected to recruit up to five volunteers *each*.

Other important aspects of the programme are:

- An Information, Education and Communication (IEC) component, which aims to raise disability issues within Afghanistan, and also in the wider aid community (in Pakistan and beyond) through newsletters, radio broadcasts, posters, videos, leaflets and discussions. For example, CDAP organises regular national workshops on disability in Afghanistan for which it brings together about thirty agencies.

- A budget from which it can fund other agencies working in disability. Through this mechanism it gains a much wider picture of what is going on in the field of disability in Afghanistan than it would through its own programme alone.

Under a new UNDP integrated programme, CDAP has now started to target vulnerable people other than disabled people.

How far can this programme connect with local communities in a way which respects their values but also acts as a catalyst for change? In order to answer this question it is necessary to consider two sets of values: first, some of the cultural values in Afghanistan which have a direct bearing on development work in general and disability in particular (discussed in the next section); secondly, developmental values that are relevant to disability, common in much current global discourse about disability, and central to the conceptualisation of CDAP (discussed subsequently).

CULTURAL VALUES IN AFGHANISTAN

The ethnic nature of the conflict in Afghanistan is related to where people perceive their identity to lie; this is inevitably bound up with values – whether cultural, ethnic, or religious. This fact alone indicates that there is no single "Afghan culture". There are, for example, differences between the culture of rural and urban communities, even within the same ethnic group; and there is a marked contrast between the cultures of different cities such as Mazar, Kandahar, Kabul, and Herat. It is also difficult to disentangle "culture" from "politics". The Taliban, for example, who insist on rulings such as shaving under the armpits and having a beard at least six inches long, indulge in a political manipulation of culture in the name of religion. Although the Taliban are mostly Pushtun, their particular brand of politicized culture and religion is not supported by many Pushtuns, especially the more educated. Here, it should be noted that the following analysis contains several specific references to Pushtun culture, which looms large in many outsiders' perception of Afghanistan. However, about half of Afghanistan is not Pushtun.

The complexity of talking about "culture" in Afghanistan has been compounded by the fact that eighteen years of conflict have seen some traditional value systems reinforced, while others have broken down. So, on the one hand, ethnic identity has become more not less important. On the other hand, the extended family system has eroded as many husbands are killed, leaving thousands of widows. Furthermore, the fact that three million

Afghans have experienced different cultures through being refugees in either Pakistan or Iran has also had an important impact on cultural attitudes and expectations. It has, for example, demonstrated to many of them that education is the key to development – of the individual and his or her family. Indeed, the lack of education in Afghanistan is one of the main reasons why many Afghan refugees are reluctant to return. At the same time, the monastic-style education of large numbers of Afghan boys in the Quranic schools of Pakistan spawned the Taliban (which means "students" or "seekers").

With these complexities and caveats in mind, attention turns to some dominant features of Afghan culture: Islam, the extended family, the community, and social structures of segregation.

Islam

The one thing that is common to all Afghans is their commitment to Islam as both a belief system and as a social programme.

If great numbers believe a prophet is authentic and they are in agreement on the means to apply the messenger's teachings in their lives, the result is order and social progress. Unity of belief is linked to collective well-being (Tamas 1996).

Islam brings with it a sense of social responsibility, evident in such things as *zakat* and *ushr* – forms of charity to those who have less. Helping deprived people, which includes disabled people, is a religious (and therefore charitable) duty through which the giver accrues credit for the hereafter. Islam brings a strong sense of morality. People are respected and earn status provided they keep to the moral code. Islam also provides a meaning system, a source of hope, and a gathering point. The mosque is the centre of the community.

Family

The typical Afghan village house consists of a high-walled compound enclosing a complex of inter-connecting mud buildings which accommodate the extended family. From five to thirty people (if not more) may live in this space. Walking though an Afghan village, one is conscious that most activities go on behind these compound walls, and are private. Interaction in public spaces is much less than in an Indian village, for example.

In common with many other poor societies, survival in a subsistence economy like that of Afghanistan depends primarily on cooperation and mutual support within the kin group. The extended family is the prime source of social welfare. Contributing to the family is prized much more highly than making one's own way in the world. Anybody in receipt of a regular income is duty-bound to contribute to the common family fund; dereliction of this duty is despised, and for the vast majority of Afghans, is unthinkable. If a family member cannot contribute because he or she is disabled, this has an important bearing on their status in the family.

In traditional rural Pushtun society the survival of the family – or at least the degree to which it flourishes – is related to its *status*, which in turn is related to its *reputation*. Reputation is determined principally by relations between the sexes, which means that men protect the family's "honour" by not allowing women to interact in the public domain. Fear of disgracing one's family honour in some way, however slight, serves as a very powerful force for social and also religious conformity.

The guardians of family honour are the senior men in the extended family, who command the obedience of all other family members. Power resides very definitely in these men, and it is used. While these values are strongest in Pushtun society they are also reflected to a lesser degree in the other ethnic groups of Afghanistan. Significantly, an inability to marry because of disability would deprive a man of the possibility of ever reaching such a position, and therefore reduces his status, actual and potential.

Community

In Pushtun society community decisions are traditionally made by a *jirga*, a permanent council of respected and powerful male elders. Power comes primarily from the number of male relatives a man has (not necessarily from wealth). In all parts of Afghanistan, the concept of a *shura* also exists; this is a council formed for a particular purpose. When the central government is strong, these two types of council, *jirga* and *shura*, tend to be weak. When the central government is weak, the *jirga* and *shura* tend to be strong.

At the village level people are inclined to give their allegiance first to their own community (through the authority of the council) and second to the government. Local tribal and ethnic loyalties are therefore reinforced through this mechanism. In the present era, marked by the existence and activities of development agencies, it is common for development agencies to "consult the community" through a *shura* which either already exists or which is created for the specific purpose of relating to the development agency. The concept of "good governance" in the modern sense (an explicit objective of some UN agencies) is not easily understood by people who have had traditional community decision-making mechanisms for hundreds of years. (The relations between these councils and the CBR committees and disabled people's organisations formed within the CDAP programme will be discussed below.)

Segregation

In effect, there are (at least) two levels of discourse in Afghanistan: one private, one public; one female, one male. Power belongs to the public sphere to which women do not have access. *Jirgas* and *shuras* do not include women as members, although in some parts of the country there are separate women's councils (for example, there are women-only CBR committees in the CDAP programme, and as mentioned above, community fora in Mazar are run by women).

The discussion on gender relations in traditional societies, especially Muslim ones, is complex and is the point where indigenous values clash most obviously with "foreign" values. It is normal in the west to portray Afghan culture as inherently oppressive of women. But most Afghan men and probably many Afghan women perceive the differential treatment as ensuring respect for women, by protecting them from harassment and from what they regard as the demeaning task of having to engage in wage-earning in the public domain. The idea (frequently quoted in the west) that disabled women suffer the double disadvantage of being disabled and of being female was firmly rejected by well-educated women working for the CDAP disability programme. They did not accept that being a woman was in itself a "disability" (CDAP 1998).

According to anthropologist Benedicte Grima, a Pushtun woman's identity and her emotions are culturally determined (Grima 1993). As for the veil as a symbol of oppression, Grima's and other anthropological studies of Pushtun communities reveal that a Pushtun village woman would no more consider going out without her *burqa* than she would consider going out naked. She regards the veil as an essential part of her public identity as a woman. This does not apply in all parts of the country; in the northern, predominantly Uzbek city of Mazar, for example, women attend a co-ed university dressed in western clothes, unveiled (see Grima 1993 and Doubleday 1988 on Afghanistan constructions of gender).

Integration

It is very difficult for a foreigner to determine what the words "social integration" mean in a context where segregation is the norm; where most interaction occurs within the private space of the home; and where women in many Afghan communities only interact socially at events such as weddings and funerals. Who is marginalised? What is the measure of marginalisation?

A "western" analysis might insist that a Pushtun woman's acceptance of the veil as part of her identity means she has internalised oppression. The same is true of disabled people: accepting an inferior position in the social hierarchy "as the normal state of things" might be constructed as evidence of internalised segregation. Moreover, the general belief that a process of integration must start with changes in perception by the person segregated is particularly difficult in the context of Afghanistan. Attempts to "modernise" the country by various rulers (most recently by the Communists in the 1970s) have been the main cause of conflict, especially where changes to the role and status of women have been pushed.

Clearly, a detailed understanding of social relations and values – especially the meaning and relevance of integration in a society that practices and values social segregation – is enormously important for the design of social development programmes. A programme which aims to "integrate disabled and other marginalised people into their own communities" (UNDP 1997) cannot possibly measure whether it has reached that objective unless it understands, and has defined, what both marginalisation and integration mean in that particular cultural context.

DISABILITY AND DEVELOPMENTAL VALUES

The following paragraphs outline a view of disability and developmental values that are common in global development discourse. How they apply to Afghanistan and the CDAP programme will be examined later.

Disability is particular in development terms because it amplifies and illuminates a range of issues that are at the heart of development discourse and ethics, such as notions of normality, equality, empowerment, rights, survival, the individual versus the collective, discrimination, and social support systems (Coleridge 1993).

Development is about the process of change. Charity, despite its good intentions, is counter-development because it does not promote change; it perpetuates the *status quo* of inequality. (It may however be the prelude to developmental awareness.) Development is a self-generating process which must start with the person or group who are the subject of development. Nobody can develop anybody else, although others can create a favourable or unfavourable climate for our development. We can all either enable or disable each other's development by our attitude towards each other.

Development is closely connected to the idea of empowerment, which means having a belief in our own intrinsic worth and the self-confidence and self-esteem that flow from that. If we think we are not worth much, then we cannot develop. Low self-esteem is the hallmark of a person who has internalised oppression. Of all people, disabled people tend to be most disempowered because they are caught in a vicious circle whereby negative social attitudes create low self-esteem which produces a type of behaviour that in turn fosters negative social attitudes. The only way out is for disabled people to start the process of change in themselves.

The medical model of disability does not take this view. It says that the disabled person must try to overcome their disability by some means or other in order to join in with the mainstream. This implies that the disabled person is intrinsically of less value because of their disability. This has devastating implications for the disabled person's ability to grow and develop. It is very insidious, and is present in just about every encounter between a disabled person and other people, especially professionals. In the former communist countries, as an extreme but at least frank example, anybody working with disabled persons is called a "defectologist". Disabled people are regarded as defective in the medical model.

The social model poses the opposite view. It says that even though the person has an impairment that cannot be changed, she or he is still of equal intrinsic worth. It is society that must come to terms with their disability and accept them as they are.

So we can choose between two basic models of society: a closed, exclusive model where beauty, fitness, and uniformity are most valued and abnormality is rejected, or an open, diverse, and embracing society where difference is valued and people are accepted for what they are, regardless of their functional ability or appearance.

However, disability is not only a social issue and the social model cannot be used to the complete exclusion of the medical model. Deafness, for example, is a barrier itself, regardless of surrounding attitudes. One cannot say that all problems faced by disabled people stem from negative social attitudes; impairment is also a factor. That is why disability is not exactly parallel to race or gender as a social issue. There is a need for a rehabilitation process which does indeed try to lessen the handicap.

In summary, there is a need to think of disability as a development and social issue in which the rights and needs of the disabled person can be met by inclusive rather than exclusive social attitudes, coupled with an individually-focused rehabilitation process where necessary. How can this view of disability be applied in Afghanistan?

DISABILITY, LOCAL VALUES, AND CBR IN AFGHANISTAN

The original design of CDAP, written in 1994, was a classic example of an external, non-consultative project formulation, written by three western development specialists from Sweden and Germany who did not visit Afghanistan during the formulation stage. The present project document, written in early 1997, had the benefit of a major evaluation of the programme conducted in the summer of 1996. However, that evaluation did not seek to probe cultural relevance explicitly. This task belongs to ongoing monitoring of the programme, and must be built in to its management and implementation strategy. This means, as stated at the beginning of the paper, that its staff must be trained as social animators, to raise questions, to be objective and reflective about their own culture, and not simply to deliver a packaged service.

One senior worker in CDAP has identified what he calls a **CBR conflict zone** in the programme, where local concepts of disability, culture, poverty, the nature of CBR, and local social values meet (Wahdat 1998). The following paragraphs explore this conflict zone and summarise conclusions that can be drawn so far on whether the programme is in tune with local values and whether it can be used for stimulating and animating a development process that is wider than disability.

We have already identified a number of factors leading to the segregation of disabled people, in particular the importance of being able to **marry** in order to conform to social norms of acceptance. Where this is impossible, the individual lives in a kind of liminal limbo. Not only may a disabled person not be able to get married, but the presence of a disabled person (male or female) in a family may affect the marriage chances of other members of the family (because disability is regarded as shameful) and cause resentment towards the disabled person within his or her own family.

Apart from the crucial matter of marriage is it possible to identify other **attitudinal factors** affecting disabled people in Afghanistan? It is often thought in the west that disabled people get a particularly rough deal in poor countries like Afghanistan, and extremely negative myths are perpetuated, for example that disabled children are killed at birth. Attitudes to disability in Afghanistan have never been systematically researched, but all one can say at this stage is that anecdotal evidence points in the opposite direction from these myths. In rich countries like America it seems that disabled people get their worst treatment from the wealthy. 'Successful' Americans obviously feel more threatened by disability as a 'defect', and therefore a departure from what they aspire to, than people of lower social status do. Discrimination against disabled people seems to occur, according to American researchers, in direct proportion to wealth (Murphy 1987). In a country as poor as Afghanistan it may be that there is less discrimination towards disabled people than there is in America. Poverty is a great leveller. On the streets of an Afghan town it is common to see a disabled child being pushed along in a crude cart by other children, with no sense of embarrassment. Amputees are such a common sight that they are accepted as part of the normal scene in a bazaar. The caring and concern shown by both mothers and fathers towards their disabled children, especially the mentally retarded, never fails to impress. The main problem is not neglect but over-protection, under-stimulation, and ignorance of how to help the child develop.

However, this does not mean that it is better to be a disabled person in Afghanistan than in America. Most obviously, the survival rate of disabled Afghans is low, as a result of inadequate or non-existent health services, not because their families reject them. There is, for example, almost no treatment for spinal injuries, which means that many paraplegics and most quadraplegics die within a year of injury from pressure sores or urinary complications. Some disabilities are more "acceptable" than others. Amputees, partly because their ability to communicate and reproduce is not impaired and partly because they may be regarded as having made a sacrifice in war, are easily accepted. Other disabilities, especially congenital ones, are often regarded as a shame, and are largely absent from public view. It is common for parents to claim that their child became mentally retarded after a rocket attack in order to conceal the congenital nature of the disability.

Disability is still generally seen as a medical problem or one brought about by divine punishment of a person's bad luck, which can be removed only through either medical or religious intervention (or both). The quest for a cure has often been protracted, expensive, and hopeless. Such attitudes (by no means unique to Afghanistan) make it difficult for a CBR programme, which offers no cure, to gain early respect.

The notion of **empowerment**, as described in the section on disability and developmental values above, is very problematic in Afghanistan. The word is inappropriate. In a seminar on cultural values with the CDAP management team already referred to, the word "empowerment" was rejected by all the participants on the grounds the power in Afghanistan means power over somebody else. It is not regarded as win-win, only as win-lose. One can only be empowered at the expense of another. The group favoured the word "enablement" instead. But even this is a concept not easily understood in a situation where people may not aspire to individual development at all, imbued with cultural values that are dominated by the need for collective family survival and kin-group solidarity.

The formation of disabled people's organisations has brought "**rights**" into the consciousness of many disabled people at the village level. By rights they usually mean equal access to what limited services are available, especially health and education. Disabled people's organisations tend (as elsewhere in the world) to be dominated by men with mobility impairments, which in Afghanistan means amputees. Given that many of these will have been disabled in war and are therefore ex-soldiers they are often forceful, and are not obviously lacking in self-esteem. The main problem is to achieve representation of other disabilities in the disabled people's organisation.

The attitude of people with other impairments, especially sensory, is often depressed. This is particularly true of women.

CBR by its nature is long-term, time-consuming, usually not very visible, and with few material inputs. What is the general **community view of a CBR programme**? How do they compare it with other aid and development programmes which bring more material benefits? Does a programme lose credibility and value in the eyes of the local community if it is dealing only with "ideas and paper"? A common response from CBRCs and disabled people's organisations, as well as from individual disabled people, when asked for their recommendations to improve the programme, is that it should deliver some kind of "incentive", by which they mean material handout. The employment support element of the programme, which gives skill training and loans to disabled people, is what many adults see as its main value. CBRCs also regularly ask that such loans and training be extended to very poor non-disabled people such as widows.

What **status** do **CBR workers** hold in the community? Are they respected for what they do? If yes, is that because others admire them for working with disabled people? Is religion a major motivating factor for them? How far can they be catalysts for wider change in the community? As already noted, the potential for a CBR programme to make a contribution to development on a scale wider than disability rests on these field workers. Their selection and training is therefore of crucial importance. It is worth stressing that the physical energy required to be a CBR worker (MLRW in this programme) in rural Afghanistan is considerable. To cover a population of 15-30,000 they have to travel large distances in extremes of climate on roads which in many cases hardly exist, either on foot or on a bicycle, or in one case on a horse. To keep up the level of visiting required day after day, month after month and year after year, in numbing cold and blistering heat, demands a very special kind of commitment. The astonishment perhaps is that a CBR programme works at all under these conditions.

When questioned on their **motivation** for the job MLRWs frequently report that religion does play an important role, coupled with a desire to serve their community. Getting to know their community brings its own rewards for many, who see their status rise by the fact of having to mobilise people. Employing disabled people as MLRWs presents a problem because of the physically taxing nature of the job, but a few MLRWs are disabled.

The **mechanisms for dialogue** with local communities are the individual families, and the CBRCs and DPOs at village and district level. The membership of the CBRCs is drawn from local health workers, teachers, disabled people, parents of disabled children and other interested persons. Sometimes they are congruent with local *shuras* dealing with general development issues in their own community, sometimes they are independent of these *shuras*. Disability is not a power issue; it is not something which people fight over. These CBRCs represent neutral territory. Dialogue with these groups is likely therefore to yield a closer reading of what people think and feel about development issues generally, and they can be used as an entry point for such discussions. At the same time their members see their membership as giving them more status in the community than they had before, as well as experience of organising, debating, and deciding. They count for something in their own eyes, and in their own communities. Disability does indeed open pathways to a different view of development that is not based either on power or materialism (Coleridge 1993).

Separate female CBRCs exist in both Taliban and non-Taliban held areas. The sense of personal and group empowerment in these all-women committees is probably greater than it is for men because women have so few opportunities outside the home to have any influence on community affairs.

To illustrate the role of these committees, the minutes of a (male) CBRC in Herat in January 1998 reveal that over two meetings they discussed the following issues: finding a place to run a vocational training course in tailoring for disabled women, raising the money to provide lunch for the trainees, identifying a skilled person to act as trainer, the lack of textbooks in schools, home schooling for girls, malnutrition in several families. They arranged the training course successfully, and identified women who could provide home schooling for girls. As can be seen, their discussions were not limited to disability issues. They were obviously and justifiably proud of the two achievements of arranging the tailoring course and home schooling for girls. The field worker, who had instigated the formation of this committee, remained in the background, observing and encouraging, a genuine but discreet change agent. Something was happening in this community that was indeed developmental. The word 'empowerment' came immediately to mind in observing this process, even though it may not translate well into Farsi.

CONCLUSIONS

People feel threatened when their values are attacked or start to disappear. When there is fighting everywhere, when the economy is in ruins, when the future holds no hope for one's children, to see one's whole value system also threatened means that the sky has fallen in. The core values described for Afghanistan, in particular Islamic charitable duty, the strength of the extended family, honour, well-defined roles for men and women, and respect for senior males, bring order and predictability to a society living in a harsh and unpredictable environment. It is perhaps inevitable that poverty, war, and destruction stimulate the emergence of leaders who preach the loss of traditional values as the cause and a return to traditional values as the cure. The same phenomenon has occurred in Europe and elsewhere. For foreigners to challenge these values as 'counter-developmental' is not likely to be met with a positive response, especially when 'western values' are not necessarily seen as producing a more cohesive society. Development programmes have to take Afghan values as the given starting point and work within them.

If development is about moving forward on a path towards greater understanding and control over our lives, a process which is more than the provision of material benefits is necessary. Material benefits, even though they are absolutely necessary in a country as poor as Afghanistan, do not amount to development. Culverts, bridges and wells, though vital, do not in themselves make people more inclusive, democratic, or peace loving. A shift in perceptions is necessary. A process must be engaged in which centres on aiming to change perceptions, not to change culture. Changing perceptions is the key to altering behaviour. An enormous difference to the way we live our lives can be created by a shift in perceptions about things we have always taken for granted or never questioned (Zeldin 1994). The difficulty is that our perceptions are conditioned by our cultural background, and changing them is not something that most humans do spontaneously. Some outside trigger is required. Seeing development as the creation of self-sufficient communities who do not need outside influence is not only unrealistic; it is a flawed model. We all need external stimuli to enable us to grow and develop (Zeldin 1994).

The role of a development worker is to give people the confidence that they do have the ability to develop themselves. At the same time he or she needs to challenge perceptions, from within the culture. Well-trained field workers working within their own cultural context are in a much better position to challenge perceptions than foreigners. The role of foreigners is to ask the questions of the field workers but not to provide the answers; these must be provided by local people from reflecting on their own context and values. Foreigners can ask the questions in different ways, which include providing the materials and the experiences which challenge field workers to change their own perceptions. Discussions on cultural values need to be a regular and normal part of the process of running a development programme and not ignored or left aside as 'too sensitive'. In this way a thinking, questioning, experimenting cadre of field workers can be created who are true catalysts for change within their own culture.

A CBR programme is at base about changing perceptions. Evidence from the CDAP programme shows that changing perceptions about disability can be an important step on the road to deeper understanding about more general development processes. As one field worker in Herat recently said during a discussion about development, 'If we had started a CBR programme twenty years ago in Afghanistan we would not need the UN today.'

ACKNOWLEDGEMENTS

This paper was first presented at a conference at Queen's University, Kingston, Canada, on: 'Disability Issues: Global Solutions and the Role of Community Based Rehabilitation', March 5-6, 1998. I am very grateful to the following for comments and invaluable insights on early drafts of this text: Tine Staermose (ILO Islamabad), Jagoda Paukovic (Justicia et Pax, Netherlands), Farooq Wardak (National Programme Manager, CDAP), Omar Daudzai (Programme Officer, UNDP Afghanistan), Hayatullah Wahdat (Project Officer for Communication, CDAP), Carol Le Duc (UNICEF, Afghanistan), Dr Will Boyce, (ICACBR, Queen's University, Ontario).

REFERENCES

CDAP (1998), Minutes of staff seminar on cultural values, 2 February 1998.

COLERIDGE, P. (1993), *Disability, Liberation, and Development*, Oxford: Oxfam Publishing.

DOUBLEDAY, V. (1988), *Three Women of Herat*, London: Jonathan Cape.

GRIMA, B. (1993), *The Performance of Emotion among Paxtun Women*, Karachi: OUP.

MURPHY, R. (1995), "Encounters: The Body Silent in America", *in* B. Ingstad & S.R.Whyte, (eds), *Disability and Culture*, Berkeley: University of California Press.

TAMAS, A. (1996), *Spirituality and Develoment: Concepts and Categories. Dialogue on Spirituality in Sustainable Development*, Ottawa: Canadian International Development Agency.

UNDP (1997), *Poverty Eradication and Community Empowerment*, Project document for the UNDP funded integrated programme in Afghanistan 1997-9.
WAHDAT, H. (1998), "Mission Report to Wardak and Ghazni January 1998", CDAP internal report.
ZELDIN, T. (1994), *An Intimate History of Humanity*, London: Minerva.

Researching Disability

In this final section of the book, discussion moves away from action and towards research – although everything that is said in the following contributions has direct relevance to the implementation of disability and development programmes.

All too often, disability and development professionals are funded to "go in and do", without first identifying:

a) what already happens in the locality (outsiders often assume that there is a blank sheet on which to write at will);

b) what local needs are – not just for disabled people, and not just in relation to individual impairments and rehabilitation (e.g. income generating opportunities for *all* might be the best way to support disabled people and the wider community);

c) local concepts and meanings of "impairment"; and

d) ways in which "disability" is constructed through local culture, values and structures (where disability means social exclusion, diminished personhood, lack of access to opportunities like education, earning, or having a family, etc).

It is important for outsiders to consider the past as well as the present; to prioritise learning from local disabled people; and to recognise that there are many ways of learning about local views and responses – through oral testimony, media, historical records, sacred texts, language, proverbs, policy, actions, and so on. It is also important to think about ways of doing research (see Stubbs), analysing data (see Stone), and using the results to inform action.

OVERVIEW OF CONTRIBUTIONS

Making Connections: Using Stories from China's Villages and Newspapers

Emma Stone uses stories to highlight the value of making connections between stories or voices and wider contexts (cultural, structural, policy). Use of different sources and "extraordinary" as well as "everyday" stories is encouraged. The complexities of disability in the majority world are lost if such connections are not made.

Disability Policy & Provision in Jordan: A Critical Perspective

Majid Turmusani explores disability policy, provision and legislation in Jordan, and considers the current situation of disabled people, dominant social attitudes, and the involvement of western organisations in disability-related provision. He offers a useful account of disability services, constraints faced, and the limitations of existing policies and provisions to address the needs of disabled people in Jordan.

Ghosts and Germs: Cerebral Palsy in Nepal – A Preliminary Exploration of Cosmology and Disability

Rebecca Saul and David Phillips explore cultural perceptions of disability in Nepal. They draw on local language and beliefs, and on family explanations and responses to impairment. Connections are made between responses and a "rural-cosmopolitan continuum". Saul and Phillips point to the subtleties of labelling and the complexities that exist in a context of pluralistic belief and healthcare systems.

Can Formal Disability Services be Developed with South Asian Historical and Conceptual Foundations?

M. Miles uses sacred texts and historical records in search of clues on responses to disabled people in South Asian history. He also considers conceptual differences that are often missed when western professionals work in the majority world (e.g. "child" and "play" are *concepts* rooted in *culture*), and he criticises the imposition of western schemes on majority world settings.

Engaging with Difference: Soul-searching for a Methodology in Disability and Development Research

Sue Stubbs draws on her experiences as a practitioner doing research with a local team. Among other issues, Stubbs explores the dangers of linking research rigour to written evidence, when oral culture and testimony is the dominant means of communication in many communities. This paper provides a fitting end to the book – a powerful reminder that the best learning comes from listening to people who live in the majority world, rather than from reading western or western-influenced literature.

DISCUSSION POINTS

- What sources of data can be used to get a better understanding of disability in the majority world? Are there any problems linked to the data sources you could use?
- What research questions would you ask if you were doing research on disability in the majority world?
- What are the characteristics of good disability research (process, outcomes) on the majority world? And how can they be achieved?
- Do you think that "disability", as defined in western disability studies (i.e. social discrimination, <u>not</u> impairment and <u>not</u> located in the individual) applies outside the minority western world?
- Are there any dangers in applying a social model approach to disability in the majority world? Are there any dangers in failing to apply a social model approach to a majority world setting?
- How, if at all, can learning about cultural, social, structural and historical aspects of disability make any difference to disabled people's lives and services?
- What evidence is there in these contributions of a globalisation of disability, and/or a globalisation of disability-related services?
- What practical steps can be taken to limit the dangers of increased exposure to western ideas, slogans and services?

CHAPTER 11

Making Connections: Using stories from China as an example

Emma Stone

INTRODUCTION

Where do we look for understanding or "data" on disability in majority world settings? How do we respond to and analyse the voices we hear, the things we see, the stories we read? Do we look hard enough for links between individual stories and the broader social, structural and cultural contexts in which those stories are situated? Do we actively seek out stories that challenge our own outsider assumptions?

In a recent paper on developing research agendas for disability research in the minority world, Len Barton (1999, p. 37) reminds us that "making connections" between voices and contexts, between stories, situations and structures, is a core component of the research task. My main aim in this paper is to illustrate how such connections be made when studying, researching or working on disability in the majority world. I have written it with students of

Disability Studies and Development Studies and future researchers. Along the way, I hope to offer a few insights into disability and development in China.

The stories used are only the tiniest fraction of data generated over nine months of fieldwork in China, in 1995 and 1996. I have written elsewhere of my experiences of doing disability research, methods I used and difficulties I faced (Stone 1997, Stone & Priestley 1995).

STORIES FROM CHINA'S VILLAGES

The first three stories are from China's villages, from parents who have a disabled child. These stories are far from unique. I heard variations on the same theme time and again.

Xiao Lin's Family

Xiao Lin is a 10 year old boy who lives in Taozhou township with his mother, father and elder sister; he has a visual impairment. The discovery was made when Xiao Lin was at nursery school and it was confirmed by examination at Shanlin County Hospital. The doctors said there was no cure, but the parents heard of other doctors and went to Wuhu and to Shanghai for further opinions. The family travels to Shanghai every year to see if anything more can be done. To date, they estimate that they have spent 10,000 yuan on medical and associated costs and that is significantly less than they would have spent had the Lin family not got relatives in Shanghai who could do all the telephoning and put them up.

Xiao Lin's parents have heard that it is possible to have an eye transplant but that such treatment is very expensive – probably 100,000 yuan. But it is not something they have completely rejected as a possibility: "we will put all we have into helping him".

Xiao Lin attends an ordinary primary school in Taozhou. His results are good but his mother is anxious that the next school might reject him because of his impairment.

The family has a respectable apartment, good social connections with the local government (Xiao Lin's grandfather was a senior member of the County Government) and a good standard of living compared to others in the town. Still the search for medical help has necessitated more economic activity on the part of the household. Xiao Lin's mother has had to set up a business making and selling breakfast dumplings before going to her regular day job. All of her wages and her husband's (a departmental head in a charcoal company) have been saved to pay for their son's medical treatment.

(Research Notes from a semi-structured interview with the Lin household, Shanlin County Research Project, Anhui Province, Data Code TZ-CD-6, Nov 1996.)

Xiao Zhen's Family

Xiao Zhen is a 6 year old girl with a hearing impairment. She lives with her mother, father and younger sister in a small rural hamlet. Her parents are poor and only have a basic education. The main family livelihood is the household plot. Additional income is made through tricycle-based deliveries. Xiao Zhen is not school-age but she finds it upsetting to see her sister attending school with other children: the family's home is situated only yards from the hamlet school. Xiao Zhen's mother does not know whether her daughter will be able to go to school or whether the family's financial circumstances will permit any form of special education. It is hard enough finding the money for books for the elder daughter (who does not have an impairment).

Almost all the farm work is done by Xiao Zhen's mother. Xiao Zhen's father is seldom at home. Xiao Zhen's mother says "he has never bothered with his daughters". Xiao Zhen's mother blames herself for her daughter's deafness [which resulted from misused antibiotics to cure a fever, see Alison Callaway's paper in this book]. Xiao Zhen's parents took her to Shanlin County Hospital and were told that the condition was incurable. A hospital in Nanjing told them the same thing. Shortly after, Xiao Zhen's father caught tuberculosis, so the family had no more money to spend on Xiao Zhen.

Recently, Xiao Zhen's mother saw a programme on television about a hospital in Hefei which claimed good results in curing deafness. So she plans to sell their grain and use the money to take her daughter to Hefei to see doctors there. "Whatever hospital I've taken her to, the results haven't been good – I am always making inquiries and wanting to find out about somewhere good to take her for an examination ... all that I want it to cure my daughter's illness".

(Research Notes from a semi-structured interview with the Zhen household, Shanlin County Research Project, Anhui Province, Data Code TZ-CD-5, Nov 1996.)

Xiao Guo's Family

Xiao Guo got a fever in infancy. After he recovered, his family discovered that his legs were weak and he could not walk or stand up. Xiao Guo's parents sought help from the local doctor, and the doctor discovered that he probably had polio. The doctor advised that they go to the county hospital, where the diagnosis was confirmed. Then they went to a hospital for infectious diseases in Tianjin City. The expenses – both medical and residential – were huge. So, they sold their own house – a four-roomed house – to cover what they owed in medical expenses. They had built their house for 1500 yuan but could only sell it for 1600 yuan, so they went to the county bank and took out a loan; the government provided some assistance. They still owe 3000 yuan. Xiao Guo's father is self-employed in fish rearing. Xiao Guo's mother stays at home to look after Xiao Guo, and she also farms the household plot. The family now live in a one-room house.

(Research Notes from a visit to the Guo family home, Heping County Research Project, Tianjin Municipality, Transcript Code NH-13, April 1996.)

MAKING CONNECTIONS

Everyone who reads this paper will probably have heard stories like those told by Xiao Guo's, Xiao Zhen's and Xiao Lin's parents, whether or not they have been to China. There is something in these stories that seems to ring true across many different cultures and countries. And yet ... still there is something that ties them to China in the 1990s. The stories are the product of a complex interplay of different factors and processes, past and present, past refashioned into present, partly global yet indisputably Chinese.

In the sections that follow, I outline some of those factors and processes. The discussion is intentionally brief because my aim is to encourage others to make similar connections in their own areas, rather than provide a detailed analysis of disability in China (that is the subject of past and planned publications).

SOME STARTING POINTS

What do the stories of Xiao Guo, Xiao Zhen and Xiao Lin's families tell us immediately?

- Parents revealed a high degree of care, commitment and concern for their child, irrespective of social or economic status – with the apparent exception of Xiao Zhen's father who seemed disinterested in his daughter.
- All the families had invested significant time, resources, energy and anxiety into seeking a cure for their child. Family members took on additional income generation, ploughed all their earnings into medical treatment and, in one case, incurred considerable indebtedness and sold a primary asset to meet medical costs.
- A large number of medical and rehabilitation professionals were consulted – in the local area, the nearest rural town, and much further afield (e.g. Shanghai). This was expensive, but was felt to be worthwhile to secure the best possible chance of a cure.

These starting points prompt further questions.

- Why is it so important to find a cure for a child's impairment, even to the extent of risking indebtedness for the entire household?
- Has it always been so important to find a cure? Is it more important now than in the past?
- Have families always made long journeys to access medical and rehabilitation services?
- Do family responses to impairment vary according to the child's gender?

In turn, these questions suggest avenues for further research, for example:

- Social and cultural views of impairment and people with impairments.
- Social and cultural views of the child (girl child, boy child), in relation to the family and notions of adulthood or personhood.
- Household expectations and household economic strategies.
- Concepts and availability of curative medicine and rehabilitation.

Add to this list the importance of exploring wider structures and changes in society, economy, policy and provision (local and national) – all of which will impact on the above (see also Momm & König 1989 for a useful framework for baseline studies).

When making connections, all these areas need to be considered in relation to each other, in combination, and with an eye to the past as well as the present. As this is done, a more complete story begins to emerge, one that is more closely woven into the particular social, cultural and structural fabric of China's villages in the 1990s.

THE BEGINNINGS OF A MORE CONNECTED STORY

The starting points, questions and areas for further inquiry provide a good framework for contextualising the stories of Xiao Guo, Xiao Zhen and Xiao Lin's families. While space does not permit me to write my own version of a more connected story in any detail, it is probably helpful to fill out the framework (or parts of it) to give a feel for what this might entail.

Wider Socio-Economic Changes and their Impact on the Household

China is one of several countries "in transition" – a term used to describe countries that were once aligned to a Communist bloc but are now engaged in capitalist or quasi-capitalist development. The notion of a country in transition is helpful in so far as it reminds that China has abandoned certain structures, modes and ideologies of development that dominated from the 1950s to 1970s (rural collectives, mass movements, revolutionary struggle, barefoot doctors). Less helpfully, the notion of transition implies an active movement towards a clear destination. Yet, the sobering reality is that China might actually have arrived.

It is possible to see China as a (pretty big) microcosm of the world in the 1990s. The widening gap between the minority and majority worlds is played out within China's vast borders, between city and village, between coastal and inland provinces. For some people, China's new road to development has brought many opportunities – above all the chance to own and profit. For others, the dismantling of China's "iron rice bowl" (guaranteed, if basic, social security, employment, schooling and healthcare) has put their lives at risk. For most, the experience of China's economic reforms has been bitter-sweet. The loss of the iron-rice bowl means greater insecurity and expense; but this has been sweetened by the chance to make money, move around, and consume. Development in China is a double-edged sword.

Competition in the labour market is severe. Unemployment constitutes a very real threat to most households. The costs to the household of basic living, schooling and health care have sky-rocketed. After decades of "free" schooling and healthcare, families – including rural families – now have to pay fees. All of this makes for a more insecure environment in which to raise a family and run a household. It is also a more pressured environment, because the opportunities for families to make money and gain status *are* there, and everyone knows someone who has done well in the new China.

Family Perceptions of Impairment – Past into Present

In China (and perhaps elsewhere), a new-born baby or child might usefully be conceptualised as "lineage capital" and "economic capital".

The notion of "lineage capital" harks back to the Chinese past, and enduring cultural and cosmological legacies that tied the body to familial and socio-cultural expectations. The expectations were from and for the whole family (including ancestors and unborn descendants), to be realised through individual family members and their fulfilment of core obligations. In the past, these obligations were: marriage, production of male children, correct performance of ancestral rituals, and provision for family elders. Through these, the individual attained the socio-cultural status of personhood. The core obligations were broadly similar for men and women (although a woman would always have diminished personhood compared to a man). Key differences included the fact that a married woman's obligations were to her husband's family, not her own; and that a woman's full personhood depended (to a much greater extent than that of her husband) on bearing a son. Impairments were a threat to the fulfilment of family obligations, partly because of social and legal regulations that prevented people with certain impairments from participating in rituals or from getting married (and thereby having children).

In the 1990s, many of these obligations remain highly relevant to perceptions of and responses to childhood impairment. Moreover, some of them have been intensified through increased economic opportunities and insecurities. Enter the concept: "economic capital".

For the Guo, Zhen and Lin families, impairment potentially undermines the entire household's capacity for economic survival and longer-term security:

- loss of household labour if the individual is not or is not perceived to be "productive";

- loss of household labour if a "productive" family member becomes a "carer"; and
- sometimes exorbitant costs of medical care and cure seeking.

Arguably, the potential economic impact of impairment on the household is greater now than it has been since the creation of the People's Republic of China in 1949. Moreover, current public discourse in China is replete with references to ensuring that disabled people "become an asset to society instead of a liability" (CDPF 1988). The same perception shapes a household's response to impairment. Most families are prepared to invest heavily to prevent the anticipated economic hardship.

Available Support Systems and their Impact on the Household

China's new road to economic development has also engendered the break-up of collective forms of social organisation. The non-kin and collective support systems established during the 1950s to 1970s have been eroded as work units and rural collectives have been progressively dismantled or sidelined under the socio-economic reorganisation spearheaded by Deng Xiaoping since 1978. Meanwhile, family support systems, which had been undermined by the introduction of work units, neighbourhood committees and rural collectives, have been further weakened since the 1980s, as family size has decreased and internal migration has increased. There is little by way of a safety-net for those who have no neighbourhood-based or kin-based support systems. State-social welfare entitlements are wholly inadequate in much of China, especially in rural and remote areas. Where disability-related support is provided, it tends to be on an *ad hoc* basis, mostly to coincide with festivals and state holidays, rather than as a reliable weekly or monthly payment.

In this context, families are understandably concerned about their capacity to support a disabled family member, particularly as other family members get older and die.

Family Responses to Impairment: Prevention through Cure

Prevention *is* a cure. Families invest time, resources and energy to educate, rehabilitate and ideally, cure their child. The bottom line is that the best guarantee of a good future – for the family as much as for the child – is perceived to be a cure.

The search for a cure is often expensive and protracted. Families may begin with a visit to a local doctor but cure-seeking seldom stops there. The poorest families journey to hospitals outside the county; more wealthy families travel further afield to Shanghai or Beijing. Even within the locality, a family will pay for an examination at the local county hospital in addition to visiting several different doctors and clinics in the area.

The hope for complete "recovery" (*kangfu*, sometimes mis/translated as "rehabilitation") and the long-standing nature of medical help-seeking in Chinese cultures (Kleinman *et al* 1975, Kleinman 1980) protract the search for a cure, even when informed that a condition is incurable. The situation is made more complicated by the multiplicity of health and therapeutic systems which form the Chinese medical landscape; and by the strong social expectations that doctor-swapping will probably be necessary, and that a family should never give up their search (see Kleinman *et al* 1975). A high degree of perseverance is expected which may ultimately work against the child's interests. Opportunities for schooling and social participation may be lost through time taken up by medical treatment, not to mention the impact on self-identity and esteem that protracted medical help-seeking may have. The search for a cure can also work against the household's long-term interests.

The costs of medical care (fees, treatment, travel and accommodation expenses, time out of everyday income generation) can be prohibitive and are borne almost exclusively by the families. Occasionally, a poor family might receive assistance from the government, or doctors and hospitals might agree to reduce fees. Household poverty does not automatically reduce the drive to find a cure, since a cure is seen as a way of avoiding perennial poverty for the whole household. Further indebtedness in such circumstances is not uncommon.

Additional Pressures: The "One-Child Policy"

The fear of indebtedness often diminishes in the face of additional pressures that bear down on parents, especially mothers. Some of the heaviest pressures are related to what might be called a "cult of the perfect child", which has swept through China on the back of the one-child policy and which articulates with the enduring social and cultural importance of having a long line of ancestors and descendants. (The phrase "one-child policy" is now inaccurate but is used here for convenience, see Davin 1990.)

There is no doubt that the 1980s and 1990s have been a boom-time for the child. Children have become the object of a massive consumer market. They have acquired the collective nickname of "Little Emperors". Moreover, given that most couples are expected to abide by a one-child policy, the onus on having a perfect (for which read healthy, intelligent, attractive, non-impaired) child is becoming even more intense. This pressure combines with already negative social attitudes towards impairment – related in part to the bleak prospects associated with impairment (less chance of marriage, employment, education, social status, etc.). The result is a context in which disabled foetuses are more likely to be aborted; disabled babies are more likely to be abandoned, often purposefully, at the door of Chinese hospitals and welfare institutions; and parents of disabled children do their utmost in search of a cure – even to the point of producing impairment (see Callaway in this book). Somewhat paradoxically, this situation has been exacerbated by growing disability awareness.

Additional Pressures: Disability Awareness

The last two decades have also seen the formation of the China Disabled Persons Federation, the emergence of Deng Pufang (the late Deng Xiaoping's eldest son, a wheelchair user) as its champion, and a range of top-down initiatives to challenge negative attitudes, change disabling language, and promote disabled people's participation in society (Stone 1996). In the 1990s, China's population is far more "disability-aware"; but disability awareness too has proved something of a double-edged sword.

The Chinese government and mass media have made significant steps forward in highlighting the poverty and discrimination that many disabled people and their families face. The government has called for an end to this through maximising the opportunities that disabled adults have to support themselves (via education, employment, rehabilitation, equal opportunities), and through minimising the perceived risk to the state and burden to society and families that disabled people might bring (via rigorous and well-publicised prevention strategies). Thus, there is a Law for Protection for Disabled People (1990), and there is also a (basically eugenic) Law on Maternal and Infant Health Care (1994).

Increased disability awareness might have fostered a more supportive environment for some disabled people, but it has also added to the already intense pressures on families with disabled children to seek a cure – to shield their child and themselves from disadvantage.

A Rehabilitation Business: Demand and Supply

Increased disability awareness has also contributed to a boom in the rehabilitation business and health care generally. This has been apparent in China throughout the 1980s and 1990s, and constitutes a refashioning, if not an intensification, of long-standing interests in the body and health. "Traditional" Chinese medicine (a convenient but misleading term) has long had an interest in impairment – and many parents turn to Chinese medicine practitioners in their search for a cure. But western-style rehabilitation is also on the menu – hailed within China as a "new" area of medicine, imported from the west.

The growth of a western-style rehabilitation industry in China has been spurred on by the rapid globalisation of the rehabilitation business, and the increased involvement of western and international professionals and organisations in promoting rehabilitation medicine and technology in the majority world. The fact that some of this outsider involvement may be welcomed and much-needed does not detract from the cumulative – and potentially counter-productive – impact that such involvement can have on family perceptions of and responses to childhood impairment, let alone on disabled children's lives and identities.

Add to all this the innumerable television and radio programmes, popular magazines and tabloids which focus on healthcare, beauty, fitness, and also the identification and cure of "diseases". The popular magazine *Health* is one such example. It regularly features apparently legitimate (sometimes fraudulent) advertisements for western and Chinese medicine: Diabetes cure! Epilepsy cure! Mental illness cure! Deafness cure! Paralysis cure! And so on. Books targeted at families, especially parents, on common diseases, treatments and home-based rehabilitation are widely available and relatively cheap.

The rehabilitation industry in China may still be small but it is expanding rapidly, and its expansion is in no small measure attributable to growing grassroots demand from parents that want to do the best for their family.

Multiple Dimensions

In addition to these overarching factors and processes, a parent's or family's perceptions of and responses to their child's impairment may vary widely according to the interplay of a host of different variables, including:

- Child's gender, age, type and severity of impairment.
- Parents' background: literacy, education, employment.
- The family's support networks: local and regional; kin-based and non-kin based; social contacts (e.g. local government, school); contact with disabled children and adults.
- The family's information networks: literacy, radio, television, telephone, internet; contact with relevant individuals, organisations or networks.
- Household assets: land, profitable sidelines, house, savings, access to credit.
- Household locality: rural, peri-urban, urban; proximity to services.

BUT, and this point cannot be made loud enough, the connections between these variables and specific outcomes are not always straightforward. For example, illiteracy will probably impact on the household's access to information, services and opportunities; but there is no simple correlation between parental illiteracy and neglect of a child (both Xiao Guo and Xiao Zhen had parents with very low levels of literacy). Similarly, evidence from China's orphanages points to the socio-cultural undesirability of a girl child with an impairment (see for example articles in *The Observer* 1996), but by no means all disabled girl children are rejected by their families or within their families. Finally, poverty may reduce opportunities but it does not reduce the pressures on a parent to search for a cure or access "special/ist" services.

TO SUMMARISE SO FAR

Obviously, the above is just a taster of some of the connections that could be made to understand what has gone on "behind the scenes" of the three stories told by Chinese parents. It illustrates, I hope, that stories from the majority world demand and deserve careful analysis. In this way, a story ceases to be one that could have taken place anytime, anywhere.

Producing a more connected story deepens one's understanding of the pressures – past, present, social and economic, personal and public – that can inform the actions and beliefs of individual families. Only then does it become possible to listen properly and act appropriately. Research that makes connections has a much higher chance of producing useable knowledge – the kind of knowledge that will prevent outsiders from formulating inappropriate action plans. For example, the three stories from China's villages, and the wider connections that were made, raise many issues that need to be recognised because they would influence the process and outcome of any disability-related intervention.

- "Child-focused" interventions may conflict with the fact that a child exists in relation to her/his family, and that most family responses are ultimately family-focused.
- Gender as a variable in shaping a child's life chances.
- The intense pressures on families (mothers in particular) to search for a cure – at almost any cost, even when a condition is deemed "incurable".
- The likelihood that families will explore several different options at the same time (e.g. Chinese medicine and also western-style rehabilitation techniques).
- Information needs are huge; recognising also that any response to information needs will result in yet more leads that families feel bound to follow.

These are just a few pointers that spring to mind. But they are helpful because they set family demands in context. Parental suggestions for more high-tech rehabilitative and curative services may be based less on the lack of such services in the region, and more on the costs of accessing existing services and/or the families' "failure" to find a cure.

STORIES FROM CHINA'S NEWSPAPERS

From villages to newspapers ... and no doubt the use of Chinese newspaper stories in a "research paper" will raise eyebrows. After all, we are talking about a country known for severe restrictions on freedom of the press. What will raise eyebrows even more is that these stories set out the voices of Chinese disabled people who are dissatisfied with the way in which they have been treated because of their impairment.

The stories that follow are not at all representative of Chinese media outpourings on disability (even though both gained national coverage) or of actions taken by Chinese disabled people. Rather, they represent new undercurrents of change, the still small voices that are growing louder and demanding more.

The stories also challenge western ideas – about where to look for data, and about the nature of stories on disability in the majority world. For example, when people heard about my research, I got the following responses: "that must be depressing" (a Professor in East Asian Studies); "you don't see any disabled children, they're all in orphanages" (a final year student of Chinese, after a year in China); and "they practise eugenics" (an activist in Britain). There is some truth, but only partial truth, in these statements.

It is all too easy to slip into stereotypes and compound myths (see Kisanji 1995a, 1995b, Ingstad 1995 on western myths and constructions). Seeking out different stories and using different sources can be a helpful way of reminding yourself, and others, that little is straightforward, and that where there are people, there are forces for social change.

"Why can't an ugly student go to university?" (*Beijing Youth Daily*, Oct. 1995)

The story of Yang Hongwei is about a young man who moved successfully through the mainstream school system, gained high grades in final exams (in excess of the standard requirements of Chinese university entrance), applied to several universities but was rejected by all of them on the basis of an "ugly" appearance.

Yang had encountered a certain amount of prejudice prior to that point, but had also been strongly supported by family members and local teachers, who urged him to apply for higher education. By all accounts, he was an exemplary pupil. However, even the appellation of "Three Good Student" did not stop universities from rejecting him:

> the student's bodily impairment will cause difficulties for his study and therefore we will not accept him (Lanzhou University);
>
> we have many activities and contacts with those outside the college, and we are afraid that admitting this kind of student would have a negative influence on these and on other students studies (Zengzhou University).

Faced with these rejections, Yang Hongwei complained to the local, provincial and national Education Commission and finally took the story to the press with the questions: "are universities in the business of education or aesthetics?" and "should you select on the basis of academic grades or external appearance?"

How far the story is a disability story is up for debate. On the one hand, "ugliness" does not slot easily into the restrictive, functionalist and five-fold definition of impairment that has been standardised in China since the 1980s. As a result, the local Disabled Persons Federation felt that Yang Hongwei was not, strictly speaking, a disabled person. However, the barriers faced by Yang Hongwei were clearly comparable to those faced by prospective students with state-defined impairments, and on that basis the local and provincial Disabled Persons Federations agreed to take up his cause.

As a result of Yang's media campaign, Yang was given offers by various universities around China, received a considerable number of letters of support and financial donations, and was offered the chance for free plastic surgery in a Beijing hospital and (according to some sources) in America. Yang redistributed the donations to students in hardship, put university on hold for a while, and took up the offer of plastic surgery in Beijing. His mother explained in a follow-up article in the *Beijing Youth Daily* (21 February 1996) that the chance for a more acceptable appearance could not be passed by since "after college, he will have to make his way in the world, get a job, make a life".

On the broader scene, the story opened debates on disabling barriers to students with impairments and prompted at least one provincial Education Commission to co-opt someone from the provincial Disabled Persons Federation to act in cases where disabled students were rejected by universities on the basis of (state-defined) impairment.

"Who will safeguard the legal rights of disabled people?" (*Legal Daily*, Feb. 1994)

We are 77 disabled people from the city of Rui'an in Zhejiang Province.

This article is best described as an open letter, written by a group of disabled people to the Chinese public, in which general and specific grievances against macro- and micro-level injustices are set out with uncompromising clarity. The first few sentences of the letter describe the increased hardship and poverty faced by disabled people who (the letter states) have been severely disadvantaged by the economic reforms of the 1980s, increased economic competition and labour markets – particularly in rural areas. The letter continues to detail a series of specific incidences involving several disabled people in Rui'an and senior personnel of the Rui'an Municipal Traffic Police.

The incidents began following official decrees in June 1993 that registered disabled people could purchase a "welfare-vehicle" (*fuliche*; a three-wheeled motorbike with space for a backwards-facing passenger or goods) to use for mobility. After saving to get the money together, several disabled people were able to buy a welfare-vehicle. The following month, they went to the municipal traffic police to get the appropriate road licence, only to be flatly refused by the officer-in-charge on the basis that the vehicles bought were "not road-worthy, a pile of scrap". A number of disabled people, whose livelihoods and mobility depended on the vehicles, resorted to driving them without a licence. They were caught, detained, and their vehicles were smashed. On top of a fine, some were beaten whilst in custody. The letter claims that this type of incident happened over 70 times between July and the end of October 1993. It continues:

> On 29th September, the aforesaid officer-in-charge mobilised the traffic police, intercepted and detained over 100 welfare-vehicles. On 4th October, he notified disabled people that they should go to collect their vehicles. He forced the disabled people to carry a signboard [*gua paizi*, a humiliating act associated with the Cultural Revolution], to sit on their vehicles and be photographed. Then, in front of a crowd, he insulted the disabled people. When they asked him to stop, the officer-in-charge of the traffic police cursed them in front of everyone, saying: "You go home and ask your mothers why you were born a cripple".

Following this incident, the disabled people and disabled colleagues sought redress, sought someone who would take an interest in the case, but found no-one. In the meantime, the officer-in-charge supplied licences to non-disabled people who used welfare-vehicles for personal profit. In the end, disabled people in Rui'an were given two options: to rent their licences for the exorbitant sum of 200-300 yuan per month, or not use their vehicles at all. The letter concludes:

> We make a desperate cry to society: think hard about the appeal we are making as disabled people. Safeguard disabled people s legal rights, in accordance with the law, and quickly put a stop to the illegal behaviour of the officer-in-charge from Rui'an City Traffic Police.

I have no idea of the final outcome of the letter. I would suspect that, given recent anti-corruption campaigns, action was taken in favour of the disabled people of Rui'an.

LEARNING FROM LESS ORDINARY STORIES

The fact that these stories are a) not representative of Chinese media images on disability, and b) describe actions that are not necessarily representative of China's disabled population writ large, need not detract from the invaluable insights they offer into the experience and construction of disability in China.

For starters, in these two stories, we learn about:

- Experiences of discrimination based on impairment, and indicative of "disability" as disadvantage and discrimination. Whilst the actions described may not be everyday occurrences, there is plenty of evidence from other sources that the experiences that prompted them are not so unusual.
- The difficulties of exercising rights that exist on paper (such as rights conferred through the State Council's "Regulations on Education for the Disabled", effective since 1994), balanced by the doors that are opened because such rights do, at least, exist on paper.
- An apparent alliance of interests between the highest levels of the Chinese state and the disabled people involved. The actions taken do not constitute "political dissidence", since the appeal is for the realisation of rights that have been granted by the government and enshrined in state policy and legislation.
- The use (infrequent but increasing) of the Chinese media to turn up the volume on disabled people's own demands, to name and shame those who have denied them their rights, and to win public support to take on higher authorities and officials. (Incidentally, Yang Hongwei's story attracted international and internet attention, including anger from overseas Chinese students that Yang had been rejected by universities.)
- The restrictive definition of who is, and who is not, a "disabled person" – and how definitions correspond to individual impairment rather than social barriers. Further research would reveal that state definitions of impairment have existed for centuries in China, but have also been influenced by the promotion of the World Health Organization International Classification of Impairment, Disability and Handicap (Stone 1999).
- The power of dominant and disabling constructions of "normality" (again, linked to state and socio-cultural definitions of normative bodies and

behaviours, and intensified by the availability of medical and cosmetic techniques to "normalise" appearance and function).

- The reappearance of charity fundraising in China, after decades in which charity was denounced as western, capitalist and bourgeois. It is now no problem for people to donate to "good causes" and "disadvantaged individuals" such as Yang Hongwei.
- The emergence, in some places, of a shared identity as disabled people, who experience socio-economic disadvantage and negative attitudes based on their impairment.

Signs of a shared identity as disabled people may well be more evident among the privileged strata of China's disabled population: generally male, younger, with physical impairments often acquired in later life, with some education, some employment and some income, living in the cities. And yet, there is something very powerful when reading about the collective action of the 77 disabled people from Rui'an. Here, it is important to note that the China Disabled Persons Federation does not have a membership base and is therefore not an organisation of disabled people, although it is led by disabled people at the national exective level. This means that the action and solidarity of the 77 people from Rui'an occurred outside any state-sanctioned organised structure. That is not only exciting; it also puts the lie to those who would argue that disability movements are a creation of western politicised individuals.

These stories make for thought-provoking reading. They are at once inspiring and depressing. They bring out the everyday reality of disability as social disadvantage and oppression. But they also point to new, less usual but potentially significant undercurrents of change. Earlier, I said that the government's programme of raising disability awareness was a double-edged sword. I think these stories add an extra dimension to that statement. Top-down and state-led initiatives may have limited power to transform a disabling society (assuming – and one probably shouldn't – that such is the intention). But who's to say where this might lead, especially when individual voices become collective voices.

SOME POINTERS FOR STUDY AND RESEARCH

Where do we look for understanding on disability in the majority world? How do we respond to the stories we find? Do we look for links between those stories and their broader contexts? Do we seek stories that challenge our own outsider assumptions?

Sources

The best source on disability is disabled people themselves. The value and validity of listening to the voices of disabled people has become a central feature of much disability research in the UK (see Barnes & Mercer 1997, Clough & Barton 1998) and elsewhere (e.g. Coleridge 1993, Ingstad & Whyte 1995, Kisanji 1995).

There may also be other relevant sources. The range and nature of those sources will depend entirely on the specific area context. In some areas of the majority world, with a strong oral culture and tradition, there may be little to be gleaned from written material (see Sue Stubbs' paper in this book). In my own case, China has one of the longest and strongest traditions of written culture in the world. Language, text, inscriptions, proverbs; local and national government policies; novels and poetry written by or about disabled people; teaching manuals on education and rehabilitation; books on the sociology of disability; newspaper articles; dedicated disability magazines; brochures on disability initiatives, and so forth. None of which are particularly "easy" to analyse (you have to be very careful about how you use state propaganda, policies and statistics, for example); but all of which can offer insights and new angles.

At the end of the day, the search for understanding isn't really about what you get. It's about how you get it, how you use it, and how far you make the crucial connections.

Making Connections

I've probably said enough on this already! I only hope that this paper encourages rather than deters prospective researchers on disability in the majority world.

The sheer range of possible connections that can be made is especially daunting given that the social study of disability in the majority world is still new. There's not much past research to fall back on – which means you will have to juggle between breadth and depth. All the more important, then, that you take the time to set up your own framework of possible variables, factors and processes. Not all majority world stories will be as complicated as stories from China – several decades of rapid social and structural change, a sudden conversion to western-style capitalism, and an equally sudden interest in disability from the highest echelons of the Chinese state. But I would suspect that the realities of disability in the majority world generally, especially in urban and peri-urban areas, are much more complicated than outsiders assume and that researchers have hitherto suggested.

A parting comment on drawing up research agendas: yes, look to culture and cosmology, "traditional" attitudes and responses – these are crucial. But don't neglect institutions and ideologies, local and national provision and policy, modes of production and structures of social organisation, the existence of old and new professions and interests. All of these – be they indigenous, imported or imposed – are part of disability in the majority world.

CONCLUSION

Disability in China is a social issue; a cultural issue; a development issue. The lived experience and construction of disability cannot be divorced from the particular social, cultural and development context in which it is located. And that holds whether you live in Beijing or Bombay or Birmingham.

The implications of this for disability research and action in the majority world are far-reaching. In this paper, I have underlined the importance of "making connections" between individual stories and the wider contexts in which those stories are situated, produced and find meaning. I have also pointed to the insights that can be gleaned from hunting out extraordinary, as well as everyday, stories and using a mix of sources.

None of these suggestions are new (that much is clear from many of the contributions to this book and other excellent texts on disability in majority and minority worlds). Yet still it demands to be said – not least because it remains the case that far too little attention is paid to the experience and construction of disability in the majority world, even less that recognises the complexity, changes and contradictions that characterise majority world realities.

ACKNOWLEDGEMENTS

The research on which this paper is based was funded by an ESRC Postgraduate Studentship for PhD research, supervised by Dr. Colin Barnes

(Disability Research Unit, Department of Sociology) and Dr. Delia Davin (Department of East Asian Studies), University of Leeds.

REFERENCES

BARTON, L. (1999), "Developing an emancipatory research agenda: possibilities and dilemmas", in Clough, P. & Barton, L. (eds), *Articulating With Difficulty: Research Voices in Inclusive Education*, London: Paul Chapman Publishing.

BARNES, C. & MERCER, G. (1997) (eds), *Doing Disability Research*, Leeds: The Disability Press.

CALLAWAY, A. (1999), "Translating Theory into Practice in a Different Cultural Context: implementing a bilingual approach for Deaf children in China", in this book.

CDPF (China Disabled Persons Federation) (1988), "China's Five Year Work Programme for the Disabled (1988-1992)", Beijing: CDPF.

COLERIDGE, P. (1993), *Disability, Liberation, and Development*, Oxford: Oxfam with ADD.

DAVIN, D. (1990), "Never Mind if it's a Girl, You Can Have Another Try!", *in* Delman, J., Ostergaard, C. & Christiansen, F. (eds), *Remaking Peasant China*, Aarhus: Aarhus University Press.

INGSTAD, B. (1995), "Mpho ya Modimo – A Gift from God: Perspectives on 'Attitudes' toward Disabled Persons", *in* Ingstad, B. & Whyte, S.R. (eds), *Disability and Culture*, Berkeley: University of California Press.

INGSTAD, B. & WHYTE, S.R. (eds) (1995), *Disability and Culture*, Berkeley: University of California Press.

KISANJI, J. (1995a), "Growing up Disabled", *in* Zinkin, P. & McConachie, H. (eds), *Disabled Children & Developing Countries*, London: MacKeith Press.

KISANJI, J. (1995b), "Attitudes and Beliefs about Disability", *in* O'Toole, B. & McConkey, R. (eds), *Innovations in Developing Countries for People with Disabilities*, Chorley: Lisieux Hall.

KLEINMAN, A. *et al.* (1975) (eds), *Medicine in Chinese Cultures: Comparative Studies of Health Care in Chinese and Other Societies*, Washington: U.S. Government Printing Office for Fogarty International Centre.

KLEINMAN, A. (1980), *Patients and Healers in the Context of Culture: an exploration of the borderland between anthropology, medicine and psychiatry*, Berkeley: University of California Press.

MOMM, W. & KÖNIG, A. (1989), *From Community-Based Rehabilitation to Community-Integration Programmes: experiences and reflections on a new concept of service provision for disabled people*, Geneva: International Labour Office.

STONE, E. & PRIESTLEY, M. (1996), "Parasites, Pawns and Partners: disability research and the role of non-disabled researchers", *British Journal of Sociology*, Vol. 47 (4): 699-716.

STONE, E. (1996), "A Law to Protect, A Law to Prevent: contextualising disability legislation in China", *Disability & Society*, Vol. 11 (4): 469-484.

STONE, E. (1997), "From the Research Notes of a Foreign Devil: disability research in China", *in* Barnes, C. & Mercer, G. (eds), *Doing Disability Research*, Leeds: The Disability Press.

STONE, E. (1999), "Modern Slogan, Ancient Script: disability in the Chinese language", in Corker, M. & French, S. (eds), Disability Discourse, Buckingham: Open University Press.

STUBBS, S. (1999), "Engaging with Difference: Soul-Searching for a Methodology in Disability and Development Research", in this book.

THE OBSERVER (1996a), "Scandal of China's Orphanages", *The Observer*, 7 January 1996 (C.Field).

THE OBSERVER (1996b), "The Tragic Life of a Child Called No Name", *The Observer*, 14 January 1996 (special correspondent).

FURTHER READING ON CHINA

CROLL, E., DAVIN, D. & KANE, P. (1985) (eds), *China's One-Child Family Policy*, Basingstoke: Macmillan.

DASSU, M. & SAICH, T. (eds) (1992), *The Reform Decade in China: from hope to dismay*, London: Kegan Paul.

DWYER, D. (1994a) (ed), *China: The Next Decades*, Harlow: Longman Group.

HINTON, W. (1991), *The Privatization of China: The Great Reversal*, London: Earthscan.

LEUNG, J. (1994), "Dismantling the Iron Rice Bowl: Welfare Reforms in the PRC", *Journal of Social Policy*, Vol. 23 (3) pp. 341-361.

PARISH, W.L. & WHYTE, M.K. (1978), *Village and Family in Contemporary China*, Chicago: Chicago University Press.

UNSCHULD, P. (1985), *Medicine in China: A History of Ideas*, Berkeley: University of California Press.

WHITE, G. (ed) (1991), *The Chinese State in the Era of Economic Reforms: the road to crisis*, London: Macmillan.

WHYTE, M.K. & PARISH, W.L. (1984), *Urban Life in Contemporary China*, Chicago: Chicago University Press.

WONG, L. & MACPHERSON, S. (1995) (eds), *Social Change and Social Policy in Contemporary China*, Hong Kong: City University of Hong Kong, Dept. of Public and Social Administration.

CHAPTER 12

Disability Policy and Provision in Jordan: A critical perspective

Majid Turmusani

INTRODUCTION

This paper provides an outline of current disability provision, policy and legislation in Jordan. Reference is made to the emergence and development of these policies and services, especially the part played by western/international organisations in this process. Background information on Jordan, the current situation of disabled people and dominant social attitudes to disability is also presented by way of context. The findings are based on secondary literature, and on empirical data generated whilst working towards a Ph.D. on "The Economic Needs of Disabled People in Jordan".

SETTING THE SCENE

The historical development of the Jordanian state is inseparable from the flight of refugees from other countries in the region, including 800,000 Palestinians who fled to Jordan from conflict in the West Bank and from the Gulf War (Wilson 1991). By the early 1990s there were already 1.1 million refugees registered with the United Nations Refugees Work Agency (UNRWA) in Jordan. As a result, Jordan has become the focus of international attention and foreign aid

Also over the past few decades, Jordan has experienced its share of rapid socio-economic development and socio-economic crisis. The major economic crisis of the latter half of the 1980s resulted in a significant drop in the general standard of living (ESDP 1993). This was compounded by the return (due to the Gulf War) of 300,000 Jordanians in 1990 – economic migrants whose return meant not only a rise in the overall population (to over 4 million people), but also a marked reduction in national revenue in the form of lost remittances. The Gulf War also led to increases in water shortages, in unemployment (to 20%) and in the number of people under the poverty line (to 6.6%). The overall scene, therefore, is one of economic constraints for a growing number of Jordanians as well as Jordan's huge refugee population.

In Jordan, the Gulf War and ongoing conflict on the West Bank have also impacted on the number of disabled people in the country. There has been a rise in the number of people with conflict-related impairments (especially among the refugee community), while the capacity of government and localities to respond to the needs of disabled people is under strain (Acton 1983, UNICEF 1993, Turmusani & Sime 1994). There are, however, no accurate figures on the number of disabled people in Jordan (ESCWA 1994). If one assumes that at least 4% of the total population has an impairment (see Coleridge 1993 and Helander 1993), this would suggest that there could be some 170,000 disabled people in Jordan. Evidence from a recent survey conducted by the Department of Statistics in 1991 states that 11% of families reported having a disabled family member. This would give a total of 66,000 families in Jordan with one or more disabled family members (UNICEF 1993, Zu'bi 1991). Of course, such statistics are open to question, not least since socio-cultural values are known to play a major role in determining who is identified (by self, family and others) as "disabled" and what is counted as an "impairment" (Johnson 1991). For example, the only nationwide survey to date on impairment in Jordan (conducted by the Queen Alia Fund) focused solely on the incidence of visible impairment (QAF 1979). It is only recently that impairments like speech difficulties and learning difficulties have been considered at all when defining who is and who is not a disabled person in Jordan.

Whilst it may not be possible to get an accurate count of the number of disabled people in Jordan, it is certainly possible to get a good understanding of the problems that many of them confront every day.

THE SITUATION OF DISABLED PEOPLE IN JORDAN

Recent research on disability in Jordan and empirical data gathered during fieldwork in 1996 all point to the serious disadvantages faced by disabled people in Jordan in relation to every area of life, including education, health, training and employment (Barghouthi and Al-Dean 1994, ESCWA 1994, Hinchcliffe 1994, Zomu't 1993).

The design of transport systems and public and religious buildings is such that they are inaccessible to many disabled people (Khatib 1994); while access to information is also greatly restricted (there is only one sign-language television programme for deaf people each week, and the range of reading materials for blind people is also very limited – see Hinchcliffe 1994).

The economic situation of disabled people in terms of employment and welfare support also leaves much to be desired. The Centre for Strategic Studies estimates that national unemployment among Jordanians could now be as high as 22-27% (CSS 1998). It is widely accepted that the rate of unemployment among disabled people in Jordan is even higher, and that disabled people are far more likely to live in poverty. Here, the absence of a welfare system and the absence of positive policies to promote the employment of disabled people serve to compound these existing inequalities. Barriers to employment are especially severe for people with a label of "mental retardation", people who have cerebral palsy and deaf people (Khatib 1989).

There is a severe shortage of specialised centres, personnel, funds and facilities to support disabled people – especially in rural areas. There is also practically no support from governmental and non-governmental bodies to disabled people who wish to live independently in the community, although the Queen Alia Fund has started to change this with a small programme to support disabled people who live in their own home through providing adaptations such as appropriate toilets and a ramp (QAF 1994). Generally, however, what little assistance there is takes the form of residential accommodation.

This situation is far from unique to Jordan. Similar conclusions have been drawn in relation to disabled people worldwide ... both in the west (see Barnes 1991, Dalley 1991, Oliver 1990 for example) and in developing countries (see Coleridge 1993, Helander 1993 and contributions to Zinkin & McConachie 1995). The overall picture is one of inadequate services, socio-economic structures that exclude disabled people, and a lack of access and equal opportunity. It is also one of negative social attitudes.

SOCIO-CULTURAL ATTITUDES TO DISABILITY: AN OVERVIEW

An analysis of dominant socio-cultural attitudes to disabled people in Jordan throws up some insightful, even contradictory, evidence. On the one hand, it is possible to identify an Islamic version of the philosophy of equal rights for people with impairments. For example, there is an episode in the Holy Qur'an which tells of God reprimanding his Prophet when he turned his back on a blind man who asked for advice and knowledge (Ali 1994: Surah Abasah verses 1-5, also Miles 1995). On this basis, it might be argued that God wishes all members of Islamic society to receive equal treatment, irrespective of impairment. On the other hand, however, there are several verses in the Qur'an and Hadith that reveal a much less accommodating, even discriminatory, attitude to disabled people (Turmusani 1998). Unfortunately, evidence collected during fieldwork and from other sources within Jordan would seem to suggest that negative rather than positive attitudes to impairment are the more dominant – especially in rural areas.

Islam is the dominant faith for more than 92% of the population. A core message of Islam is that anything that occurs and everything that exists in the world can be attributed to the will of God. Accordingly, impairment may be explained as an act of God, designed to test the faith of individuals and their capacity to accept that fate with gratitude and patience. This perception of disability as a test of the faith and as God's will plays a major part in shaping attitudes towards disabled people.

There is also evidence that Arab societies (including Jordan) have tended to treat disabled people as people with no prospects and no potential (Khatib 1989), and have viewed impairment as something shameful and as an ordeal to be endured by the family. Thus, for fear that knowledge of an impairment within the family might incur difficulties in securing marriages, many families have denied the existence of a disabled family member (see also Coleridge 1993). Guilt and pity may also prompt some parents to "hide" their disabled children, with the result that access to appropriate services (where they exist) is even further restricted.

Disabled people constitute, and/or are perceived to constitute, an inevitable and significant drain on family resources and a potential source of damage to family status. Such attitudes have also been evident in the media: until recently, the media in Jordan has portrayed disabled people as passive and dependent, thereby perpetuating a negative image (Khatib 1994).

There are some signs of change. Public attitudes towards disabled people in Jordan seem to have improved over time, at least towards some sections of the disabled population. The changes are particularly apparent in relation to people with sensory and less severe physical impairments (rather than people with "mental retardation"), and in relation to men rather than women (see Quryouti 1984 and Florian & Katz 1983 on the status of people labelled as "mentally retarded").

Although the position of women in Jordan has improved in comparison to other Islamic countries, women still occupy a different status to men. In some parts of the country, women are considered to be awra (i.e. women's faces and bodies must not be exposed to public view) and are not allowed freedom to choose a husband, express an opinion or live on their own. The situation of disabled women, especially those who are labelled as "mentally retarded", is even worse since disabled women are often viewed as an endless burden on their families – both morally and financially. In southern Lebanon for instance, it has been reported that a disabled girl was left to die following an Israeli military offensive on her village and family home. The father was reported to say that he preferred to save the family cow rather than his disabled daughter because the cow was more useful (Habib 1998). Generally, where a disabled woman is the focus of family concern, this is less out of concern for her well-being, than for the protection of family honour.

In summary, negative attitudes towards disabled people and discrimination against them have a long history in Jordan.

DISABILITY-RELATED PROVISION IN JORDAN

Institution-based and community-based (see Coleridge 1993) services are provided by and/or funded by professionals working for international and national non-governmental organisations, government and the private sector. These include: early detection services, special education services, rehabilitation services, vocational training services, sheltered workshop services, employment schemes and community-based rehabilitation programmes. There are 72 centres for disabled people which are run by NGO, government and private sectors; and they provide services to around 7,000 disabled people (less than 2% of the total population of disabled people). In this paper, I focus on services related to employment and community-based rehabilitation. All the statistics were gathered during fieldwork in late 1996.

Employment schemes and services

The importance of employment for disabled people is a key issue (Barnes 1991, DAA 1995). Often, self-employment is regarded as preferable to sheltered employment, while open employment is the most favoured option. However, the barriers to open employment in Jordan are significant. Several schemes have been set up with a view to increase the number of disabled people in work. Currently, two government bodies in Jordan are responsible for employment policy and creation of economic opportunities for disabled people: Ministry of Labour and the Vocational Training Corporation. Other organisations, especially NGOs, are also involved.

- Vocational training services are conceptualised in Jordan as an integral part of special education, irrespective of market demands or employment opportunities. The services offer low quality and limited skill development, often with inappropriate supervision. Training opportunities are very limited: only 276 disabled people – all between 14 and 24 years old – were in receipt of this service in 1996 (that is, less than 4% of the total population of disabled people who receive services). Of the 9 vocational training units in the country, 3 target "mentally retarded" people; 2 target deaf people; 2 target people with a physical impairment; and only 1 unit is open to people with different impairments. Most of the trainees are men. All of the centres are located in cities.
- There are 4 sheltered workshops in the country and, again, they are all located in big cities. They employ around 83 people with mild impairments – people who have graduated from vocational training programmes. According to Hinchcliffe (1994), the working conditions in these sheltered workshops are poor. The workshops are run by the voluntary and international non-governmental sectors, not by the state. Even though sheltered workshops are considered by many to be an unfavourable option (ILO 1989), there are still very long waiting lists of potential employees.
- The Friendship Society for the Blind started the first scheme to set up self-employment projects for blind men, primarily in Amman. In the 1980s, the

National Aid Fund started to provide micro-credit loans for husbandry projects, and support to purchase aids and equipment. This support was also open to disabled people and, in contrast to other schemes, operated in rural areas. In 1992, the General Union of Voluntary Societies and the United Nations Development Programme established a self-employment scheme targeted at disabled people. Unfortunately, disabled people were not involved in the design and delivery of this project – this was reflected in the low attendance record of disabled people (GUVS 1994).

- In 1994, the National Council for the Welfare of Disabled People established a new department with responsibility for promoting the open employment of disabled people in public and private sectors. It is reported that about 150 disabled people have been employed in the private sector, although this is mostly a result of personal contacts rather than legal incentive or enforcement (NCWDP 1994).

Community-based rehabilitation schemes and services

Community-based Rehabilitation (CBR) has been put forward as one way to increase the availability of services to disabled people in developing countries (see Coleridge 1993, Khatib 1994, Daoud 1991, Andrew 1991). The key principals of CBR are low-cost and simple technology, the use of local resources, and community participation (Twible & Henley 1993, Ingstad 1995, Helander 1993). In Jordan, the eight CBR programmes – serving a total of 500 people – which are currently under way or in the planning stages have been spearheaded and funded by international agencies and organisations. Where local NGOs are involved, their role has been limited to delivery rather than design and management of services.

- In the early 1980s, the first CBR project in Jordan was set up and run by the United Nations Refugee and Work Agency (UNRWA) in a refugee camp. Nowadays, UNWRA runs six CBR programmes – all in refugee camps.
- In 1991, UNICEF funded a pilot CBR project in 13 villages of Mafraq district, following recommendations made at the Jordanian/Swedish Medical Association conference in Amman (QAF 1994). The only part of the original project that is still active is a mobile clinic unit, which is administered by a local NGO (with funding from UNICEF). The mobile

clinic provides medical rehabilitation services to some parts of Mafraq district.

- In 1995, the Holy Land Institute for the Deaf started a CBR project for people with hearing impairments in Salt District in central Jordan (HLID 1994).

Other Schemes and Services

- There is no welfare system in Jordan, although the National Aid Fund has some responsibility (more on paper than in reality, it seems) to provide support for disabled people to provide grants for individual rehabilitation purposes.
- There are no organisations controlled by disabled people, although it is interesting to note that Deaf people in Jordan have recently started to set up their own social clubs (Hinchcliffe 1994).
- There is a Jordanian Federation for Handicapped Sports, but it is the only cross-impairment organisation related to sports and recreation opportunities for disabled people. It is based in Amman and has very limited resources and capacity.
- A few workshops produce disability aids and equipment (e.g. wheelchairs).

All of this looks bleak. The good news is that – on paper – things should get better as a result of recent legislation which sets out the facilities and services that disabled people and their families should start to expect to get. These are discussed shortly. Before that, it is important to consider some of the main problems that have impacted on the provision of services, their appropriateness and their effectiveness.

SOME LIMITATIONS AND CONSTRAINTS

Several of the services exist more in name than in reality. For example, the National Aid Fund has a remit to provide financial support to people in poverty, including disabled people. Support might include a micro-credit loan or a grant towards meeting rehabilitation needs. However, access to this support depends on a number of conditions and criteria, including politically-related allocation prorities. Procedures are long and complex. The potential geographical distribution is very wide.

Advocacy and self-organisation of disabled people exists in only limited form. Despite the fact that the right of disabled people to participate in decision-making relating to their life is guaranteed by recent legislation (see below), the reality falls far short of the idea. The government seems to prefer professionally-run services for disabled people; and where there have been attempts to form organisations of disabled people or to set up consultations, these have failed. At the time of data collection in late 1996, there was only one parents' society – which was inactive – and a failed attempt by some disabled people to set up their own organisation (the failure seems to have arisen from a leadership conflict among the membership).

The lack of a mobilised "voice" of disabled people in local areas and nationwide, combined with the preference of those in government, voluntary and private sectors to deploy professionals rather than adopt a community-based approach which involves disabled people, has had a negative impact on the appropriateness of services provided. One example is the inappropriate voluntary sector scheme to promote self-employment among disabled people: the buildings used were inaccessible with no appropriate facilities, and disabled people were not consulted as to the type of employment they wanted – so attendance was very low (see Turmusani & Sime 1994). Another related issue lies in the failure of those running vocational training schemes to consider local market demands, with the result that training provided does not equip individuals with the skills they need to thrive in the local economic and competitive labour market.

The government's preference for professionals is reflected in a range of schemes to provide skills and training to those professionals who already work with disabled people, in order to enable them do their job better – for example, through supporting professionals to gain postgraduate academic qualifications in special education and through the provision of in-service training and local or overseas exchanges. A major problem, however, is how to retain those who have been trained – since many higher-level professionals turn to employment in the private sector or overseas rather than receive the lower salaries on offer in government and voluntary sector work in Jordan. A more promising approach – although it is firmly based in a "medical model" of disability, is the creation of an Occupational Therapy College (a new joint-project between GUVS and Royal Medical Services, with funding from the British Government). This is one of the leading professional institutions in the country; and there is a high demand for graduates both within local communities and further afield.

The severe shortage of appropriate services, personnel, funds and facilities in disability-related work in Jordan (see above) means that the few disability projects that do exist operate under significant constraints. They have to learn to do a lot of work with very few resources. This is compounded by an apparent lack of planning, co-ordination and co-operation between the agencies that are involved in disability and rehabilitation programmes in Jordan, which further restricts the potential impact of these services to benefit disabled people (Hinchcliffe 1994). This lack of co-ordination results in the unnecessary duplication of services and an inefficient use of limited resources (WPACDP 1983). It is more than likely that low capacity, lack of planning and lack of consultation, and over-stretching capacities in terms of geographical spread were the root causes of programme failure in the CBR project in Mafraq district (see above).

THE DEVELOPMENT OF DISABILITY POLICIES IN JORDAN

A medical model of disability, exemplified by many professional practices, western NGOs and international agencies, has penetrated the local culture and affected attitudes towards disability in Jordan. Clearly, this is not to say that negative attitudes towards impairment and disability have only emerged since the 1960s (when international agencies and organisations became active in disability in Jordan) ... the information on "traditional" attitudes outlined in the previous section is proof enough of that. It is, however, to argue that the ways of working and the scope of projects implemented by western organisations have influenced the attitudes and shaped the responses of the Jordanian government, voluntary and private sector, as well as families and individuals.

In Jordan, as in many countries, rehabilitation services for disabled people have been initiated in the wake of war and conflict. The increased incidence of conflict-related impairment, and the reduced capacity to meet the needs of disabled people, have often been the catalyst for more state and, significantly, international involvement in the lives of disabled people (see Ingstad 1995). In Jordan, disability-related provision began in the 1960s and was led by foreign NGOs which provided institutional (residential) care for severely deaf and "mentally retarded" people. In the 1970s, government and voluntary organisations followed suit and began to get involved in western-style institutional provision for "mentally retarded" people. In time, western-style institutions which specialised in institutional care, special education, vocational training, and rehabilitation began to spread throughout Jordan (Khatib 1994). No matter how well intentioned these international and local initiatives might have been, there is little doubt that the result of western influence has been a view that equates "institutions" and "special" with "disability provision", and which thereby promotes the marginalisation of disabled people in society, and their exclusion from "mainstream" services and provision.

A further legacy of western influence is the degree to which disabled people and related services have been seen as the tasks of non-governmental organisations and the voluntary sector, rather than the responsibility of the government. The existence of comprehensively funded services for disabled people has encouraged reliance on these (mostly international) NGOs and agencies, and therefore discouraged the development of formal state-run and state-funded services. None of this is to deny the important contributions that have resulted from western and international involvement in disability (e.g. rehabilitation, care services, training) – it is simply to point out that these contributions have been at a cost.

The nature of service provision has impacted on family responses to disabled people. There is now a stronger view that disabled people are no longer a family responsibility alone: communities and government also have some responsibility to meet the needs of disabled people. This view has certainly been influenced by western involvement in establishing residential centres for disabled people, thereby taking over what had previously been the sole responsibility of the family (see Mallory *et al* 1993 on the impact of western, especially colonial, influence on attitudes towards and provision for disabled people in developing countries). From my research and experience, it seems that poorer families may now be more inclined to send severely disabled family members to residential institutions out of a belief that such western-style and (often) western-funded institutions provide better services than can be offered by the family.

The level of international interest has not reduced. Indeed, it received a boost in the International Year of Disabled Persons (1981) and the subsequent United Nations Decade of Disabled People (UN 1994). 1981 was also, however, a turning point in Jordan in terms of the government's agenda for disabled people and public awareness of disability. It can be argued that, since then, state and voluntary sectors within Jordan have taken steps to provide disabled people with more appropriate services, with a view to enabling them to contribute to society and also to meet Islamic obligations in providing equal opportunities regardless of someone's mental, physical, or economic condition. But there is a very long way to go, since services are still provided to less than 2% of the total population of disabled people in Jordan (Khatib 1994, UNICEF 1993).

Finally, it should be noted that the Monarchy of Jordan has played an important role in supporting disability policies and legislation. The involvement of members of the Royal Family in public life, especially in disability issues, has speeded up the introduction of disability legislation and, through organisations like the Queen Alia Fund and the Al-Hussein Society for Physical Handicap, has provided additional services. Here again, however, the influence of international agencies is clear.

It is clear that both foreign and indigenous forces have contributed to the emergence and development of non-family responses to disability. The interplay of these forces has resulted in a complex set of policies, programmes and practices that reflect both local values and values that originated in very different sociocultural contexts. I would argue that a medical approach to disability has been paramount, and that this has largely been introduced through western involvement in disability in Jordan. What is required now is a transformation of this approach to what has been called a social model of disability, which focuses on social solutions rather than individual solutions (see Crow 1996, Barton & Oliver 1997, Barnes 1991 & 1996, Oliver 1990 & 1996, Lunt & Thornton 1994, and Turmusani 1999 among others).

LEGISLATION AND DISABILITY IN JORDAN

The International Year of Disabled Persons was also the first time that thought was given to legislation as a means of improving the situation of disabled people in Jordan. Since 1981, many attempts have been made by parents and activists who work in western NGOs to formulate appropriate legislation under the supervision of the Ministry of Social Development, and with the support of Their Royal Highnesses Ra'ed Ibn Zaid and Firas Ibn Ra'ed. Eight years later, in 1989, a Provisional Law for the Welfare of Disabled People (No.34/1989) was passed. Then, in 1993, the provisional bill was passed and Law No.12/1993 for the Welfare of Disabled People came into existence.

The mission statement of this Law is to ensure the rights of disabled people for services and provision which will promote their integration into society and affirm their rights:

> This law affirms the right of disabled persons to education, training, employment, rehabilitation, medical treatment, sports and recreation, transport, aids and equipment and materials, support services and participation in decision making as far as the resources allow. This law establishes a body called the National Council for the Affairs of Disabled Persons to implement the law (see NCWDP 1993).

In order to make these rights a reality, there is a strong need for all relevant parties (including government, NGOs and the private sector) to co-operate and co-ordinate their efforts; to enforce implementation of the law; to involve society and raise awareness of disability and the law, and so forth.

The definition of a disabled person is:

> any person with a permanent, partial or total impairment in any of his senses or physical, psychological, or mental abilities to the extent that the ability to learn, to be rehabilitated or to work, is limited in a way which inhibit him/her short of fulfilling his/her normal daily requirement in circumstances similar to those of able-bodied persons (NCWDP 1993).

Some impairments, such as dyslexia, are not included.

Hinchcliffe (1994) has criticised this law on the basis that many of the "rights" established depend on the discretion of the Minister of Social Development. Also, representatives of disabled people are appointed by the Minister rather than by other disabled people or groups they might represent. The high turnover of members of the various government ministries and organisations, who have been appointed to debate the implementation of the law, will lead to a low-level of commitment and consistency in decision-making and in enforcing the law. Finally, the law is clearly based on a "welfare" rather than a "rights" perspective, thereby setting the scene for continued dependency on others, especially on welfare and disability professionals (Turmusani 1998).

It is arguable that nothing will change until serious mechanisms (and resourced mechanisms) are in place to implement rights such as the right to employment. The right for employment of disabled people in Jordan is guaranteed by the new law, and there are several sections of the law which discuss the opportunities and support that disabled people should expect to access. However, evidence from fieldwork shows that disabled people's participation in the economy remains very limited and the majority of disabled people – including those who are well-trained or qualified – are unemployed or employed in low-skilled, low-paid work. The preference for employing non-disabled people remains strong. The situation is little different whether in the public or the private sector.

CONCLUSION

There is a growing awareness of the substantial contribution disabled people make, and can make, to their local communities and society in general. All too often, development plans bypass disabled people and, when they do take account of disability, tend to treat disabled people as "separate" and "special". I have argued that this is the case in Jordan.

In Jordan, disabled people are marginalised and experience socio-economic disadvantage as well as negative socio-cultural attitudes. Existing disability-related provision, policies and legislation are inadequate, poorly-resourced, more apparent on paper than in reality, and underpinned by the view that institutional, special and medical provision, run by professionals with little involvement of disabled people, constitutes the most appropriate form of disability provision. Even when discussion turns to employment schemes, it is clear that most of the limited opportunities that exist are in low-level jobs, set apart from other employees. Moreover, the increase in service provision since the 1960s (e.g. residential centres, employment schemes, CBR outreach) is minute compared to the needs of 98% of disabled children and adults who do not receive support in the 1990s. The distribution of priorities and approaches to disability in Jordan must change if Jordanian state and society are ever to meet these present demands (Turmusani & Sime 1994). In my view, existing policies, provision and legislation will only contribute to disabled people's empowerment if the following factors are in place and prioritised:

- Support to disabled people to promote their self-organisation and self-advocacy.
- Increased access to financial and other resources – for individual disabled people, groups of disabled people, and also for service providers.

- Promotion of a social model of disability among disabled people, society in general, service providers in government, voluntary and private sectors and, of course, among those western NGOs and international agencies that are still working and will continue to work with disabled people in Jordan.

With these factors in place, and with co-ordination and collaboration, disability policy and provision in Jordan could be greatly improved.

REFERENCES

ACTON, N. (1983), 'World Disability: The Need for a New Approach: A Cry for Health', in O. Shirley (ed) *Poverty and Disability in the Third World*, Frome: Third World Group and AHRTAG.

ALI, A. (1994), *The Meaning of The Holy Qur'an* (transl), Maryland: Ammana Corporation, Brentwood.

ANDREW, L. (1991) "The Role of Institution in CBR in Jordan", in *Community Based Rehabilitation: Proceedings of the 3rd Seminar of JSMA*, Amman: JSMA.

BARGHOUTHI, M. and Al-Dean, H. (1994), "Family Role in the Rehabilitation and Taking Care for the Disabled", in *The Role of Family in Integrating Disabled Women into Society*, Amman: ESCWA.

BARNES, C. (1991), "Institutional Discrimination Against Disabled People and the Campaigning for Anti-Discrimination Legislation", *Critical Social Policy* 12 (1), pp. 5-22.

BARNES, C. (1996), "The Social Model of Disability: Myths and Misconceptions", *Coalition*, August, pp. 25-30

BARTON, L. & OLIVER, M. (eds) (1997), *Disability Studies: Past, Present and Future*, Leeds: The Disability Press.

COLERIDGE, P. (1993), *Disability, Liberation and Development*, Oxford: Oxfam.

CROW, L. (1996), "Including All of Our Lives: Renewing the Social Model of Disability", in Barnes, C. & Mercer, G. (eds.), *Exploring the Divide: Illness and Disability*, Leeds: The Disability Press.

CSS (1998), *Unemployment Among Jordanians*, Jordan: Centre for Strategic Studies, University of Jordan.

DAA (1995), *Overcoming Obstacles to the Integrating of Disabled People*, Copenhagen, Denmark.

DALLEY, G. (ed) (1991), *Disability and Social Policy*, London: Policy Studies Institute.

DAOUD, A. (1991), "UNRWA Experience in CBR in Jordan", in *Community Based Rehabilitation: Proceedings of the 3rd Seminar of JSMA*, Amman: JSMA.

ESCWA (1994), "The Situation of Disabled Women and Their Social Integration in the ESCWA Region", in *The Role of Family in Integrating Disabled Women into Society*, Amman: ESCWA.

ESDP (1993), *Economic and Social Development Plan: 1993-1997*, Amman, Jordan: Ministry of Planning.

FLORIAN, V. & KATZ, S. (1983), "The Impact of Cultural Ethnic and National Variables on Attitudes Towards the Disabled in Israel", *International Journal of Intercultural Relations* 7, pp. 167-179.

GUVS (1994), *The Annual Report: The General Union of Voluntary Societies (GUVS)*, Amman: Co-operative Society for Press Workers.

HABIBI, L. (1998), *Gender and Disability: Women's Experience in the Middle East*, Oxfam UK and Ireland.

HELANDER, E. (1993), *Prejudice and Dignity: An Introduction to Community Based Rehabilitation*, New York: UNDP.

HINCHCLIFFE, A. (1994), *Explanatory Report on the Situation of Disability in Jordan*, Amman: Disability Development Action (DDA).

HLID (1994), *The Holy Land Institute for the Deaf*, Salt, Jordan.

ILO (1989), "Vocational Rehabilitation and Employment of the Disabled People in ESCWA Region", in *The Capabilities and Needs of Disabled Persons in the ESCWA Region*, Amman: ESCWA.

INGSTAD, B. (1995), "Mpho Ya Modimo – A Gift from God: Perspectives on 'Attitudes' Towards Disabled Persons", in Ingstad, B. & Whyte, S.R. (eds), *Disability and Culture*, Berkeley: University of California Press.

JOHNSON, R. (1991), "The Health Transition: The Cultural Inflation of Morbidity During the Decline of Mortality", *Health Transition Review* 1(1), pp. 39-68.

KHATIB, A. (1989), "Disability Situation in Jordan", in *The Capabilities and Needs of Disabled Persons in the ESCWA Region*, Amman: ESCWA.

KHATIB, A. (1994), "The Role of NGO's in Integrating the Women into the Society", in *The Role of Family in Integrating Disabled Women into Society*, Amman: ESCWA.

LUNT, N. & THORNTON, P. (1994), "Disability and Employment: towards an understanding of discourse and policy", *Disability and Society* 9 (2), pp. 223-238.

MALLORY, B., NICHOLLS, R., CHARLTON, J. & MARFO, K. (1993), *Traditional and Changing Views of Disability in Developing Societies*, University of New Hampshire, World Rehabilitation Fund IEEIR.

MILES, M. (1995), "Disability in an Eastern Religious Context: Historical Perspectives", *Disability and Society* 10(1), pp. 49-69.

NCWDP (1993), *Law for Welfare of Disabled People No 12 for the Year 1993*, Amman: The Jordan Printing Press.

NCWDP (1994), *Proceedings of the National Council for the Welfare of Disabled People*, Amman, Jordan.

OLIVER, M. (1990), *The Politics of Disablement*, Basingstoke: Macmillan.

OLIVER, M. (1996), "Defining Impairment and Disability: Issues at Stake", in Barnes, C. & Mercer, G. (eds), *Exploring the Divide*, Leeds: The Disability Press.

QAF (1979), *National Survey of the Handicapped in Jordan*, The Queen Alia Fund, Amman: Jordan Press Foundation.

QAF (1994), *The Annual Report: The Queen Alia Fund*, Amman: Jordan Press Foundation.

QURYOUTI, Y. (1984), "Special Education in Jordan: A Present Status of Needs Assessment Study", unpublished PhD dissertation, Michigan State University.

TURMUSANI, M. (1998), "Some Cultural Representation of Disability in Jordan: Concepts and Beliefs", working paper presented at the Expert Meeting on Local Beliefs and Concepts of Disability in Different Cultures, Bonn, 21-24 May 1998.

TURMUSANI, M. (1999), "The Economic Needs of Disabled People in Jordan: from the Personal to the Political Perspective", *Disability Studies Quarterly* 19(1).

TURMUSANI, M. and SIME, J. (1994), "Evaluation Report on the Disability Provision in Jordan", Amman: GUVS.

TWIBLE, R. and HENLEY, E. (1993), "A Curriculum Model for a Community Development Approach to Community Based Rehabilitation", *Disability and Society* 8(1), pp. 43-57.

UN (1994), *The Standard Roles on the Equalisation of Opportunities for Persons With Disabilities*, New York: United Nations.

UNICEF (1993), "Priorities for Childhood Disability Program in Jordan", A report by Gulbdan Habibi on a visit to Amman, Jordan, 3 December.

WILSON, R. (1991), *Politics and Economy of Jordan*, London: School of Oriental and African Studies.

WPACDP (1983), *The World of Action Concerning Disabled People*, Rehabilitation and Employment Convention number 169, 1983, Geneva: United Nations.

ZINKIN, P. & McCONACHIE, H. (1995) (eds), *Disabled Children and Developing Countries*, London: Mac Keith Press.

ZOMU'T, Y. (1993), *Vocational Rehabilitation of the Disabled*, Amman: Press and Publication Publishers, the Church Council.

ZU'BI, A. (1991), *Disabilities in Jordan: Characteristics and Some Demographics Factors*, Amman: DSS.

CHAPTER 13

Ghosts and Germs: Cerebral Palsy in Nepal – A preliminary exploration of cosmology and disability

Rebecca Saul and David Phillips

INTRODUCTION

The need for cross-cultural studies of disability has often been stated but seldom acted upon. It was nearly thirty years ago that Edgerton, in a highly influential paper, made the intellectual case for increased study of disability within and between societies, both developing and developed (Edgerton 1970). His hope that such studies would soon be undertaken has not been borne out (Manion & Bersani 1987). This dearth of studies has not been just because of indifference: there are substantial methodological problems to overcome too, and even highly experienced researchers undertaking field studies for many years have raised questions about validity in studying disability in another culture (Miles 1992). Nevertheless, even studies with problematic methodologies or with limited exposure to another culture can enhance understanding if their findings are treated with caution and circumspection. More importantly, studies in other cultures can give insights into our own culture and can lead to questioning and development of taken-for-granted academic understandings.

The present study was conducted in this spirit: as a short-term, tentative exploration, envisaged as a feasibility study rather than a research project. It would be implausible to conceive of this study as a fully-fledged cross-cultural study, nonetheless it has provided insights and facilitated the formulation of tentative conceptual frameworks which can then be refined (or replaced) before being rigorously and empirically tested.

DISABILITY IN NEPAL

Nepal is an independent kingdom on the southern slopes of the Himalayas, situated between Tibet and India. It is predominantly rural (only nine per cent of the population live in towns or cities), has a population of around 23 million people and, although one of the poorest countries in the world, is undergoing rapid economic development. It has an ethnically and culturally diverse population with a wide range of religious beliefs, including Hindu, Muslim, Buddhist and folk religions. It also has diverse medical and health-belief systems, including Sanskrit-based ayurvedic medicine, Tibetan medicine, homeopathy, acupuncture, unani (Greco-Arabic medicine), various types of spiritual healers (shamans, tantric Buddhist healers, exorcists, traditional midwives), as well as Western allopathic medicine (Durkin-Longley 1984, Streefland 1985).

While perceptions of illness in Nepal have received some ethnographic attention (McHugh 1993, Acharya 1994) there has been very limited research on either the prevalence of or cultural beliefs about disability. Where literature does exist, there are a large number of inconsistencies. For instance, the estimates of the proportion of disabled people in the total population of Nepal ranges from less than one percent, to three percent (His Majesty's Government 1993). Other small-scale studies estimate the prevalence to be as high as 13% (BPEP/DANIDA 1995, ICS/DANIDA 1995).

On the basis of data for other developing countries with similar demographic and socio-economic profiles to Nepal, there are estimated to be over 60,000 children in Nepal who have cerebral palsy. Furthermore (based on information from Professor Bhatuk Rajbandari, Director of the Nepal Cerebral Palsy Self-Help Group), it is estimated that less than a thousand of these children receive any type of biomedical therapeutic assistance, such as physiotherapy or speech or occupational therapy; and that less than 200 receive schooling, whether in "special" schools or in mainstream schools. Evidence from the Kathmandu Valley suggests that there are no reported cases of young people with cerebral palsy living past the age of twenty years. The situation in the rest of the Nepal is unlikely to be very different.

To date, there have been very few ethnographic studies of disability in Nepal and none specifically about cerebral palsy or similar conditions. On the basis of a year's fieldwork in 1976 and 1977 in rural settings near Kathmandu, Peters concluded that learning disabilities are recognised, labelled and stigmatised (Peters 1980). Richardson, during a two-month study tour of rural areas north and west of Kathmandu, estimated that around one per cent of the population had physical disabilities (Richardson 1983). Richardson's data collection methods were highly impressionistic and so his estimate needs to be treated with caution, but he made the interesting observation that high levels of physical impairment and disability were often coupled with low levels of handicap (Richardson 1983).

Two other studies are relevant although they do not directly address issues of disability. Streefland, in an exploration of the interface between western and traditional medical systems, points out that ideas, beliefs and practices which are characteristic of a specific medical system are often deeply embedded within the culture of an ethnic or religious group (Streefland 1985). Pigg, after undertaking fieldwork from 1985 to 1988, concluded that modernisation and development have profoundly affected people's perception of medical realms and healing (Pigg 1995).

THE STUDY: AIMS & METHODOLOGY

The study aimed to explore the cultural beliefs and actions concerning cerebral palsy and similar conditions of: parents and families of children with cerebral palsy; medical, healing and other professionals working with the children; and, where possible, the children themselves.

Fieldwork was undertaken in Nepal between October and December 1997 by Rebecca Saul, who had previously undertaken two and a half years of applied and cultural anthropological fieldwork in Nepal. Data was collected in two locations: Kathmandu, the capital city (for four weeks: 30 interviews) and Janakpur, a medium-sized urban centre in South-east Nepal, just north of the border with India (for two weeks: 10 interviews).

In Kathmandu, the research population mainly comprised: staff, parents and children at the Self-help Group for Cerebral Palsy (hereafter SGCP) school and rehabilitation centre; families who were part of the outreach programme run by the SGCP; and staff of other organisations working in the disability sector. Several of the teachers at the SGCP school were themselves parents of children attending the school; field methodology included observing, interviewing and holding discussions with these mothers/teachers. The use of SGCP as a base permitted access to families from outside Kathmandu, when they brought their children to the rehabilitation centre for diagnosis, therapy or annual check-ups. There was also ample opportunity to have discussions with the Nepali staff at the centre. In addition to the school and rehabilitation centre, the SGCP runs an outreach programme to follow-up families who have visited the centre, and to establish new contacts with families who are referred to SGCP (by medical institutions and social services in Kathmandu, or by concerned neighbours and family members). These outreach visits enabled Rebecca to revisit several of the families on her own after an initial introduction by the home visit staff.

In Janakpur, as in Kathmandu, the Janakpur school for disabled children was the main means by which contact was made with children with cerebral palsy and their families. The school is supported by funds from the local Hindu temple, although children of all faiths attend. The school is built on temple land and has three teachers, a carer/cook/housekeeper, and a gardener – who also brings disabled children to school on his bicycle. Between eight and fifteen children with various disabilities, including cerebral palsy, attend the school at any one time. As well as play and learning sessions, the children also make candles and chalk to sell in local bazaars in order to purchase equipment for the school.

Since the study was designed as an exploratory study, a central objective was to test our methodological approach. This included mobility mapping and ranking, ethno-histories and biographies of disability, art and story-telling, as well as participant observation, focus group discussions, unstructured and semi-structured interviews. We were particularly keen to develop ways of involving the children themselves in the research through conversational interviews and role playing.

In the course of the study, some important ethical issues arose from cultural and religious differences. For example, we learnt that one question which should never be put to adults who do *not* have a disabled child (e.g. some school teachers, physicians, carers, etc.) is: "How would you feel/cope if you had a disabled child?". The reason for this is the strong Hindu belief in self-fulfilling prophesies (see below).

THE FINDINGS

The principal findings which emerged from the study relate to: the rural-cosmopolitan continuum; the causes of childhood disability; local understanding about disability in terms of normality and deviance; and pluralism of beliefs. These are explored in turn.

RURAL-COSMOPOLITAN CONTINUUM

Nepal is an extremely heterogeneous society in terms of religion, demography and social geography, and is also in the throes of rapid, but uneven, development. Thus it has a wide range of cultural beliefs and cosmologies. Based on our, as yet, tentative understandings of the cosmologies of different people and groups within Nepali society, we suggest that conceptualisations of disability can be placed on a continuum which ranges from "rural", through "urban", and on to "'cosmopolitan" (see Redfield 1947, Mahale 1983, Bell 1992 and Beggs, Haines & Hurlbert 1996). This is not an exclusively geographic model in the sense of rural dwellers having a rural ideology, and urban dwellers having an urban ideology (Streefland 1985). For example, there are a large number of people living in urban centres in Nepal who continue to adhere to a rural cosmology, and there are many Nepalis with cosmopolitan world-views who live in rural areas. Rather, it implies that the various ways in which people understand and deal with disability are influenced by their income, education, mobility, exposure to outside ideas and technologies, as well as other factors such as caste and ethnicity.

Broadly, a rural cosmology can be seen as one firmly based in traditional values, often strongly influenced by beliefs in ghosts, spirits and witchcraft.

An urban cosmology will often be influenced by systematic belief systems based on the written word, often associated with Hindu, Muslim or Buddhist teachings and with ayurvedic medicine.[1] People with cosmopolitan cosmologies have been exposed to modernity in all its facets and will be informed about western biomedical teachings (such as germ theory) and will have a detailed awareness of: mother and child vaccinations; information about maternal nutrition; and therapies, such as physiotherapy, occupational therapy and speech therapy. They will also be aware of different types of medical services outside Nepal and the Indian sub-continent in places such as Hong Kong and Brunei, where the Brigade of Gurkhas had been based. (It should be remembered that Nepal is an independent sovereign state which has had a unique connection with Britain and the British armed forces through the Brigade of Gurkhas – which has Nepali and British officers and Nepali other ranks.)

In using this framework we do not assume that a cosmopolitan cosmology is the same as a "western" (biomedical) cosmology. It will generally be characterised by some degree of adherence to Hindu religious beliefs and practices, including ayurveda and astrology (indeed, cosmopolitans in Kathmandu often have strong beliefs in astrological influences). There are also other dimensions to understanding: some aspects of an individual's or family's beliefs may be embedded in traditional folk understandings, while others may have their origins in cosmopolitan experiences and encounters. Thus the boundaries between cosmologies are blurred and individuals often simultaneously hold several different (and sometimes contradictory) beliefs from all three points on the rural-cosmopolitan continuum.

THE CAUSES OF CHILDHOOD DISABILITY

Perceptions about the causes of childhood disability vary greatly but there are a number of general and fairly widespread beliefs about pre-natal and post-natal causes. Pre-natal causes include:

1. parental sins in a previous life;
2. the child's sins in a previous life;
3. the results of accident, poor food, or unsuccessful attempts at abortion through the use of large amounts of medicine by the mother during pregnancy;

4. a "self-fulfilling prophesy" where thoughts about or visions of disability entered the mother's mind during pregnancy;
5. contamination through the mother coming into contact frequently or continuously with a disabled child during her pregnancy;
6. mother's ill health during pregnancy, which may or may not have supernatural causes; and
7. astrological mischance via an inauspicious alignment of stars and planets at the times when the child was conceived and born, as well as when the parents were conceived and born.

We can look at these perceived causes within the rural – cosmopolitan framework. Explanations one, two, and six (and, to a lesser degree, explanations four and five) are consistent with a rural cosmology: they find their meaning in often highly specific regional and cultural understandings. Explanations three, four, five, six and seven are in line with urban cosmology and can be seen as a composite of, perhaps even a transition between, rural and cosmopolitan cosmologies. Explanations three and six are cosmopolitan in orientation: they are grounded in biomedical understandings, as well as a more literate knowledge of Hindu teachings. To a lesser extent, cosmopolitans sometimes subscribe to explanation seven.

Post-natal causes include:

1. childhood illness;
2. possession or a curse; and
3. the child being contaminated or "infected" by contact with an already disabled child: "rok satné", literally: to trade or exchange disease – an explanation not uncommon among South Asians in England (Shah 1992).

Childhood illnesses are the most common explanation given by those who adhere to a cosmopolitan cosmology (explanation one). The rural folk explanation is more likely to be that the child or mother was possessed or cursed, or that the child was contaminated (explanations two and three). Childhood illness or contamination are more likely explanations for people with an urban cosmology (explanations one and three).

During the course of collecting disability biographies, parents mentioned all of the above explanations for their children's disability, as well as a few idiosyncratic or highly individual reasons. Sometimes both pre-natal and post-natal explanations are combined, as can be seen from the following examples:

I was pregnant in the village and was ill for six months during the pregnancy. I did not eat much and maybe this was a cause. Also, my father-in-law give me joreebuthi [herbal medicine] and I think that it was bad for me. Rai mother, Kathmandu.[2]

Our son was normal at birth and we did not see any abnormality until he was several months old. He became ill and was admitted to Kanti Hospital [in the Kathmandu Valley]. It was there that we believe he was switched for a disabled baby. Maybe, though, because our son was ill with pneumonia and was weak and defenceless he was attacked by a ghost in the hospital [this latter explanation is supported by the grandmother]. Brahmin mother and father, Bhaktapur, Kathmandu Valley.

My son got encephalitis when he was two years old. That is why he has CP. There are no other explanations. Newar mother, Kathmandu.[3]

This is the hand of God; it is God's will that Sunu has CP. Muslim uncle, Janakpur.

UNDERSTANDING DISABILITY: DEVIANCE AND NORMALITY

'The complexity in explanations of the *causes* of disability is mirrored – and even amplified – in relation to beliefs and understandings of its *nature*. As well as differences in cosmologies on the rural-cosmopolitan continuum, there are varying perceptions of different manifestations of disability. One key issue is that of "deviance" from the "norm". People may perceive some but not other disabilities as "normal" within their own society. An important element of this discourse concerns the categories of "non-normal" and "yes-disabled" suggested by Devereux (1963) and developed by Sachs (1995). "Non-normal" refers to deviance not yet categorised; "yes-disabled" refers to a specifically recognisable deviance which fits into an indigenous category. Devereux and Sachs conceptualise these statuses as mutually exclusive, but we found that this does not adequately reflect the range of rich and complex folk conceptualisations among Nepalis. In order to make a start it is necessary to create a new category which encompasses both the non-normal and yes-disabled categories (see Figure One).

Figure One: Non-Normal, Normal and Yes-Disabled

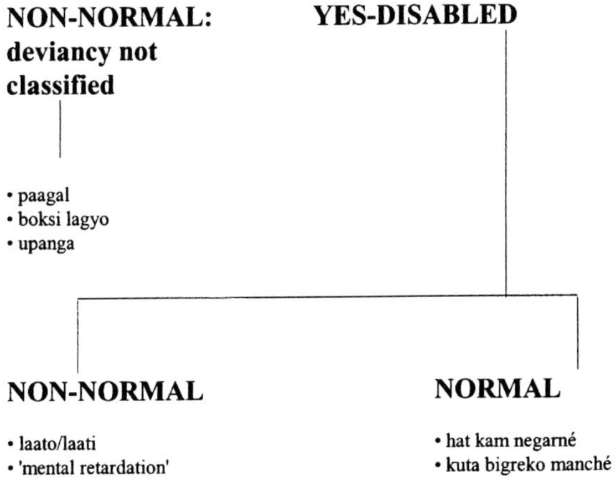

Non-normal: deviancy not classified

People who exhibit forms of bizarre behaviour such as extremely poor personal hygiene, lack of normal modesty and verbal ranting are often referred to as *paagal* – literally crazy. Alternatively, a person exhibiting similar behaviour but of a more disturbing or violent nature may be considered to be possessed by a witch: *boksi lagyo*. In these, as yet undetermined states, it is still possible that the deviation from normality may be temporary (see Stone (1986) for a discussion of indeterminate status in relation to a sudden onset of non-normal behaviour classified as *man bigrayo* – literally broken mind).

Yes-disabled and non-normal

The category *laato/laati* in Nepal, meaning literally deaf and dumb males and females respectively, is often applied to people with a wide range and variety of disabilities, including communication difficulties (such as speech impediments) and learning disabilities. *Laato/laati* are generic terms covering specific permanent conditions which are seen as both disabling and deviating from normality in terms of either demeanour, behaviour or speech.

Yes-disabled but normal

People who, for example, have suffered from polio or who are crippled or have had limbs amputated, are placed in this category. Unlike the previous two categories of *paagal* and *laato/laati*, it is the disabilities (physical rather than mental), rather than the people, which are named and this is a reflection of their "yes-disabled but normal" status. People who have a crippled leg are described as *kuta bigreko manché* (man with a broken leg); if someone has a crippled arm, the disability will be described as *hat kam negarné* (arm which doesn't do work), etc. Even though their *bodies* do not meet normative standards, their behaviour, demeanour and speech fall within normative limits and they therefore retain their "normal" status.

These three examples are all consistent with rural Nepali cosmologies but there are other, different conceptualisations from the urban and cosmopolitan cosmologies (see Figure Two). For example, a cosmopolitan is unlikely to characterise a person as *paagal* or *boksi lagyo*. A cosmopolitan term for non-normal behaviour presumed to be beyond the person's control is *upanga* – a catch-all term for an as-yet undiagnosed or unrecognisable condition that can be explained within a western biomedical framework.

Laato/laati are terms for non-normal and yes-disabled statuses which are commonly used within rural and urban cosmologies, and to a lesser extent by cosmopolitans. But cosmopolitans will use the term *swasta mansthit* (or its western equivalent "mental retardation") in situations where to western eyes a person unambiguously has severe learning disabilities, and this term is increasingly being used by urbanites too. The cosmopolitan yes-disabled but normal category is more straightforward in that a western biomedical term (or its shorthand version) would normally be used: e.g. cosmopolitans virtually universally refer to cerebral palsy as "CP".

People with learning disabilities, but no physical disabilities are normally referred to as "MR" – mentally retarded – by biomedical practitioners, and mental retardation is called *swasta mansthit* by other cosmopolitans. These diagnoses are sometimes added on to describe learning disabilities which accompany physical disabilities. Cerebral palsy is called *mastiska pancha ghat* (brain paralysis) by cosmopolitan lay persons, but is generally referred to as CP by educated urbanites and professionals who work with such children.

Perhaps specific terminology for different types of disability is not necessary for those with a rural cosmology, because it serves no purpose in terms of diagnosis, referral, treatment or therapy. There are no real options for biomedical treatment either in rural areas, or among those whose lack of education or money are effective barriers to accessing services if they do exist locally. Terminology becomes more specific as one moves progressively from rural to cosmopolitan, as it becomes more necessary to identify and gain access to specialised ayurvedic and biomedical health care resources.

Figure Two: Cultural Categories of Disability

<table>
<tr><th></th><th>Rural</th><th>Urban</th><th>Cosmopolitan</th></tr>
<tr><td>Non-normal:
deviancy
not yet
classified</td><td colspan="2">Paagal (crazy)
Boksi lagyo (witch-possessed)</td><td>Upanga (catch-all term
for non-specified
disability - with a
western emphasis)</td></tr>
<tr><td rowspan="2">Non-normal and
yes-disabled</td><td colspan="2">Laato/laati
('deaf/dumb' - but generic meaning)</td><td>Specific to impairment:
(often with biomedical
label)</td></tr>
<tr><td></td><td colspan="2">Swasta mansthit
"Mental retardation"</td></tr>
<tr><td>Yes-disabled
but normal</td><td colspan="2">Specific to impairment -
descriptive of impairment
(e.g. hat kam negarné,
kuta bigreko manché)</td><td>Specific to impairment:
often with biomedical
label (e.g. CP)</td></tr>
</table>

Figure Three identifies those conditions classified in each of the normality/disability categories for each cosmology. All cosmologies treat the “non-normal: deviancy not yet classified” category in the same way. This category includes undiagnosed debilitating mental illness and socially unacceptable odd behaviour. In contrast, there are some subtle differences between the three cosmologies in relation to the “non-normal and yes-disabled” category: all cosmologies include learning disabilities, and these may be accompanied by physical disabilities, in this category; but treatment of communication difficulties varies. In a rural cosmology, communication disabilities are unequivocally situated within the “non-normal and yes-disabled” category, but this is not the case in a cosmopolitan cosmology (so long as there are no associated learning disabilities). The situation is less clear-cut in the urban cosmology where the extent of the communication difficulty and the presence of any associated physical disability are taken into consideration. A similar situation arises in the classification of the "'yes-disabled but normal" category, as evident in the final row in Figure Three.

Other commentators have also noted the particular attention paid to communication difficulties in Nepal. They were explored in some detail in Peters' 1980 study. Peters undertook research among the Tamang, the largest ethnic group in Nepal, in two sites: a small market town and a village, both about eight kilometres from Kathmandu. He found that categorisation of people as *laato/laati* was "based partially on insufficiency of intelligence and behavioural adaptation, but primarily on speech incompetence" (Peters 1980, p. 352). Individuals with less severe speech impediments were called *adha-laato/adha-laati* (literally half-dumb, i.e. mildly yes-disabled and non-normal). He argues that competence in communications is important in the ritual life of the rural Tamang where clarity in enunciating mantras is essential in performing the rites necessary to fulfil the householder's role. Peters also stated that the Tamang believe *laato/laati* to be caused by "bad karma" (consequences of bad actions by parents or patrilineal kin in previous lives), in contrast with other mental disorders which were ascribed to supernatural causes such as witchcraft, spirit possession or soul loss and were therefore, in principle, amenable to cure by traditional ritualistic means (see also Stone (1988) for a discussion of indigenous Nepalese classifications of curable and non-curable conditions).

Figure Three: Conditions Classified in Cultural Categories

	Rural	**Urban**	**Cosmopolitan**
Non-normal: deviancy not yet classified	Undiagnosed debilitating illness Mental illness Socially unacceptable odd behaviour		
Non-normal and yes-disabled	Learning or communication difficulty: can be accompanied by physical disability	Learning difficulty: can be accompanied by physical disability; Physical disability along with communication difficulty	Down's Syndrome; Some cerebral palsy; Diagnosed learning difficulties: can be accompanied by physical disability
Yes-disabled but normal	Physical disability with no learning disability or communication problems	Physical disability with no learning disability or communication problems; Mild communication disabilities	Physical disability with no learning disability; Some cerebral palsy; Communication disabilities

The placing of people within the three normality/disability classifications (illustrated in Figure Three) is a result of mediation between various actors. Most children with cerebral palsy go through several classificatory stages, beginning with either normal or non-normal, and ending up as either yes-disabled and non-normal, or yes-disabled but normal, depending on the socio-cultural, economic and educational characteristics of the child's family; the diagnosis; and the severity of the disability. There is no folk term for cerebral palsy in Nepal; children with undiagnosed cerebral palsy are either termed *laato/laati*, *boksi lagyo* or *upanga* depending on the biography and severity of the disability. The following case study illustrates this negotiation and the movement between conceptual categories of disability.

> We took Sunu to many hospitals and doctors in Nepal and India. Even after they told us in Patna [India] that he had CP, we continued to talk to western physios and doctors who visited Janakpur. Our friends and neighbours advised us that, with such cases, a hole should be dug and the child placed in it, with his arms resting outside the hole and supporting his body. They said that his body and legs would then straighten until his feet touched the bottom of the hole. This would cure him if it was done for one to three hours every day. The doctors told us to ignore this advice, which we did. Besides, we think that he has been attacked by a ghost. We paid much money to Hindu sadhus [ascetics] and Muslim holy men who said that they could cure Sunu, but they were just charlatans. Our neighbours and distant relatives sometimes ask us if Sunu is getting better, or if we have found a cure, but now we know he has CP so it will be very difficult for him to get better. We need to wait until the big western doctors find a powerful medicine to help Sunu. But he is getting weaker, worse, and maybe it will be too late for Sunu. *Muslim grandfather, Janakpur.*

While some community and family members (and also some traditional practitioners) believe that the boy has been attacked by a ghost (*bhut*) – a potentially curable, non-normal, condition – others believe instead that he is *laato* – an incurable, yes-disabled and non-normal, condition. The close family, based on a biomedical diagnosis, have accepted that Sunu has cerebral palsy, but are unsure of whether this yes-disabled condition is curable or not. Sachs writes: "among Turkish migrant families it seems that when someone is seen as non-normal, there is still the possibility of correcting this state into a normal state but when the person is classified as yes-disabled, it is a permanent state and there is nothing else to do" (Sachs 1995, p. 212). This, as the above case illustrates, is not always true in the Nepal context.

PLURALISM

Sunu's case study exemplifies the different beliefs that can be held simultaneously by different family members or even by the same person. Very little has been written about plurality of beliefs about the *causes of disability,* although Stone (1988) writes movingly of a family's pluralistic attempt to explain a teenage son's sudden severe mental disorder. There is, however, a considerable literature about plurality of beliefs and practices related to *illness and healing* in Nepal (Oswald 1983, Parker 1988, Subedi 1989, 1992).

Parents often access a number of different practitioners and healing systems in dealing with their disabled child. Anthropologists have described how traditional healers, unlike western-trained physicians, share conceptions of illness and curing with their patients. Patients may consult traditional healers because they understand afflictions that biomedical practitioners deny are real, such as possession. Also, biomedical services can be geographically or financially inaccessible to patients, forcing them to rely on traditional healers when they might otherwise seek biomedical solutions. Finally, people may describe an illness-specific pattern of therapy to the outside investigator, but follow a multiple-use pattern (pluralistic) as they try anything that may provide relief (Durkin-Longley 1984). Parents often turn to a number of different practitioners in an attempt to make their child better.

Because many of the interview families were contacted through the biomedical system, family members were often reticent in discussing the alternative healing modes which they accessed. It was usually during a follow-up visit, unaccompanied by professionals, that people would reveal multiple-use patterns in dealing with their child's illness and/or disability. The following cases illustrate this:

> When Prasad became ill [at the age of two years] I despaired. I called every Buddhist, Hindu and Muslim holy man I could find. Some of them were very good, and could even tell me where my house was and what it looked like before they visited. I did this for two years, spending so much money, and going every day to Pashupatinath temple and other holy places to

> perform puja [religious offerings]. When Prasad was five I took him to the CP centre, and now I know that this was just his fate, and that no one is to blame, and that Prasad will never be cured [here she is crying]. *Newar mother, Kathmandu.*

> For many months after I noticed that Santi was ill I called a dami [traditional Hindu spirit-medium] to come and expel the evil sprits who had attacked her. But this did no good, so we took Santi to Brunei, where the medical doctors told us she had CP. *Rai mother (her husband is an ex-Gurkha soldier).*

CONCLUSIONS

This has been a small-scale exploratory study and any conclusions drawn from it need to be treated with caution. We make no claims that the families interviewed are representative of families of children with cerebral palsy in Nepal as a whole. Similarly we do not believe that the empirical findings have exhausted the possible – or even the most important – perceived causes or cultural classifications of cerebral palsy in Nepal.

Any strength of an exploratory study such as this lies in its ability to illuminate an under-researched area and to encourage the development of concepts of more general significance. We believe that the rural-cosmopolitan continuum enables some of the complexities of pluralistic beliefs in developing countries to be unpacked. Even within an indigenous setting there are complex and sometimes contradictory relationships between different belief systems, as well as between the health care system and cultural values and beliefs within the community it serves. People can be reticent to discuss their beliefs concerning illness, disease and disability, and their own cultural categories and definitions, because they are not the same as the dominant medical perspective – or the perspective that the researcher is assumed to have.

We also hope that this paper has illustrated to those involved in both policy and practice the need to recognise that disabled categories and identities (as well as the causes behind them and the interventions sought for them) are culturally constructed. In one's own cultural context indigenous categories are, by definition, acceptable because they stem from the dominant cosmology and are widely held. The relationship between non-normal and yes-disabled sheds some light on the subtleties of labelling different statuses.

We believe that the conceptual frameworks that we developed to contextualise and to try to help explain our findings are of some heuristic value. While both frameworks need further conceptual refinement based on further research, it is our intention that they be a contribution to the oft-heralded but as yet nascent field of cross-cultural disability studies.

END-NOTES

[1] Ayurvedic medicine has a complex and rigorous theoretical base and is rooted in the religious teachings and world view expressed in the Vedic scriptures of the Indian Sub-Continent.

[2] Rai is the name of an ethnic group indigenous to East Nepal. They have their own indigenous religious belief system, but nowadays generally adhere to Hinduism, especially if they live as an ethnic minority in areas of high Hindu concentration such as Kathmandu.

[3] The Newar are an ethnic group, centred in the Kathmandu Valley area, who adhere to both Hinduism and Buddhism.

ACKNOWLEDGEMENTS

Leigh Fiorentino, Sharon Macdonald and Robyn Piggott gave us help, encouragement and support. Without them the project would never have got started. Rebecca was helped and supported in Nepal by Arundati Pradhan, Suresh, Professor Bhatuk Rajbandari, Bob and Fran from VSO, and by her partner, Tim. We also gratefully acknowledge financial support from the British Academy (Grant SS-4264/APN6331).

REFERENCES

ACHARYA, B. (1994), "Nature, cure and indigenous healing practices in Nepal: a medical anthropological perspective", *in* M. Allen (ed), *The Anthropology of Nepal*, Mandala.

BEGGS, J., HAINES, V. & HURLBERT, J. (1996), "Revisiting the rural-urban contrast – personal networks in nonmetropolitan and metropolitan settings", *Rural Sociology* 61(2), pp. 306-325.

BELL, M. (1992), "The fruit of difference: the rural-urban continuum as a system of identity", *Rural Sociology* 57(1), pp. 65-82.

BPEP/DANIDA (1995), *Disabled People of Nepal*, Kathmandu: DANIDA.

DEVEREUX, G. (1963), "Primitive psychiatric diagnosis: a general theory of the diagnostic process", *in* I. Galdstone (ed), *Man's Image in Medicine and Anthropology* (pp. 337-371), New York: Institute of Social and Historical Medicine, New York Academy of Medicine.

DURKIN-LONGLEY, M. (1984), "Multiple therapeutic use in urban Nepal", *Social Science and Medicine* 19(8), pp. 867-872.

EDGERTON, R. (1970), "Mental retardation in non-Western societies: towards a cross-cultural perspective on incompetence", *in* H. C. Haywood (ed), *Social-Cultural Aspects of Mental Retardation: Proceedings of the Peabody-NIMH Conference* (pp. 523-559), New York: Appleton-Century-Crofts.

HIS MAJESTY'S GOVERNMENT (1993), *Population Census 1991*, Kathmandu: Central Bureau of Statistics.

ICS/DANIDA (1995), *Disability Survey of Kanchanpur District, Kathmandu*, Kathmandu: DANIDA.

MAHALE, P. (1983), "Relevance of folk-urban continuum in studies of complex societies", *Man in India* 63(2), pp. 197-205.

MANION, M. L. & BERSANI, H. A. (1987), "Mental retardation as a Western sociological construct: a cross-cultural analysis", *Disability, Handicap and Society* 2(3), pp. 231-245.

McHUGH, E. (1993), "Culture and the transformation of suffering among the Gurings of Nepal", *in* C. Ramble & M. Brauen (eds), *The Anthropology of Tibet and the Himalayas*, Zurich: Ethnological Museum of Zurich.

MILES, M. (1992), "Concepts of mental retardation in Pakistan: towards cross-cultural and historical perspectives", *Disability, Handicap and Society* 7(3), pp. 235-255.

OSWALD, I. (1983), "Are traditional healers the solution to the failures of primary health care in rural Nepal?", *Social Science and Medicine* 17, pp. 255-257.

PARKER, B. (1988), "Ritual coordination of medical pluralism in highland Nepal: implications for policy", *Social Science and Medicine* 27(9), pp. 919-925.

PETERS, L. (1980), "Concepts of mental deficiency among the Tamang of Nepal", *American Journal of Mental Deficiency* 84(4), pp. 352-356.

PIGG, S. (1995), "The social symbolism of healing in Nepal", *Ethnology* 34(1), pp. 17-36.

REDFIELD, R. (1947), "The folk society", *American Journal of Sociology* 52, pp. 293-308.

RICHARDSON, S. (1983), "Physical impairment, disability and handicap in rural Nepal", *Developmental Medicine and Child Neurology* 25, pp. 717-726.

SACHS, L. (1995), "Disability and migration: a case story", *in* S. Reynolds Whyte & B. Ingstad (eds), *Disability and Culture* (pp. 210-225), Berkeley: University of California Press.

SHAH, R. (1992), *The Silent Minority: Children with Disabilities in Asian Families*, London: National Children's Bureau.

STONE, L. (1986), "Primary health care for whom? Village perspectives from Nepal", *Social Science and Medicine* 22(3), pp. 293-302.

STONE, L. (1988), *Illness Beliefs and Feeding the Dead in Hindu Nepal: an Ethnographic Analysis*, Lewiston, NY: Edwin Mellon Press.

STREEFLAND, P. (1985), "The frontier of modern western medicine in Nepal", *Social Science and Medicine* 20(11), pp. 1151-1159.

SUBEDI, J. (1992), "Primary health care and medical pluralism exemplified in Nepal: a proposal for maximizing health care benefit", *Sociological Focus* 25(4), pp. 321-328.

SUBEDI, J. (1989), "Modern health services and health care behavior: a survey in Kathmandu, Nepal", *Journal of Health and Social Behavior* 30, pp. 412-420.

CHAPTER 14

Can Formal Disability Services be Developed with South Asian Historical and Conceptual Foundations?

M. Miles

EXPERT FOR EXPORT

During 12 years' disability resource and service development work in Pakistan and region plus a two-year handing-over period (1978-1992), the inappropriateness to South Asia of much European disability ideology, planning and strategy became apparent to myself and Christine Miles; and also the difficulties experienced by Asian field leaders to base policies and plans on their own cultures and concepts, either independently or with some blend of appropriate foreign elements. Elsewhere I describe some of the background and development work (Miles 1986, 1990b, 1993a), and the planning efforts and intentions of government and NGOs (Miles 1986, 1990a, 1993b), while criticising the incautious export/import of European theories and methods (Miles 1985b, 1996a, 1997a).

The 1980s saw very few published appraisals of third world disability service planning and practice. The people involved were sufficiently busy staying alive, raising funds and coping with the wondrous schemes foisted on them by representatives of aid organisations and UN agencies. Disability development publications during this period are mostly of the "What a great job we do" type, intended to sustain funders' interest and repel challenges from newer claimants, e.g. street children, genitally mutilated girls, whose minders coveted a piece of the aid pie. However, relevant parallel fields of research had slowly been progressing. For example, the beginnings of anthropology of mental retardation in non-western cultures were documented by Edgerton (1970, 1984). Groce wrote model studies in historical anthropology of deafness (1985) and mental retardation (1986). Broader cross-cultural disability themes were noted by Scheer & Groce (1988). Disability anthropology studies begun in the mid-1980s have now appeared in Ingstad & Whyte (1995). Burck (1989) in Zimbabwe wrote one of the rare ethnographic studies associated with disability service development. Through the 1980s, Sultana Zaman (Bangladesh), Molly Thorburn (the Caribbean), Robert Serpell (Southern Africa), and David Werner (Mexico), together with colleagues produced disability studies and guides blending rigour, ethnography and practical social concern. Cross-cultural variations in concepts of personhood were investigated by Shweder & Bourne (1982) and in connection with disability by Dossa (1989); while studies of child development and of cross-cultural psychology became global enterprises with their own dedicated journals. Concerns with disability in culturally diverse families in Europe and North America also developed implications for "countries of origin" (e.g. Gartner, Lipsky & Turnbull 1991, Harry & Kalayanpur 1994, Kalayanpur 1996). A more extensive literature review appears in Miles (1996c). However, these nascent fields of knowledge were practically unknown in our remote corner of Pakistan. A decade later, after considerable growth, they remain unknown to many field participants and aid programs under the "Community Based Rehabilitation" umbrella.

For many years, European aid to economically weaker countries has had a component conceptualised as "transfer of knowledge and skills". With some such notion my wife and I went to Pakistan, invited by local people. In the course of "transfer" efforts, we discovered that all along there had been a vast unseen "conceptual" dimension requiring not merely "adaptation for cultural differences", but an entire rethinking and rebooting with concepts nearer those in the minds of Asian colleagues. The *reconceptualisation* of planning and strategy that emerged from our own experiences was called Information Based Rehabilitation (IBR), a phrase that has generally been misunderstood. Briefly, IBR is not an alternative or additional *strategy*, it is an effort to examine existing services and development strategies in terms of information, understood in the modern "information society" sense, i.e. as *concepts, knowledge, skills, and design, with feedback*. An examination of these features illuminates what is happening, for example where different strategies might be mutually strengthening rather than competitive or exclusive (Miles 1989, 1993a, 1996a).

THE CONCEPTUAL DIMENSION

The importance of the conceptual dimension slowly dawned on Christine Miles in connection with school staff whom she was training and guiding. During five or six years of daily work together with them in school, and in counselling parents from a wide catchment area, she had become fluent in Pushto, Urdu and local dialects. She began to realise that concepts of "the child", "learn", "teaching", "play", which during the past two centuries became basic to European work with children having learning difficulties, developmental delays or multiple impairments, were understood by her Pakistani staff in ways substantially and significantly different from what she had supposed; and by many families were understood differently again (C.Miles 1991, Miles & Miles 1993). She also realised that some of what was now becoming clear to her had actually been mentioned by staff in the first year – she had been unable to hear it, precisely because the differences were at the conceptual level. It had been difficult for staff to express. During the first year they all had been seeking common ground rather than exploring differences; so after trying a few times to raise conceptual issues, staff desisted. (As the Centre's administrator, a step back from the professional front line, it took me even longer to understand the issues and their significance). Returning to England in the 1990s, Christine met the reverse image. After years of learning how these key concepts appear to Pakistanis, she observed monolingual and largely monocultural British teachers, trying to teach British Pakistani pupils said to have "severe learning difficulties", with minimal awareness of the children's linguistic, cultural and conceptual background, or of their actual skills and learning ability in their mother tongue (C.Miles 1993).

The Pakistan experiences strengthened our desire for a greater understanding of the South Asian conceptual world of disability and social responses, so that the *development* (rather than *transfer*) of knowledge and skills should be appropriately rooted in indigenous conceptual bases. Some understanding could perhaps have been acquired from the results of anthropological, psychological, or sociological studies – but the research capacity hardly existed in Pakistan in the 1980s, as admitted in evaluations by senior social scientists (Hashmi 1989, Inayatullah 1989). At Pakistan Government request we did some practical studies, but for lack of resources and research experience they were of a pilot nature (Miles 1983, 1985a). We noted such social research as existed, e.g. studies at the National Institute of Psychology on cognitive development and on childraising practices (e.g. Pervez & Durrani 1989, Pervez 1989, Shah & Pervez 1994). The anthropology of Pakistani childhood has yet to match the vigorous achievements of Blanchet (1996) and colleagues in Bangladesh, though there are many similarities and resonances. Occasionally we discovered material from earlier decades, long out of print, such as an account of integrating blind children in ordinary schools in the 1960s (Grant 1963), and a thesis on the education of mentally retarded rural children (Haider 1971), which confirmed ideas gleaned painfully from many sources. Through the 1980s, such meagre disability studies as appeared in Pakistan mostly concerned enumeration. Some data was gathered in the 1981 National Census, but it was obviously weak and no published study appeared until Afzal (1992). Efforts were made to discover quick, cheap methods of finding and assessing children with disabilities, biomedically defined. These studies, while perhaps necessary, were little use for the construction and expression of a culturally, historically and conceptually valid knowledge base. Many Pakistanis were uneasy about the indiscriminate importing of European and American methods and equipment, but were preoccupied by concerns other than challenging foreign intervention or developing indigenous alternatives.

Since 1990 some useful qualitative studies on disability have been undertaken; yet most of them are over-dependent on western theoretical structures, and remain unpublished. The formal knowledge base, i.e. what has been written and circulated about disability within Pakistan, has not adequately been gathered and documented. A bibliography listing 420 items on disability in Pakistan has elicited amazement among people considered "expert" in this field, though a comprehensive bibliography might be two or three times longer. Similar responses have met ongoing bibliographies on disabilities in Zambia and neighbours, on Syria, Lebanon, Jordan and region, and on Bangladesh. These responses, from various regions, highlight the problems of assembling a formal knowledge base where there are inadequate libraries and publishing facilities. Even if people report experiences or formal research, many of those who should read the results find no opportunity. This is discouraging to researchers. It also reinforces the idea of "expertise" as something locked in the minds of particular people, often university staff, whose time must be hired, yet with little hard evidence of what they actually know or its application. When an organisation buys a report from such an expert, the few copies tend to remain in office cabinets, instead of being filed on the Internet, rewritten for peer review, journal published and thus opened to public debate.

Fortunately a few of our Pakistani colleagues could apply their minds both to digest some European ideas and to integrate them into their thinking and practice. They gave the greatest assistance in adapting, translating, publishing and later revising practical manuals in Urdu covering education and therapy with children in the main "disability categories". Yet hardly any could both do so and also explain how they integrated the different concepts. To construct effective bridges between substantially different conceptual worlds probably requires years of ordinary residence (i.e. not in a "foreigner" enclave) and daily work in both worlds, plus fluency in the languages and also strong communication abilities. Between the disability service fields of Pakistan and Britain, we know no single person who can yet construct such bridges; at best there are a few joint efforts by people with some of the necessary qualifications. Flaws in the present chapter demonstrate our own difficulties in communicating across the gulfs. Had we returned to UK after five or six years, we could have posed as "experts" on special educational needs in Pakistan – without ever discovering the conceptual world. Perhaps some other returned expats have learnt faster; but our perception is that many people in disability aid have spent two years here, three years there, and are then deemed "expert", without realising the fundamental flaws in their understanding. People from developing countries may also easily spend a few years in Europe or North America without reaching a critical understanding of the conceptual differences underlying the practical work they have seen.

By 1990, Pakistani colleagues had taken over our work, so we returned to Britain – without really having satisfied, after 12 years, the need for a deeper understanding. In Britain, Christine Miles was able to undertake research involving Pakistani children with learning difficulties and their mothers – even in the British context, the isolation of many of the mothers (through cultural restrictions on women's mobility, and the stigma of having produced a disabled child) was such that their thought patterns seemed little different from those met in Pakistan (C.Miles 1996). I began studying Asian disability histories, reviewing background factors such as the historical responses of Asian religions toward disabilities and disabled persons, historical records of practical responses to mental handicap and to blindness, as well as specific studies, e.g. of goitre, cretinism and iodine in South Asia, and microcephaly at a Punjabi shrine (Miles 1995, 1996b, 1997c, 1998a, 1998c). Some efforts have been made, using academic and popular media (Miles, Chandran & Balasundaram 1995), to share the process and findings with Asian colleagues. There was never any research funding or salary to share with them.

SOME CONSTRUCTIONS FROM EXPERIENCE AND RESEARCH

This chapter has the following agenda:

- Material from historical studies noted above, and its implications.
- A glance at recent disability service trends, and their mis-selling in South Asia.

The historical material is a small selection from Sanskrit and Tamil classics, roughly 2,000 BC to 600 CE, and a glance at the 19th century. Methodological issues in the studies are discussed elsewhere (Miles 1998b).

In relation to the question posed in the title, "Can formal disability services be developed with South Asian historical and conceptual foundations?", it is recognised that many Europeans may doubt the relevance to current planning, of historical-cultural studies from a period ending 1,400 years ago. Indeed, very few South Asians have made any significant study of their ancestors' histories – yet it is with them and all around them, at least in popularised versions, apparently forming a sort of cultural bedrock on which they might build with some confidence. A grittier view is that the surrounding heritage is less a bedrock than a bedroom, in which minds are lulled to sleep while their owners' bodies are directed by enthusiasts for *hindutva* (Lele 1996).

NOT DEAD YET

In this section, historical material is cited from Sanskrit and Tamil classics: the Vedas, Upanishads, Arthasastra, Jataka, Shilappadikaram and Manimekhalaï.

Vedas

However remote from current European thought patterns, the Vedas remain live currency for some 350 million Asian adults when it comes to deciding how society should function. ***Rigveda***, the oldest "book" still in daily use, mentions various people with disabilities, and their healing by the Aswins, semi-divine medical twins, or Soma, the 'magic potion' personified:

> He [Soma] covers the naked and heals all who are sick. The blind man sees; the lame man steps forth. [RV 8.79] (O'Flaherty 1981, p. 121).

> When in the time of night, in Khela's battle, a leg was severed like a wild bird's pinion, Straight ye [Aswins] gave Vispala a leg of iron that she might move what time the conflict opened. [RV 1.116] (Griffith 1926, p. 450).

Such claims hardly reflected everyday experience. They suggest the dominant public perception of disability, i.e. blindness and lameness were familiar misfortunes, not identical with sickness. For a blind person to see or a lame person to walk required divine intervention. (Mythological interpretations have also been suggested – they were in vogue among European scholars, before the adventure playgrounds of psychoanalysis were developed.) "Iron legs" are harder to interpret, whether Vispala was horse or human. The idea of an artificial limb or aid was clearly present, but this does not prove that non-mythological examples existed. There is some evidence of Mediterranean prostheses back to the 5th century BC. Possibly the "miraculous" part of the intervention was not that a prosthesis was supplied, but the speed with which mobility was said to be restored, or the use of iron rather than wood.

Rigvedic comparisons of mental capacity are applied directly to education by Mookerji (1947, pp. 25-26):

> As the Rigveda itself points out [x, 71, 7]: Class-mates (sakhas, i.e. those of same knowledge ... or who have studied the same Śāstras ...) may have equality in the possession of their senses like the eye and the ear, but betray inequality in respect of their power or speed of mind... this passage refers to three grades of students, the Mahāprajñāñ, the Madhyamaprajñāñ, and the Alpaprajñāñ, students of high, medium, and low ability (Brackets are Mookerji's).

While noting the mental poverty of "blockheads" who' chant the Vedas mindlessly, Mookerji countenanced their inclusion in primary school, "marked by noisy recitation and repetition of texts by pupils in the manner of frogs lustily croaking after rain" (ibid, p. 36). At secondary level however, "the collective work of the pupils in a class ceased, and their individual work commenced" (ibid, p. 36). Soon, "The more unfit were weeded out, sent back to the plough or the loom [x, 71, 9]" (ibid, pp. 36-37). *Atharvaveda* consists largely of charms against afflictions including paralysis, mania, epilepsy (Bloomfield 1897). One charm guards against the consequences of sinfully sitting with a person with bad teeth or nails, or "one who is deformed" (ibid, p. 72). At least three thousand years later, in the 1880s, the guru Ramakrishna reiterated the ancient message that people with bony or dented bodies, heavy elbow joints, hollow, yellow, squinting or crossed eyes, snub nose, thick lips, short stature, etc, have difficulty acquiring faith, or are wicked and deceitful ("M." 1942, pp. 234, 597, 766, 783). While republishing Ramakrishna, no effort was made to spin-doctor these remarks. Western advocates should understand that their Asian hosts may find remarks reported from earlier millennia more authoritative than recent European trends, however polite the hearing accorded the latter. Unfortunately this "culture-based resistance" seldom issues in culturally and conceptually appropriate plans.

Upanishads

The "advanced" Upanishadic lore dating between 600 and 300 BC abounds in philosophical speculation. Blindness appears repeatedly as a metaphor for ignorance, e.g. "like blind men led by one who is himself blind" [Katha Up. 2.5;

Mundaka Up. 1.2.8; Maitri Up. 7.9] (Hume 1931, pp. 346, 368, 456). Other disabilities were familiar enough to be cited in arguments about the essentials of life:

> One lives with speech gone, for we see the dumb; one lives with eye gone, for we see the blind; one lives with ear gone, for we see the deaf; one lives with mind gone, for we see the childish; one lives with arms cut off, one lives with legs cut off, for thus we see. [Kausitaki Up. 3.3] (ibid, p. 322).

The continuity of existence, even with senses missing, is further developed in the "Contest of the Senses" [Chandogya Up. 5.1.1-14, Brihadaranyaka Up. 6.1.7-14]. Speech, Sight, Hearing and Mind successively take a year's leave, then return to see how the others fared. They had in turn been like the blind, the dumb, the deaf, the simpleton or child, etc. When Breath prepares to leave, the others know they cannot manage without Breath, which therefore triumphs. More practically, foetal development is described in Garbha Upanishad, with details of the formation of body parts in successive months. An aetiological hypothesis also appears:

> The blind [andha], the lame [khanja], the hunchback [kubja], the dwarf [wāmana] are born to those parents whose minds are distressed [vyakulita manasā]. (Keswani & Bhide 1965, p. 70.)

Arthasastra

Kautilya's manual on statecraft and diplomacy, political economy, brothel regulation, intelligence work etc, is traditionally dated to the 4th century BC. Some of its flavour appears in the robustly chauvinist batting order for suitors at the king's court:

> ... gods and deities, hermits, heretics, Brahmins learned in the Vedas, cows, sacred places, minors, the aged, the sick, the handicapped, the helpless and women. [1.19.29] (Rangarajan 1987, p. 148.)

The legal incapacities of disabled people were manifold: they could neither inherit, nor make a valid contract, nor act as legal witnesses. Women employed in municipal brothels could decline to serve clients with physical defects; yet on the positive side, prostitutes were discouraged from adding to disfigurement, e.g. "cutting off a client's ear" in the heat of the fray (ibid, p. 354). A man should not insult his wife by calling her a cripple, and there were penalties for defamation using disability terminology, whether true, false or ironically euphemistic. The State organised a home-worker scheme by which women with disabilities, widows and so forth could earn their living from textiles. They were encouraged not to be idle, under threat of digital amputation. Some disabled people might find employment in the spy network; but spies were sometimes able-bodied people disguised as disabled. The guise of simplemindedness was recommended to entrap dishonest artisans, e.g. depositing a valuable for safekeeping, to test whether they would return it on demand. When or where these laws were effective is unknown. Indian commentators mostly believe Kautilya's work describes a functioning code of statecraft. Some western commentators disagree. The better known *Laws of Manu*, which have been the fundamental legal base during two millennia, also have some provisions for disability, largely of a protective or prohibitive nature, with little or no "social context".

Jataka

The 530 Jataka, stories of Buddha's incarnations, provide "a vivid picture of the social life and customs of ancient India" around the 3rd century BC, with continuing relevance to British ethnographies in 19th century India (Cowell 1895-1907, Vol. I, xi). Several are specifically on disability, which also appears casually in many others. Some portray "unexpected" features of disabled people, such as a warrior dwarf, a man with hemiplegia who is an ace stonethrower, a blind seapilot who sees more with his hands than other men with two eyes. Others present familiar stereotypes, such as the rich, crooked, squinting miser who drives the poor from his gate. Some incongruity appears in stories of women misbehaving with severely crippled men, and the tale of a blind old hag lusting after a young Brahmin. For deriving lessons on attitudes towards disability in ancient India, the latter story is opaque, even allowing for folkloric exuberance. Its familiar moral, for the young Brahmin studying at Taxila University, is that women are vile creatures of unbridled passion. His teacher has an ancient, blind mother, to whom "with his own hands" the teacher gives personal care and hygiene. Such filial devotion, or perhaps the physical involvement, evokes neighbourly derision, so the teacher builds a forest hut and instals himself and Mother. When the young Brahmin comes for tuition, the teacher requires him to undertake the psycho-physical care of Mother, commanding him to praise the crone's beauty while he massages her feet and back. The student obeys so diligently that Mother, instead of calling the Forest Police, imagines the young fool is in love with her. Though decrepit, passion kindles in her, to the point of plotting to axe her son. Ergo "women are depravity incarnate". The filial care initially seems laudable; yet to use Mother as a case study in the vileness of women must surely lose brownie points.

Tamil Sources

Material noted above derives from North Indian Brahminical traditions, and gives a taste of the vast stores of disability reference in e.g. the epics, drama and puranic literature. An even briefer glance must be given to Tamil antiquity, represented by *Shilappadikaram* and *Manimekhalaï*, probably from the 2nd century CE (Daniélou 1993a, 1993b). Both reflect the reforming influences of Buddhism as well as Jaina practices. With erratic storylines, they combine poetry, religious mythology, popular songs, some celebration of women's power to change events and contribute to knowledge, even an "Intelligent Girl's Guide to Philosophy" (later dismissed by the intelligent girl as completely useless). Ironic or prurient commentary is offered on sexual decadence. In *Manimekhalaï*, the whorehouse madam is enraged when her granddaughter gets religion and disgraces the family profession by her social worker antics.

The atmosphere and approaches to disability differ from those of the Sanskrit material. While the usual humpbacked maids and attendant dwarfs appear, charitable institutions and hospices for poor and disabled persons are more prominent. The nature and period of such institutions is debatable. For example, Chandogya Up. [4.1.1] mentions a MacDonalds forerunner named Janasruti, "a pious dispenser, a liberal giver, a preparer of much food. He had rest-houses built everywhere with the thought, 'Everywhere people will be eating my food'" (Hume 1931, p. 215). More formal places of care for the hungry, ill or disabled may have existed earlier in Ceylon and southern India. *Shilappadikaram* mentions a spa at Puhar where disabled people could bathe and recover health and strength, apparently without benefit of the Aswins, who were usually invoked in North Indian healings.

By contrast with the medical/Aswin and charitable-ruler dominance, the merits of card-carrying social workers are now emphasized. Aputra, surviving neonatal abandonment and a Brahminic education, denounces the cruelty of some Brahmins who plan to sacrifice a cow. Expelled, he goes to Madura and begs from the rich, distributing the proceeds "to the poor, the blind, the deaf, the infirm, the orphans, and the sick, keeping for himself only the remains" (Daniélou 1993b, p. 55). One night Aputra faces an emergency and runs out of food. The goddess Saraswati gives him a magic bowl of plenty, from which he feeds thousands. The story now takes an ironic turn. The gods are shaken by Aputra's display of virtue – they are ever vulnerable to ascetics who live on occasional gulps of air while standing on one leg for a few centuries in aid of holiness. Indra descends to sort out Aputra – who, as "a simple and innocent boy", roars with laughter and tells the god he needs nothing (ibid, p. 57). Indra then spoils the game by sending abundant rain, eliminating hunger. Instead of starving people, the squares are filled with idle layabouts. Even the villages have nobody in need. Aputra turns to Overseas Aid, but gets marooned on an island. Depressed at the loss of hungry people to feed, he decides "to give up life itself rather than stay alone and useless on this desert island with a miraculous bowl in his possession that no longer served anyone but himself" (ibid, p. 58). This makes a welcome change from the tedious monthly reports of hungry mouths filled. It also shifts Aputra offstage so that our heroine Manimekhalaï can strut her stuff. She duly receives the bowl, after venerating the Buddha and on condition that her charitable motives be sincere. An early Princess Di model, Manimekhalaï experiences the joys of anatomically correct public service:

> Around Manimekhalaï, beautiful as a doll, her pubis resembling a cobra's hood, there soon gathered the blind, the deaf, the crippled, the orphans, the idiots, the ascetics who performed severe practices, all those that were hungry, the poor dressed in rags, and hundreds of thousands of other living beings, who crowded together to approach her (ibid, p. 149).

EARLIER THAN THOU

This material is a tiny fragment of available South Asian historical disability-related material, selected here because it derives from classical literature highly regarded by Indians, illustrating some modern-sounding issues. A few thoughts arise:

1. At least 3,500 years of substantial South Asian experience and evidence exists, in which varied responses to disability and people with disabilities appear. Some South Asians will prefer to recover their own cultural heritage on disability, rather than taking lessons from large-footed, beef-eating foreigners who know nothing of it, from countries with much briefer cultural attainments (including the perfection of weapons of mass destruction and disablement).
2. Some ancient material concerning disabilities is well known, involving for example characters such as blind King Dhritarashtra and his blindfolded wife Gandhari, Ashtavakra the brainy supercrip and Hanuman the divine but crack-jawed monkey, cunning and vengeful Manthara, even Shiva the (occasional) Simpleton; while vastly more characters and episodes, such as Khujjutara the humpbacked female thief turned religious teacher, are known mainly to scholars.
3. Details in key episodes such as the intervention of humpbacked Manthara on which the Ramayana story turns, lend themselves to discussion of many aspects of disability, e.g. the portrayals linking disability with guile or evil, the "wisdom" in Manthara's hump, the abuse of disabled servants and the sexual use/abuse of disabled women. Differences between the multiplicity of Ramayana versions suggest that editors have recognised the nuances and sensitivity of some disability issues. Complaints by blind Dhritarashtra about his son's dismissive attitude towards him, and the portrayal of blindness in *Mahabharata*, precede a considerable blindness literature, down to the Bengali ballads rescued from oblivion some 80 years ago (Miles 1997b, Sen 1926-32).
4. Literary, social and religious evidence sampled above is paralleled by constructions of disability in the development of South Asian medical, psychological and legal literature. Studies of these fields are more a scholarly than a popular pursuit, yet the results greatly extend the understanding of how some Asian societies have responded to disability down the centuries. Some, perhaps many, of those responses would now be unacceptable to Asians and Europeans alike; yet the study of such material, and discussion of the moral and ethical issues, is likely to be far more illuminating to Asians, as they readily grasp the cultural subtleties and nuances.
5. The Indian material noted above is of course less directly relevant to disability policy and planning in Pakistan and Bangladesh, for which the

disability roots in Islamic history need greater attention. Yet despite "official" neglect of the Hindu heritage, these countries with largely Muslim populations have been deeply affected by the Hindu, Jain and Buddhist presence. Even more have they been affected by the cultural inferiority complex still deeply ingrained, according to long-running studies by Garg & Parikh (1995), among the sort of modern, educated urban Asians who should be the first to shake it off. Each of these strands requires book length treatment; here, only a few of the oldest components have been sketched.

A GLANCE AT FORMAL SERVICE DEVELOPMENT

Social responses to disabled people, by way of formal services, date from antiquity as noted above.

Charity and "Welfare"

The basic format of wealthy people setting up kitchens for feeding hungry crowds, and rulers providing shelter or hospices for severely disabled or chronically sick people, can sporadically be documented, but not quantified, at intervals from 500 BC to the present. The early jurist Brihaspati [XVII: 10-12, 22-23] mentioned what may have been a village cooperative, the surplus from which

> shall be bestowed on the idiotic, the aged, the blind, to women or children, to afflicted or diseased persons, to persons having issue, or the like (worthy persons) (Jolly 1889, p. 349).

This glimpse, plus oddments in the Jataka, suffice for politicians to conjure the ghost of a blissful, self-sufficient, village "welfare state" in which every need was met with benevolence, before the brutal British destroyed it – or perhaps it was the brutal Persians or Moghals, since visitors to India from the thirteenth to the eighteenth centuries fail to report widespread bliss. Perhaps it never existed for anyone to destroy. In the *Report of the Indian Famine Commission* (1880, I, p. 60) British officers indeed considered that

> Native society in India is justly famous for its charity. It is owing to the profound sense which is felt by all classes of the religious duty of succouring,

> according to their means, the indigent and helpless who have claims on them as members of the family, the caste, or the town or village, that in ordinary times no State measures of relief are needed.

Yet the result merely "sustained existence" in armies of paupers, many of them disabled, who would die a little later in famines or epidemics. Their condition and prospects were not improved by indiscriminate personal charity. How far there was improvement when urban Indians began to participate in organised British charities is debatable (Sanyal 1977); as also its converse, e.g. the fluctuating participation of the British in administering Muslim charitable trusts (Rashid 1978, pp. 11-36). Neither can be pursued here.

Early records of organised European charitable work in India run from Portuguese hospitals and orphanages in the 16th century (Meersman 1971) including an institution for needy and deaf people as early as 1589 (Gracias 1994, p. 137 and personal communication), via an occupational disability compensation scheme at Madras in 1764 (Penny 1904, pp. 385-89), to a lengthy "refutation of the charge of indifference to the interests of the Natives" by senior administrator Charles Lushington (1824, p. 6) detailing benevolent institutions initiated by the British. Of immediate interest, however, is the introduction of new policy, method and technique, which would begin to differentiate professional-developmental-progressive models from the mere charitable maintenance of disabled paupers.

Mission and education

The Rev. Andrew Bell believed strongly in method, technique and achievement, while running the Military Male Asylum school at Madras, 1789-97. Bell increasingly used older children to teach and monitor the younger. This saved staff salaries, the boys achieved far more, and discipline problems became rare. Asylum regulation No.23 stated that

> any boy lame, or deformed, or whose faculties may be deemed unequal to the elements of letters, shall be admitted, or rejected, at the discretion of the Select Committee, who will be guided in their decision principally by considering the probability of his becoming a permanent burden on the funds, or of his being able at, or before, the age of fourteen, to earn his own subsistence, agreeably to the plan of this institution (Bell 1807, p. 114).

Bell recalled the case of a "stupid, sluggish, and pusillanimous" boy who somehow had gained admittance. His schoolmates "made a mocking-stock of him, and treated him with every insult and indignity ... it appeared to me that ere long he would be rooted and confirmed in perfect idiotism, of which he already had the appearance" (ibid, p. 74). Bell admonished the boys, telling them that they could either drive the victim to complete idiocy or help him forward to achieve whatever he was capable of. He challenged them to do the latter, and made it clear that he was watching events closely. He placed the weak boy under the tutorship of a steady lad; and after some time saw

> the boy's countenance more erect and brighter; his spirit, which had been completely broken, revived; and his mind, which had sunk into lethargy and stupidity, reanimated. Henceforth his progress, though slow, was uniform and sure (ibid, p. 75).

This minor pedagogical incident at Madras occurred shortly before Victor, the "wild boy of Aveyron", attracted notice in France and Jean Itard attempted his education (Lane 1979). Bell's slow learner seems familiar enough as a type well below average in ability, further hindered by emotional disarray and liable through ill-treatment to become fixed in "idiocy". He was rescued by changing his schoolmates' behaviour and giving steady encouragement and a supportive environment, within an achievement-oriented school. Victor's situation, by contrast, was and is extremely rare, and thus a less appropriate experimental ground for developing educational methods with severely disabled children. Itard is Eurocentrically considered the "father of special education for the mentally and physically handicapped" (ibid, p. 285); yet the commonsense approach of Bell, and doubtless of many earlier educationists, may have had far broader application and might have avoided some of the labelling and segregation of children less abnormal than Victor. India indeed had "jungle children", one of whom was closely observed at the Dacca Asylum in the 1840s by Medical Superintendent Green (1856-57, p. 408). Yet there have been thousands of children at the level Bell described, for each "Victor".

Bell's recollected incident, and the beginning of formal technique in teaching blind children in India, both occurred in military orphan asylums. Parents themselves were probably less urgent at this period in putting their disabled child to school. Asylum superintendents, however, had disabled orphans on their hands and meant them to become self-supporting, rather than a "permanent burden on the funds". In 1838 or 1839 the Calcutta Military Orphan Institution asked the London Society for Teaching the Blind to Read to send Lucas's embossed material for its blind orphans. Later it stated that their "joy and satisfaction were great" (*Annual Report of the London Society for Teaching the Blind to Read* 1839, p. 11; 1841, p. 11). By then, William Cruickshank, a blind former pupil of the Madras Military asylum, was flourishing as a teacher in ordinary schools. In 1841 he returned to his old school as headmaster ("T." 1879). From the 1840s, the use of special techniques increased, with Moon script eclipsing Lucas in the 1850s. During the 1860s, Jane Leupolt at Benares energetically organised education for blind children, special training for Indian teachers, and local printing of embossed materials (Leupolt 1884, pp. 243-47; Miles 1997c).

Partial Histories and Interpretations

Work with disabled children from the 1790s to 1870s has disappeared from current Indian educational historiography. The relevant documentation has been inaccessible within India, but is now becoming available from British sources (Miles 1997c, 1998c). It is important that Indians should investigate their own sources, to reach informed judgements and "own" their own histories. For example, hypotheses have been floated suggesting that European special education was developed to "control" awkward elements among the masses, and disability was "created" by European industrialisation, i.e. as people with impairments who earlier found a niche in rural labour failed to meet the demands of urban factories. These ideologically-driven propositions have little enough historical credibility in Europe (see critiques by Oliver 1986, and Cole 1989); yet South Asians should take the opportunity to test them using their own evidence, rather than relying on arguments from remote cultures.

Indian textbooks and educational histories uniformly and mistakenly suggest that special education in India began with the creation of schools for deaf children at Bombay c.1884 and for blind people at Amritsar *c.*1886. These beginnings were long considered a "creditable" missionary activity. The substantial roles of Indians in the achievements, acknowledged at the time, were later forgotten. Western notions of school integration from the 1970s and 1980s, and the buzzword "inclusion" in the 1990s, begin to suggest that the origins in India of what are now construed as damaging, "segregated institutions" can conveniently be blamed on wrong-headed foreigners, cruelly exercising professional "control" over disabled children, as part of the imperial discourse of racist superiority (etc., etc.); and if any Indians were involved, they must have been coerced. British educationists in early 19th century India keenly promoted a spirit of competitiveness or "emulation" (a key word) among schoolboys, which they found lacking in native schools. Such a spirit would sit uneasily with "inclusive" ideologies – yet matches the ambitions of the modern South Asian middle classes. Modern Indians, whether disabled or with professional or parental interest, need to be able to see through the ideological posturing, to decide what credible historical grounds there are for supporting one or other form of service provision.

It is normal enough for one social group to accumulate knowledge then use it to control and exploit a weaker group. There are plenty of examples in Asian and European history – but such examples do not prove that a particular type of disability service actually was developed with such motives. It is more interesting to argue from verifiable data. For example, there is evidence that Moon script could be learnt by blind people more easily than Braille, but was costlier to print. These two systems competed over several decades in India. Braille really needed a skilled teacher, whereas Moon could be learnt quickly by blind or sighted people, who could easily pass on the skill. The determining factor seems to have been the cost and availability of materials – since reading skills were useless without materials to read. By 1900, the cheaper Braille was ousting Moon; but this meant that specialist teachers were required. Efforts to teach deaf Indian children saw a similar struggle. Some deaf children were casually integrated in early missionary schools, where informal signing systems developed (e.g. Chapman 1839, p. 91). Later, oral methods were imported from Europe by Mr Walsh at Bombay (Editorial 1887). Education of deaf children then required a specialist teacher, and thus became expensive and less accessible. The results of these struggles were by no means inevitable, and the details have yet to be fully examined in the historical Indian situation. However, it was predictable that any trend favouring specialist teachers, who obviously were very scarce, would result in such people working in specialised schools where their skills would reach far more disabled children, rather than in ordinary "integrated" classrooms where their expertise would be required by very few. Many children with lesser impairments continued in ordinary schools, as they do today, with teachers either ignoring any special needs, or using commonsense methods as did Bell in the 1790s.

MODERN IDEOLOGICAL CRUSADES

Mention was made earlier of "wondrous schemes" foisted on the third world disability field by western and global agencies. The 1970s saw trends of "deinstitutionalisation" and "normalisation", the 1980s saw a strong drive on school "integration" and the hyping of the WHO model of Community-Based Rehabilitation. In the 1990s disability has become a "rights issue" following a "social model", with "inclusion" as the new version of school integration with go-faster stripes (or with a total reconceptualisation of what education is about – the viewpoint perhaps dependent on the square of the distance between the proponent and the classroom). Behind each trend and buzz-word there are innovative ideas and practices, having some merits within their original contexts, and perhaps other merits as they have outgrown their origins. Developing countries are entitled to know what is going on around the world, and could not in any case be prevented from hearing about these ideas. Yet what has repeatedly taken place has been not merely the communication of balanced information, but the "foisting of wondrous schemes", with a combination of ignorance, naïveté and dishonesty. There has been colossal ignorance and naïveté about the cultures, socio-economics and histories of the countries in which schemes have been pushed. Dishonesty appears where schemes are exported without reference to the context in which the ideas developed, and without the debates and challenges to which they continue to be subjected in their original context.

Adequate documentation of these charges would require book length. A few examples will set the scene, contrasted with some recent realism. Deinstitutionalisation and normalisation, "probably the most controversial and emotionally charged issues in the field of mental retardation" (Landesman & Butterfield 1987), together with "independent living", involve assumptions about concepts of personhood, individuality, relationships, families, the meanings and goals of life, the ethics of making choices for other people etc, all of which are open to debate within their native context. Yet the slogans, the advocacy, and the western textbooks which have passed their sell-by date and been dumped in third-world bookshops, repeatedly hit South Asia during the 1980s, without exposing the conceptual assumptions or disclosing the ongoing controversies from their places of origin. Such controversies are indeed discussed in some western journal papers (for example, from Rose-Ackerman 1982 and Baldwin 1985, through many authors to Simpson 1998); yet these have minimal circulation in the developing world.

On school "inclusion" of disabled children, Barton (1997) underlines the significance of context. He notes, in a British context, that

> Everything currently seems to be against an inclusive outcome, including the increasing marketization of educational planning and provision, the intensification of competitiveness and the increase in selection, both in terms of access and experience within schools, and a set of values which celebrate individualism thereby making the possibilities of cooperation, collaboration and difference, at an institutional and individual level, less desirable or possible.

Such realism may cause advocates of "inclusion" to seek a more welcoming context – even to the point of asking rather hopefully, "can poverty facilitate inclusion?" (Stubbs 1997). By contrast, an internal review of BRAC's much praised "alternative" schools in Bangladesh suggests that Barton's cut-throat education jungle may flourish there too. BRAC schools are intended for primary school drop-outs or non-starters, using a child-centred curriculum taught by literate but unqualified women. Evaluators found one teacher getting good results by first kicking out duller pupils, so as to keep up the achievement level – incidentally subverting half the purpose of these "rescue" schools! (Khan & Khan 1993, p. 27). The role model here is the middle-class urban Asian child, goaded onward by ferociously ambitious parents (Blanchet 1996) from its entry as a toddler to "kindergarten" – another western import which, like the "Montessori", now reproduces across South Asia the stultifying, formal knowledge factories against which Froebel battled in 19th century Europe and Maria Montessori fought worldwide for half the 20th century.

Another educational consultant to developing countries is unusually frank about the outcomes of "inclusion" back in the USA. After listing common elements identified in successful inclusion programs – none of which can by any stretch of the imagination be said to be common in Asian or African schools whether government or private – Butler (1997) notes that "The move towards full inclusion is not based on a body of solid educational evidence demonstrating clear merits over special classes." Both Barton (above) and Butler broadly favour the inclusion trend. Both are rare in presenting arguments for and against, rather than mere sales pitch. Stone (1997) is also refreshingly honest about the process of adjusting from theoretical emancipatory research and a social model of disability, toward the realities of Chinese disability politics where people see things differently. For the latter, perhaps an entry-point might be the ancient writer Chuang-tse (or Zhuangzi) who sketched an early "social model" of disability. Chuang-tse first pictures water "finding its own level", taking the shape or filling the contours of whatever land or vessel it meets. He seems to suggest that a powerful spirit may similarly assume a deformed human shape – the deformities arising from the misshapen and defective society in which the powerful spirit has taken birth (Graham 1981, pp. 80-81). Indian literature of antiquity provides a different "environmental model", in which the rottenness of society results in an increase in serious congenital impairments. If ideas from Chinese disability histories are added to those of India, it is doubtful whether modern European disability activists have any new theory to teach Asians.

The illusion of a seamless transfer of ideas between Eastern and Western (or Northern/Southern) minds without the pain and pleasure of studying cultural and conceptual history, is sustained by the willingness of educated Easterners/Southerners to use English and to keep quiet when they do not understand or do not wish to contradict. The "social magnetism" factor operates powerfully. Educated, urban Europeans visiting or working in developing countries usually have educated, urban counterparts who speak a European language and have made some progress in government or NGOs; who are often also embarrassed by their country's economic weaknesses, and may be resolutely ignorant about rural lives, cultures and talents. This is especially so for urban disabled counterparts, who have usually lacked the mobility or communication ability to learn much about their own rural population. During visits, and in the first years of expatriate work, Europeans inevitably look for things they feel they can understand, rather than pursuing the incomprehensible. Their hosts are strongly motivated to continue offering whatever the visitor responds well to, rather than insisting on what is different and difficult. This sort of well-meant and highly understandable *folie à deux* establishes and reinforces a series of largely false ideas in the minds of visitors and short-term workers, unless they determinedly seek a much broader cross-section of viewpoints and contrary evidence.

RECOVERING DISABILITY HISTORIES, CONFIDENCE AND SKILLS

Is it not merely European paternalism to suggest that Asian planners, professionals and disabled people need help to construct their "own" disability histories, or to have solid home ground on which to stand? I doubt it – but if I were to meet as many as three planners in Islamabad, Delhi and Dhaka who knew their national disability histories and were confident of achieving a viable blend of old and new, I would be content. It took years before I realised that Asian disability histories are practically unknown, and that documents, time and resources for their construction are sparsely available. Any reasonably bright Asians could have pursued the studies leading to the publications listed here – provided they had either independent means or a spouse able to earn their bread; and were willing to spend several years grubbing about in obscure corners of libraries in several countries; and realised that results in terms of changes in policy and planning might not appear during their own lifetime. Unfortunately, such conditions are unattractive. Until some groundwork is completed, bibliographies are available, and it has been shown that viable fields of study are waiting, one cannot expect much interest from funding agencies or researchers. Whether for private individual or senior government planner, the disability field is chronically short of all sorts of resources; and what there is has often been secured by particular groups, e.g. disabled urban male ex-combatants or pathetic-looking children requiring surgery. "Disability history studies" have hardly been a competitive proposition. They are not yet a "felt need", let alone a priority. Their absence is unlikely to be felt until western cultural imperialism and anglophone globalisation, which already cause some anger in Asian health and education fields, have aroused sufficient heat in the disability field too; and until enough Asians have tasted the early fruits of their own disability histories and have decided that they are an indispensable component of future planning.

On the positive side, the point must and can be reached where educated Asians know that disability histories have been studied and written about and taught like the rest of their countries' histories. In some, this should generate the cultural confidence needed for an intelligent appraisal of the strengths and weaknesses of both indigenous and western approaches. The present generation, hearing with surprise that disability histories are being studied, may still lack confidence. The next generation, growing up aware that such studies exist, should be better placed to deal sensibly with westerners offering their latest goods. They should at least reach the level of confidence that educated Asians now have, after some 160 years of struggle, about Asian traditional medicine, e.g. that it works for some conditions that are not well addressed by western practices, and its "appropriate cultural packaging" lends a powerful psychosomatic advantage. There will be other outcomes that are hard to predict; but the studies must be done anyway, whether or not there are policy and planning outcomes to applaud. Disabled people in the 21st century will have a stake in knowledge about responses to disability in the past. They too will construct parts of their identities from a selection of historical material, and will find arguments from the past to further their aims.

A further important point is that this chapter enquires only about "formal" disability services. The informal services provided to disabled South Asians by at least 100 million mothers, aunts, sisters and daughters inevitably are based on the latter's local concepts and cultures, accumulated through centuries. This would seem to be another excellent target for studies. What do they do? With what thoughts in mind? How are their services received by disabled relatives? Amidst this colossal, historically unrecorded, unpaid, daily hands-on effort, what can be learnt, what skills or techniques exist? The answer is a deafening silence. Women's efforts are hardly taken seriously. The idea that national policy could be influenced by the humble services of 100 million female carers is a feeble joke. A bibliography of over 1,500 Indian articles on mental retardation barely mentions family resources (Venkatesan & Vepuri 1995). Conventionally, professionals have viewed families as ignorant obstacles, though perhaps such attitudes are weakening. Reporting a series of research studies on Indian families with disabled members, Peshawaria *et al* (1995) believe they have broken new ground – yet even they resolutely use American research references throughout, as though results from American families must be normative for India! Culturally appropriate skills and experience lie all around, invisible, ignored.

CONCLUSION

Can formal services be developed with South Asian historical and conceptual foundations? Both the practical experience and historical studies outlined above, together with the literature cited, affirm (as indeed is intuitively obvious) that services cannot adequately and appropriately be developed in South Asia *without* such foundations. To assimilate modern knowledge and skills that may be scarce in their countries, South Asians may indeed be trained abroad, or trained in their own countries by foreigners, or may train themselves using foreign information media – or may discover modern knowledge by their own research – but the problems arise when they in turn should train the next generation. Unless they have integrated the conceptually foreign material with their own practice, concepts and culture, they are likely to find great difficulty either passing on a coherent message to the next generation of trainee professionals, or acting as competent guides or partners with disabled people or parents of disabled children.

The present chapter has been an inadequate, lightning sketch of much too vast and complicated an area of disability histories and current practices – yet that is what faces South Asians and their foreign collaborators. Vast complexity and pitifully unequal resources are the working challenges that face people in many countries, who wish to plan and develop culturally and conceptually appropriate services, to diminish the disabling forces in society and environment, and to enhance the positive features. The proposed solution – much more serious effort and research towards constructing or recovering a relevant historical-cultural base – is no quick fix. It is more probably forty years' hard graft. In the zeitgeist of the late 1990s, to spend one's time planting saplings, the fruits of which might be enjoyed by distant people's grandchildren, is a form of madness. How much crazier then to meddle with the alien histories of the weak, despised and disabled, in the hope of influencing still unborn decision-makers who will occupy a world hardly imaginable? Yet the most irrational approach of all would be to blunder on, ignoring the lessons we may learn from the past.

REFERENCES

AFZAL, M. (1992), "Disability prevalence and correlates in Pakistan: a demographic analysis", *Pakistan Development Review* 31, pp. 217-57.

Annual Report of the London Society for Teaching the Blind to Read, 1839, p.11; 1841, p.11. London.

BALDWIN, S. (1985), "Sheep in wolf's clothing: impact of normalisation teaching on human services and service providers", *International Journal of Rehabilitation Research* 8, pp. 131-42.

BARTON, L. (1997), "Inclusive education: romantic, subversive or realistic?", *International Journal of Inclusive Education* 1, pp. 231-242.

BELL, A. (1807), *An Analysis of the Experiment in Education, made at Egmore, near Madras, etc.*, 3rd edition, London.

BLANCHET, T. (1996), *Lost Innocence Stolen Childhoods*, Dhaka: University Press.

BLOOMFIELD, M. (transl.) (1897), *Hymns of the Atharva-Veda*, Oxford.

BURCK, D.J. (1989), *Kuoma Rupandi (The Parts are Dry)*, Leiden: African Studies Centre.

BUTLER, C. (1997), "Review of integrated education for children with disabilities in the United States", *Asia Pacific Disability Rehabilitation Journal* 8, pp. 31-33.

CHAPMAN, P. (1839), *Hindoo Female Education*, London: Seeley & Burnside.

COLE, T. (1989), *Apart or A Part*, Milton Keynes: Open University Press.

COWELL, E.B. (ed) (1895-1907), *The Jàtaka, or Stories of the Buddha's former births* (6 volumes, 1993 reprint), Delhi: Low Price Publications.

DANIÉLOU, A. (transl.) (1993a), *Shilappadikaram (The Ankle Bracelet)*, New Delhi: Penguin.

DANIÉLOU, A. (transl.) (1993b), *Manimekhalaï (The Dancer with the Magic Bowl)*, New Delhi: Penguin.

DOSSA, P.A. (1989), "Quality of life: individualism or holism. A critical review of the literature", *International Journal of Rehabilitation Research* 12, pp. 121-136.

EDGERTON, R. (1970), "Mental retardation in non-Western societies: toward a cross-cultural perspective on incompetence", in Haywood, H.C. (ed), *Social-Cultural Aspects of Mental Retardation*, New York: Meredith Corp.

EDGERTON, R. (1984), "Anthropology and mental retardation: research approaches and opportunities", *Culture, Medicine & Psychiatry* 8, pp. 25-48.

Editorial: School Items (1887), *American Annals of the Deaf* XXXII (2), p. 124.

GARG, P.A. & PARIKH, I.J. (1995), *Crossroads of Culture*, New Delhi: Sage.

GARTNER, A., LIPSKY, D.K., & TURNBULL, A.P. (1991), *Supporting Families with a Child with a Disability. An International Outlook*, Baltimore: Brookes.

GRACIAS, F. da S. (1994), *Health and Hygiene in Colonial Goa (1510-1961)*, New Delhi: Concept.

GRAHAM, A.C. (transl.) (1981), *The Seven Inner Chapters*, London: Allen & Unwin

GRANT, I.L.D. (ed) (1963), *Handbook for Teachers and Parents of Blind Children in Pakistan*, Lahore: Ilmi.

GREEN, W.A. (1856-57), "Contributions towards the pathology of insanity in India", *Indian Annals of Medical Science* 4, pp. 374-435.

GRIFFITH, R.T.H. (transl.) (1926), *The Hymns of the Rigveda*, 3rd edn., Banares: Lazarus.

GROCE, N.E. (1985), *Everyone Here Spoke Sign Language*, Cambridge, Mass.: Harvard University Press.

GROCE, N.E. (1986), *"The Town Fool": an oral history of a mentally retarded individual in small town society*, New York: Werner-Gren Foundation.

HAIDER, S.S. (1971), "A plan for training the mentally retarded in developing countries: Pakistan", unpublished PhD thesis, Southern Illinois University, Carbondale, Ill.

HARRY, B. & KALAYANPUR, M. (1994), "Cultural underpinnings of special education: implications for professional interactions with culturally diverse families", *Disability & Society* 9, pp. 145-165.

HASHMI, S.H. (ed) (1989), *The State of Social Sciences in Pakistan*, Islamabad: Quaid-i-Azam University.

HUME, R.E. (1931), *The Thirteen Principal Upanishads*, Delhi: Oxford University Press.

INAYATULLAH (1989), "Social sciences in Pakistan. An evaluation", *International Social Science Journal* 41, pp. 617-33.

INGSTAD, B. & WHYTE, S.R. (eds) (1995), *Disability and Culture*, Berkeley: University of California Press.

JOLLY, J. (transl.) (1889), *The Minor Law-Books. Part I. Nârada. Brihaspati*, Oxford: Clarendon Press.

KALAYANPUR, M. (1996), "The influence of Western special education on community-based services in India", *Disability & Society* 11, pp. 249-270.

KESWANI, N.H. & BHIDE, N.K. (1965), "Garbha Upanishad. A brief Sanskrit treatise on ancient Indian embryology", *Clio Medica* 1, pp. 64-74.

KHAN, N. & KHAN, K.A. (1993), *Education for Freedom. The children of BRAC's urban schools*, Dhaka: BRAC.

LANDESMAN, S. & BUTTERFIELD, E. (1987), "Normalization and deinstitutionalization of mentally retarded individuals. Controversy and facts", *American Psychologist* 42, pp. 809-816.

LANE, H. (1979), *The Wild Boy of Aveyron*, London: Paladin.

LELE, J. (1996), "Hindutva as pedagogic violence", in Crook, N. (ed), *The Transmission of Knowledge in South Asia*, Delhi: Oxford University Press.

LEUPOLT, C.B. (1884), *Further Recollections of an Indian Missionary*, London: Nisbet.

LUSHINGTON, C. (1824), *The History, Design, and Present State of the Religious, Benevolent and Charitable Institutions, Founded by the British in Calcutta and its Vicinity*, Calcutta.

'M.' [Mahendra Gupta] (1942), *The Gospel of Sri Ramakrishna* (transl. Swami Nikhilananda, reprinted 1984), New York: Ramakrishna-Vivekananda Centre.

MEERSMAN, A. (1971), "Notes on the charitable institutions the Portuguese established in India", *Indian Church History Review* V(2), pp. 95-105.

MILES, C. (1991), "Mobilising skills for special education in Pakistan: a personal, cross-cultural experience", *International Journal of Special Education* 6, pp. 201-212.

MILES, C. (1993), "Ethnic & linguistic minority children with special needs", in ALBRECHT, F. & WEIGT, G. (eds) *Behinderte Menschen am Rande der Gesellschaften*, Frankfurt: Verlag für Interkulturelle Kommunikation.

MILES, C. (1996), "Bilingual children in special education: acquisition of language and culture by British Pakistani children attending a school for pupils with 'severe learning difficulties'", unpublished M.Phil.(Ed.) thesis, University of Birmingham. Reformatted version, ERIC ED410725.

MILES, M. (1983), *Attitudes Towards Persons with Disabilities Following IYDP (1981)*, Peshawar: Mental Health Centre, & ERIC ED236826.

MILES, M. (1985a), *Children with Disabilities in Ordinary Schools*, Peshawar: Mental Health Centre, & ERIC ED265711.

MILES, M. (1985b), *Where There Is No Rehab Plan*, Peshawar: Mental Health Centre, & ERIC ED267530.

MILES, M. (1986), "Misplanning for disabilities in Asia", *in* Marfo, K., Walker, S. & Charles, B. (eds), *Childhood Disability in Developing Countries*, New York: Praeger.

MILES, M. (1989), "Information Based Rehabilitation for Third World disability", *Social Science and Medicine* 28, pp. 207-10.

MILES, M. (1990a), "Disability and Afghan reconstruction: some policy issues", *Disability, Handicap and Society* 5, pp. 257-67.

MILES, M. (1990b), "A resource centre developing Information Based Rehabilitation", *in* Thorburn, M. & Marfo, K. (eds), *Practical Approaches to Childhood Disability in Developing Countries*, St. John's, Canada: Memorial University, Newfoundland.

MILES, M. (1993a), "Service development by information, not ideology", *in* Finkenflügel, H. (ed), *The Handicapped Community*, Amsterdam: VU University Press.

MILES, M. (1993b), "Mental handicap services: practical trends in Pakistan", *European Journal of Special Needs Education* 8, pp. 45-58.

MILES, M. (1995), "Disability in an Eastern religious context: historical perspectives", *Disability & Society* 10, pp. 49-69.

MILES, M. (1996a), "Community, individual or information development? Dilemmas of concept and culture in South Asian disability planning", *Disability & Society* 11, pp. 485-500.

MILES, M. (1996b), "Pakistan's microcephalic chuas of Shah Daulah: cursed, clamped or cherished?", *History of Psychiatry* 7, pp. 571-89.

MILES, M. (1996c), "Community Based Rehabilitation: information accumulation & exchange. South Asian research notes", ERIC ED403714.

MILES, M. (1997a), "Disabled learners in South Asia: lessons from the past for educational exporters", *International Journal of Disability, Education & Development* 44, pp. 97-104.

MILES, M. (1997b), "References to physical and mental disabilities in the Mahabharata (in English translation)", *Asia Pacific Disability Rehabilitation Journal* 8(2) Suppl., pp. 2-7.

MILES, M. (1997c), "Disability Care and Education in 19th Century India: Dates Places and Documentation", revised version, ERIC ED408747.

MILES, M. (1998a), "Goitre, cretinism & iodine in South Asia: historical perspectives on a continuing scourge", *Medical History* 42, pp. 47-67.

MILES, M. (1998b), "Studying responses to disabilities in South Asian histories", paper presented at the Symposium on Local Beliefs and Concepts of Disability in Different Cultures, organised by Comparative Research & Behinderung und Dritte Welt, Bonn, May 1998 (proceedings forthcoming).

MILES, M. (1998c), "Blind and Sighted Pioneer Teachers in 19th century China and India", ERIC ED414701.

MILES, M., CHANDRAN, G. & BALASUNDARAM P. (1995), "Mental handicap in Indian history: cross-cultural action research and communication", *International Journal of Special Education* 10(2), pp. 12-21.

MILES, M. & MILES, C. (1993), "Education and disability in cross-cultural perspective: Pakistan", in PETERS, S. (ed), *Education & Disability in Cross-Cultural Perspective*, New York: Garland.

MOOKERJI, R.K. (1947), *Ancient Indian Education (Brahmanical and Buddhist)*, London: MacMillan.

O'FLAHERTY, W.D. (1981), *The Rig Veda. An anthology*, London: Penguin.

OLIVER, M. (1986), "Social policy and disability: some theoretical issues", *Disability, Handicap & Society* 1, pp. 5-17.

PENNY, F. (1904), *The Church in Madras*, London: Smith, Elder.

PERVEZ, M. & DURRANI, N. (eds) (1989), *Cognitive Development in Primary School Children of Pakistan*, Islamabad: National Institute of Psychology.

PERVEZ, S. (ed) (1989), *The Pakistani Child: Educational and Psychological Research*, Islamabad: National Institute of Psychology.

PESHAWARIA, R., MENON, D.K., GANGULY, R., ROY, S., PILLAY, R.P.R.S., & GUPTA, A. (1995), *Understanding Indian Families Having Persons with Mental Retardation*, Secunderabad: National Institute for the Mentally Handicapped.

RANGARAJAN, L.N. (transl. & ed) (1987), *Kautilya. The Arthashastra*, New Delhi: Penguin.

RASHID, S.K. (1978), *Wakf Administration in India*, New Delhi: Vikas.

Report of the Indian Famine Commission (1880), London: HMSO.

ROSE-ACKERMAN, S. (1982), "Mental retardation and society: the ethics and politics of normalization", *Ethics*, 93: 81-101.

SANYAL, R. (1977), "Indian participation in organized charity in early Calcutta, 1818-1866: a response to the poverty question", *Bengal Past and Present* 96, pp. 97-113.

SCHEER, J. & GROCE, N.E. (1988), "Impairment as a human constant: cross-cultural and historical perspectives on variation", *Journal of Social Issues* 44, pp. 23-37.

SEN, D.C. (1926-32), *Eastern Bengal Ballads*, University of Calcutta.

SHAH, M.H. & PERVEZ, M. (1994), "Profile of Pre-school Charsadda Child", study report, Primary Education Charsadda District Project, Pakistan.

SHWEDER, R.A. & BOURNE, E.J. (1982), "Does the concept of the person vary cross-culturally?", *in* Marsella, A.J. & White, G.M. (eds), *Cultural Conceptions of Mental Health and Therapy*, Dordrecht: Reidel.

SIMPSON, M.K. (1998), "The roots of normalization: a reappraisal", *Journal of Intellectual Disability Research* 42, pp. 1-7.

STONE, E. (1997), "From the research notes of a foreign devil: disability research in China", *in* Barnes, C. & Mercer, G. (eds), *Doing Disability Research*, Leeds: Disability Press.

STUBBS, S. (1997), "Poverty and membership of the mainstream: lessons from the South – can poverty facilitate inclusion?", *Asia Pacific Disability Rehabilitation Journal* 8, pp. 9-12.

'T.' (1879), "The blind schoolmaster of Palamcotta", *Church Missionary Gleaner* 6, pp. 65 & 76-7.

VENKATESAN, S. & VEPURI, V.G.D. (1995), *Mental Retardation in India (a bibliography)*, New Delhi: Concept.

CHAPTER 15

Engaging with Difference: Soul-searching for a methodology in disability and development research

Sue Stubbs

INTRODUCTION

Disability is about much more than disability. Outsiders don't know this. Most people not directly concerned with disability issues still see it as a "marginal", "specialist" issue, slightly boring, and certainly not with any major contributions to make to the big bold issues of development, research or social exclusion. The opposite is true; the potential contribution is immense.

Whether considering discrimination, development, inclusion, or research, addressing disability brings out the polarities, the extreme challenges, the range of diversity, and provides the opportunity to get to the essence of the problem. I found this to be particularly true in relation to research. Anyone who begins to read about research methodology is quickly aware of the complexity of issues and the paradoxes within all research paradigms. Researching across cultures adds to these dilemmas; and a focus on disability enlarges and illuminates them, sometimes to dazzling degree.

In this chapter, I will share with you a life-changing personal experience of research, which I carried out with colleagues in Lesotho a few years ago. Many of the challenges and questions which arose are not specific to disability or development research, but it was precisely because the focus was disability and development that the issues emerged so large and luminous. This forces a more rigorous engagement with these issues, which has the potential to lead to deeper insight, personal transformation and research that is more emancipatory than exploitative.

For those wanting more detailed information about this research, the fully referenced academic version (Stubbs 1995) is available on the EENET website or from the Save the Children (UK) Resource Unit.

BACKGROUND

My research sprang from my work as Global Disability Advisor for Save the Children UK. Part of my job was to "lead the process of policy development" in relation to disability, including issues around the education of disabled children. I was clear that this policy should be developed from the ground upwards – through our staff and partners in the 60 countries where we worked. But I felt daily and grossly inadequate for this task. This is a healthy feeling, provided it is balanced by determination to take on the challenge with integrity. I wanted the resulting policy and strategy to reflect real situations and real issues on the ground, whatever that meant. So, when the chance to take part in a flexible, research-based Masters Degree course at Cambridge arose, with a tutor who was asking similar questions, it seemed the ideal way forward.

My choice of topic – a Save the Children supported national programme on Inclusive Education in Lesotho, Southern Africa – was determined by a combination of principles, preference and pragmatics. I had visited the country twice before, and had established that our staff and partners would welcome the research. The programme itself was pioneering and potentially had much to teach others embarking on similar journeys. I wanted to learn from this programme.

The research topic was located in the broader area of the education of disabled children in countries of the South. (I use the terms North and South to refer to the broad division of countries in relation to resources and power). In my travels, I had been inspired by examples of integrated and inclusive education in the poorest countries with the fewest resources. Many seemed to be much nearer the ideals of inclusion than the so called "model programmes" of the North. Yet all the writing, research, discussion, experience-sharing was based on examples from the North. Worse still, these examples and ideas were being exported to the South, transplanted into alien cultures and contexts, frequently propped up by funding from the North (which did not last forever), and totally unaffordable in the local context.

The topic of Inclusive Education however, is not the focus of this chapter. My focus is research methodology. By this I do not mean "methods" of data collection. There is too frequently confusion between these two terms (methodology and methods) which, to me, are wholly different concepts. If I compare the research experience to an archaeological expedition, then the methods will only be the spades and technical tools used to dig up the treasures. The methodology, however, includes all the planning, the values and reasons behind the journey, the choice of companions, the choice of transport to get there, the decisions on which way to go to get there, the etiquette and behaviours agreed between colleagues during the dig. It includes the responses to objects uncovered, the decisions on what to do with them, who owns them, who should keep them, how they should be kept, and where and when; and the analysis of the importance and value of the objects at the end of the expedition.

SEARCHLIGHT ON LITERATURE

As the "literature search" is a standard requirement of formal research, and is so rarely critiqued as a methodology in its own right, my chapter will begin with this focus.

I had wondered whether I could avoid what seemed to me to be the inevitable characteristics of literature searches (often rambling, descriptive and uninformative; sometimes fastidious and gleeful digs at irrelevant details in other people's writings). Contrary to my expectations, the exercise of searching the literature was an extremely provocative experience. It placed crucial issues on the methodological agenda and provided me with a set of criteria by which to create my own research literature.

I wanted to discover what other people had written on the broad topic of the education of disabled children in "the South", and what it really had to teach me. I already knew that a literature covering three quarters of the world would be impossible to validate – how could I have any idea whether the one article on education in Mali would be complete fantasy or a careful and authentic critique? Accordingly, I felt that I had to look at what lay beyond the descriptions. What processes of reflection were the authors engaging in? What were their starting points? What beliefs and values lay at the heart of their investigations? What purposes and aims lay ahead of them?

My starting questions were:

- What does the literature contribute to our knowledge about the education of disabled children in countries of the South, particularly in Africa?
- In what ways does it present information or insights which will contribute towards the development of relevant, effective, sustainable, appropriate policy and practice?

Has Literature Anything To Do With Authentic Knowledge?

A key issue was the role and status of literature in relation to knowledge. During my introduction to research protocol, the basic question of whether or not literature is the best way of accessing valid and reliable knowledge was never raised. It was not even perceived to be a question. The issues giving rise to my own questioning were:

- *Lack of reference to indigenous knowledge*: Within the different cultures and contexts of the South, there is a huge amount of knowledge and experience relating to the education of disabled children. This exists primarily within children, parents, family and community members, teachers, education, social and health sector personnel, and local researchers. Is this knowledge reflected in the literature?
- *Alternative methods of knowledge storing/communicating*: There are many culturally diverse approaches to accessing, storing and communicating knowledge, which are more common than writing (e.g. oral history, visual records, drama, storytelling). Many of these cultures are predominantly oral cultures

- *Accessibility of Local Knowledge*: Even when local knowledge is written down (within local programmes or by local researchers), these reports and articles are often not accessible to anyone who cannot literally go and physically find them on the shelves, nor to those who do not read the written language used in the report.
- *Power inequalities*: The power in global research, including agendas and resources, is firmly located in the North. In disability research, this power is largely held by non-disabled researchers and agencies. None is in the hands of children themselves.

Once I began to track down relevant literature, the importance of my question was confirmed. I found about 180 publications (very few given the broad scope of the topic). Most were written by writers from the North. Less than one third were obviously written by writers from the South, and these were usually the articles most difficult to find. Only 5 authors were writing from their perspective as disabled people. There was only one publication which represented the views of disabled and non-disabled children, but that was based in the UK. This simple start alerted me to the danger of assuming that the content of this literature would offer insight into the actual situation of disabled children's education. It also raised further concerns.

- *Southern authors dancing to the tune of Northern academics*: Many authors from the South were writing within the Northern academic style, and many had been funded by or based in Northern academic institutions.
- *Building towers on quicksand*: There was a tendency for the same small number of Northern academic writers to be cited in all writings, with no critical examination of the facts and perceptions originally presented. These authors were assumed to have laid solid foundations on which to build a literature.
- *Validating personal experience*: There is no basis to assume that a report or piece of research that is well-referenced is any more reliable or valid than one that is written purely on the basis of personal experience. In fact, the articles I found which drew directly, confidently and critically on personal experience were by far the most informative and inspiring.

These criticisms might hold for any literature, but they are exacerbated in relation to topics which span a wide range of contexts, cultures and circumstances which might be unfamiliar to the writers; and when there are few peer reviewers with sufficient knowledge and experience to offer criticism. Beware!

10 Questions for a Literature Search on Disability and Development

There are several key questions that it would be wise to ask when searching or producing literature on disability and development. For a fuller discussion, backed by lots of references (!), please refer to my Critical Review (Stubbs, 1994).

1. *Are the facts and "hard" data reliable and can they be trusted?*
   (I came across 3 totally different statistics on numbers of disabled children in one area, all written in articles published in the same year.)
2. *Are the facts really facts?*
   (Disability statistics are a good example, since definitions depend on cultural and contextual perceptions of people with impairments.)
3. *Are key concepts examined critically?*
   (I found that concepts like "special needs" and "disability" were seldom defined, or that Northern definitions were used, without criticism.)
4. *Are concepts considered from a cross-cultural perspective?*
   (I found an assumption that key concepts had a universal meaning and were culturally immune, e.g. "education", "childhood".)
5. *Had key concepts been uncritically exported from the North to other cultures?*
   (Exportation was also selective and piecemeal. Concepts became more rigid and reified once exported. Concepts discredited in the North were still used as a basis for practice in the South, e.g. IQ testing.)
6. *Are the perspectives of key stakeholders represented?*
   (In relation to this topic, stakeholders would be disabled children, disabled adults, parents, local teachers and community members. Generally, their views were not represented – nor was this even perceived to be problematic.)
7. *If the writers are "outsiders", are they self-critical and reflexive?*
   (Researching beyond one's direct experience is difficult. Where a writer is a non-disabled adult from the North, writing about disabled children in the South, then there needs to be awareness of the issues this raises, and – at the very least – an attempt to engage with these issues and be reflexive. This was rarely the case.)
8. *Is the issue of ownership, participation in and control of research addressed?*
   (Disabled writers have argued that research which does not involve

disabled people makes no contribution to disabled people's lives. The same arguments have been made about research by the North on the South. Yet these critiques were not generally seen as an issue in the texts I found.)

9. *Is local knowledge and practice acknowledged and drawn upon?*
   (I found an assumption that communities were not doing anything in relation to educating their disabled children. Some writers challenged this, with compelling evidence that communities and teachers have been supporting disabled learners in creative ways for years.)
10. *Is there a discussion of power and resources in relation to global development?*
   (Global power and resource inequalities, agencies such as the World Bank or our own government aid departments, are all relevant to poverty, political control and resource allocation, which in turn are relevant to disability and development. Yet I found a tendency to portray the South as lacking political will, full of disease, poverty and victims – with little discussion on the underlying causes or systems which perpetuate injustice and inequality ... including in academia.)

No writing is ever going to be totally without flaws – and many of those who have written in this area have proven to be excellent practitioners and facilitators for social change. But for me the key issue remains whether a literature produces useable knowledge that firstly, can limit the damage that outside interventions can do and secondly, that leads to more effective, rights-based, sustainable, culturally appropriate, participatory development. Therefore it is important that constructive alternatives to the existing literature and research are proposed and implemented. This is what I tried to do. The critical literature search had provided me with clear criteria to inform my own research, and by which I would have to judge myself.

A DIFFERENT JOURNEY: PREPARING IT

In my research, I wanted to facilitate a valid, ethical, useful enquiry in the context of different cultures and languages, acknowledge different power relationships, reconcile different agendas, and use approaches which would be empowering for a wide range of very different people. The stipulations I set for my research were that it should:

1. Directly benefit the programme – and not at some vague point in the future.

2. Provide lessons for policy and practice at a wider level (linked to my job).
3. Meet academic criteria (linked to the Masters Degree I was taking).
4. Result in personal and professional development – especially how to engage with "difference" as an outsider and a Western non-disabled professional).

The tension between these four stipulations permeated the research, and contributed greatly to the resulting richness of insight which I was privileged to gain.

Trawling the Methodology Guidebooks

Planning the research journey became a research journey in its own right. Publications on research methodology are extensive, but none reflected the particular situation I was in. However I found helpful ideas in several bodies of literature, including new paradigm research, qualitative research, reflective practitioner research, participatory research, disability research, feminist research, case study research (to a lesser degree), and development research. This last group was the most helpful to my situation (but refer to Stubbs 1995 for more detail on what I learnt from other approaches).

Robert Chambers pioneered the broad and rapidly growing range of approaches known as PRA (Participatory Rural Appraisal) or PLA (Participatory Learning Approaches). Slim and Thomson raise key issues around doing research in oral cultures. The PRA approaches are often trivialized for advocating deceptively simple methods which can be used with non-literate communities. However, such criticisms confuse mere *methods* with the broader philosophical and ethical issues raised in the *methodology.* It was the methodology of PRA that I found useful and relevant.

PRA proposes a methodology which builds on the notion that local people are capable of sharing, enhancing and analysing their own knowledge in order to plan, act and promote their own development. It contains a moral and practical imperative for local people to analyse their own problems and implement their own solutions. It suggests a new role for outsider agencies from the North (donors or implementers) who support project work in countries of the South: a role of facilitation. PRA offers a relatively quick, effective and ethical way of doing appraisals and evaluations. Power relations and participation issues are addressed; a balance between precision and pragmatics is proposed in concepts such as "optimal ignorance" (not knowing what is not worth knowing) and "appropriate imprecision" (not measuring more than is really needed).

Preparing Oneself, Not Planning For Others

Preparation is the key – rather than planning. This may seem trivial, but I found it was an immensely practical concept. For me it meant that I could work on my values, my beliefs, my standards and parameters of behaviour, and I could develop a kit bag of tools (methods) which I might or might not use "in the field". What I could not do, sitting thousands of miles away from the location of my research project, was really plan. Moreover, I wanted the research team in Lesotho to plan the research together.

This was not an easy decision to stick to, when my colleagues in Britain were developing their questionnaires and making detailed plans. To add to my fears, I knew I would soon be far away from my tutor and my literature, with only one chance to "get it right". I had hoped to do some long-distance planning with the team, but this did not happen – primarily because the team in Lesotho had more pressing priorities and it would only be when I was on their doorstep that they would be able to give some time to the research.

LIVING IT: THE JOURNEY IN PROCESS

I will share with you an entry from my research diary soon after I landed in Lesotho:

> Monday, 13th February: I'm in Lesotho, jet-lagged and sweaty and L came to welcome me in my very own cool rondalla which will be my home for the next month. She came straight to the point, and warned me what I had let myself in for; everything takes a huge amount of organisation, plans don't always work, the Ministry wanted to know what it's all about, if it rains it will be very difficult in the mountains, the LNFOD representative (disabled person team member) got a job two days ago and is now unavailable, the Ministry has appointed a new Sp Ed team member but he has only just started work, another team member has to go for physiotherapy everyday and so cannot come on the field trips...

Even the bits I had been sure about had crumbled; the Ministry had been informed and agreed the research, but were now having second thoughts, and how about my beautifully balanced research team? I was plunged into the swirling waters of collaboration.

A research team does not make the research task any easier – but it is, I believe, absolutely vital when researching grassroots issues, designed to feed into grassroots actions, and outside one's own culture and experience. Important issues to take on board in setting up a research team are:

- All the key stakeholders should be involved in planning, implementing and analysing the research.
- The diversity within the particular context should be reflected in the team members (e.g. gender, disability, outsiders and insiders, cultural and linguistic backgrounds).
- Team members should have a representative role, not a tokenistic one. It is surprising how often a disabled person is involved but with no representative remit, and, even worse, insufficient self-empowerment to participate on an equal basis.
- Power differences must be recognised and managed. This has implications for chairing the team and for the behaviours and roles of the team's powerholders.
- A commonly agreed goal is essential, and can be a raft to hold onto when the sea of difference gets choppy.

In our research team, we found a new member of the Lesotho Disabled People's Organisation to join us and established a team of 6 people, reflecting a balance of gender, disability, outsiders and insiders, culture and linguistic backgrounds (Basotho, Zimbabwean and British). All team members wanted to improve policy and practice in relation to the educational inclusion of disabled children in Lesotho.

Mutual Ownership or My Agenda

At the first meeting of the team, it was clear that although my colleagues had welcomed the research and agreed to be involved, much more needed to be done to establish real joint ownership. One key lesson I learnt was that ownership is not developed just by telling people on Day One that this research belongs to them. Rather, developing ownership by others in the team demands giving up some of your own ownership, and an on-going commitment to shared ownership at all levels.

The PRA literature was useful here. It gave me simple sheets for planning which I could photocopy and hand out to my research team. This may seem a trivial point – but it was a way of handing over the "power" of research methodology to team members. They had access to what I had access to; methodology was demystified.

As a team, we developed a list of key research questions, topics, sub-topics and methods of data-collection. We tried to identify our own assumptions and bias. We had already decided to focus on two pilot Inclusive Education schools; one perceived as responding positively, and one which appeared to be responding negatively. All team members listed criteria which defined the terms "positive" and "negative". The schools were identified by Ministry of Special Education members of the team, who had overall responsibility for the pilot programme. This promoted more ownership, as it linked directly into their professional work. Assigning tasks to pairs within the team also promoted ownership, and brought out more in-depth perceptions and information than was revealed in meetings of the whole team.

It was also good to compile a matrix of relevant knowledge, skills and experience which different team members had between them. This brought together such diverse areas as knowledge of local language/community, knowledge of the families, ability to relate well to children, observation skills, listening skills, drawing/writing skills, story-telling skills, role play skills, report writing, organisational skills and leadership. The table demonstrated that each team member had a range of different contributions to make. We included local community members in this matrix, in anticipation of their involvement.

You WILL Be Participatory!

I had strong opinions about what sort of approaches I wanted to use. Extracting sensitive information from vulnerable people at gun-point was not one of them. However, some team members had been exposed to Northern ideas about interviews and questionnaires, and methods for extracting information which were far from participatory or empowering. I began to realise that we all needed to spend some time learning and experimenting with different types of participatory methods.

Behind this was the more fundamental issue of who the research was for and what our roles were. As a team, we were still all "outsiders" in relation to the real primary stakeholders who were: firstly, disabled and non-disabled children; secondly, their parents and families; thirdly, the classroom teachers; and fourthly, community members. I initiated a discussion on action research and our potential role as research facilitators rather than extractors of information.

The term "community participation" will make anyone in the development field cringe out of over-exposure and accumulated cynicism – and rightly so. These concepts need to be taken apart and turned into practical approaches. In my situation, there were very many communities at different levels all interacting in different ways and with different agendas. We had established our own community in the research team, with a reasonable degree of mutual understanding and ownership. We were now going to visit a remote rural community consisting of different groups of people all with different perceptions and agendas. Fortunately, the schools were signed up members of a long-term pilot project, and monitoring and evaluation was an integral part of this process. It would have been inappropriate to try to involve a school not part of any longer term project. Also, some of the team members knew the teachers and had established a good rapport already.

As the time for field work drew near, despite the progress made, my anxiety rose:

> Thursday, February 16th: I am concerned that the visit to the school will be nothing more than a series of predicable interviews on passive groups of people trying to do what is expected of them.. am I as usual, being over-ambitious?.. I feel confused about the objectives of the research; is it me gaining insights?, gaining lots of "evidence" for "them out there"?, transferring skills to the team? rehearsing the evaluation? improving the programme? helping the Sp Ed team to learn about their impact?, are these compatible? ...I am currently placing more emphasis on the collaboration and research process than research results.. (Personal research diary).

Yet the team were bored with planning, and wanted to get started. Again, Chamber's encouragement to "start, stumble, and self-correct" was helpful. My natural inclination would have been to spend the next 6 months planning!

TOOLS OF THE TRADE

There were many rich insights gained during each day of the research process, but these can be read in the unedited version (Stubbs 1995). Instead,

I want to share with you some insights about the nature of tools or methods used.

We wanted to start by finding out what the existing situation was in relation to inclusion. Classroom observation had been agreed as the "tool" to initiate this. Classroom teachers and the District Advisor would also take part in observing each other's classes. Following the observation, we had a group discussion which exceeded expectations. Teachers became very animated and engrossed in presenting their feedback and challenging each other. At this point I found I had to make what then seemed a choice between two of my research stipulations: the discussions were carried out partly in English but when they got going, they lapsed into Basotho. My "academic" stipulation implied that I should take detailed notes of all this wonderful data. But to "directly benefit the programme" required that I accept that teachers were gaining more from the discussions in their own language. I put the notepad aside.

I also began to get to grips with my role as a facilitator and supporter. Some of the feedback from the classroom observations was judgmental, based on interpretation. I could highlight the difference between describing a factual incident or sequence of events, and presenting a generalised judgement. The teacher who was being observed had the first opportunity to comment on the observation, then it became a free for all. A wide range of key issues relating to inclusion were raised: is "behaviour" a disability? What does "lazy" mean? What are the best seating arrangements? How can teachers maintain discipline without disempowering children?

Another issue that emerged from research was the distinction between non-confrontational and confrontational tools – both of which can be used participatory research. Non-confrontational tools are those methods which are taught to the primary stakeholders, who then use the tools themselves to learn about their own situation. They then present their finding to the research facilitator/team, and thereby engage in their own analysis. Non-confrontational methods include inviting people to:

- Compile their own table of successes and constraints in their work.
- Draw a programme profile, giving peaks and troughs and catalytic events.
- Draw mobility diagrams, maps or tables related to their work.
- Do small groupwork or work in pairs on analysing aspects of their work.

Some methods may involve direct engagement by the research facilitator or team, but are still not really inherently confrontational: facilitated storytelling; focus groups, with sensitive facilitation; and questionnaires.

Confrontational methods are those that require the research facilitator or team to engage directly with the person who holds the information or experience. Here, the agenda is set and controlled by the research facilitator. These tools include:

- Classroom observation (unless carried out by teachers alone).
- Structured and semi-structured interviews.

All of these approaches can be appropriate and successful in different contexts and cultures. I learnt that both confrontational and non-confrontational tools work well where the key stakeholders (the ones with the information/experience) had a high level of rapport and trust with the research facilitators, and where they themselves had a good level of empowerment and self-confidence. However, non-confrontational tools potentially work well in all situations – including where there is a low level of trust and self-confidence among key stakeholders. Confrontational tools had more limited usage: they did not work where there was not a good level or trust, or where the people concerned had low self-confidence and had significantly less power than the Research Facilitator/team members. Also, confrontational tools might not work in cultures where there is a very formal system of inspection or judgement by those in authority – since participants might feel extremely threatened and cautious.

Confrontational tools depend on the inter-personal skills and experience of the research facilitator or team member. When we carried out semi-structured interviews or facilitated story-telling (basically sitting with a parent of a disabled child and inviting them to "tell the story" of their child from birth), there was a vast difference in the results depending on the approach of the facilitator. Some people made the parent feel at ease and heard a detailed and passionate account of their experience. Others expected the parent to respond formally to the list of prompts that the team had agreed, and basically asked them questions that resulted in stilted responses. With non-confrontational tools, the facilitator needs different skills again, to be able to explain and demonstrate a method very clearly.

As always, the key is not seeing any of these tools as inherently right or appropriate without modification. Rather, any and all of them may, or may not, be the best tools in a certain situation. So, in a subsequent evaluation in China, it was deemed appropriate to use more traditional methods with government officials who would have been offended if asked to get down on the ground and draw pictures; whereas kindergarten teachers welcomed methods which were more interactive.

ENGAGING WITH DIFFERENCE

As a team, we encountered cultural differences. For example: I asked the team to meet every evening to review the day and plan the next. Some felt this was a bit over the top. We had different understandings of the term "thoroughness", which seemed to be both a cultural and a personality issue. I was the stereotypical western perfectionist, obsessed with writing it all down, doing it quickly, and staying in control. My Southern African colleagues displayed a greater degree of tolerance, a preference for face-to-face communication, plenty of pragmatism, a greater ease with the "unexpected", a totally different sense of time, and a lot of patience. What was exciting about our team was the alchemy of bringing these two perspectives together. Thus. I felt I could contribute about the rigour of the process, but I tried to let go of my less necessary obsessions with detail and timing.

We also encountered the difference of disability.

The PRA tools had not been designed to be accessible to disabled people. Even so, providing the underlying philosophy was understood, it was not difficult to be creative with the basic ideas. Many of the practical tools used in PRA involve manipulating objects such as sticks, stones, dried beans, the earth to make maps, tables, graphs etc. This offers ways of involving people with visual impairment, and can facilitate the involvement of people with learning disability. For example, a group of children with a range of impairments compiled a daily profile of their life in different segments. All were able to draw a series of pictures and then talk about them, providing a wealth of information about their daily lives, and providing them with an opportunity to have the details of their lives heard and validated.

In Lesotho, our visually impaired team member and his "aural observation" in the classroom made a unique contribution: the rest of us were so dominated by the visual, that we missed much of the interactive dialogue between teacher/pupil, and pupil/pupil, let alone the tone of voice and dominance of difference speakers. He also facilitated the focus group discussions with children to discuss their perceptions on inclusion. As a disabled role model he had the authority to ask the sort of questions that would have been inappropriate for non-disabled people to ask. He was also a role model for the teachers, particularly in the school which was resistant to inclusion.

Working with a disabled team member or involving disabled children in research really highlights the issues around participation. It might be possible to get away with thinking that girl children are participating along with boy children, or that children from different cultures are all involved (there will often be children from oppressed groups who are very clever at learning what is expected and copying the mainstream norms). But when there is a deaf or blind child or team member, when a person uses a wheelchair, when there is a child with severe learning disability using an alternative form of communication, then the extent to which a situation is inclusive becomes very evident. Until the involvement of disabled people in community participatory research which does not have an overt disability focus becomes the norm, any so called participatory research will still be fundamentally exclusive.

REFLECTING: RESEARCH AS EXPLOITATION OR EMANCIPATION?

When I came to write up the research, I made a distinction between the *collaborative analysis* which was carried out by the team, during and after the period of research in Lesotho, and my own *personal retrospective analysis* which happened back in the UK in the following months. The collaborative analysis reflected the views of the team, and I felt that it was extremely important to present this as it happened. It was not my business to tamper with it. This included the team's reflections on both the process and the resulting learning. When reading write-ups of participatory evaluations, I rarely find this distinction. The writer places their own interpretation on the research results irrespective of whether the participants have different perspectives. This is a very limited concept of participation. The analysis stage is frequently ignored, yet it is the most significant aspect of research and evaluation. Statistics and data do not speak for themselves: they will always have an underpinning philosophy and interpretation which may or may not be overt.

The advantage of being committed to write up this research in the UK meant that I was forced to carry on thinking in a systematic and critical manner long after I left Lesotho. This was incredibly valuable. Normally, after an experience of learning, we semi-consciously draw up a set of conclusions, which might include generalisations or stereotypical perceptions. The clarity of the insights and impact of the experience fades after time. However, putting one's reflections under the microscope can consolidate and clarify those insights, even produce new insights. It can create a depth of understanding which does actually transform one's values, beliefs and behaviour.

I would like to end this chapter by sharing some of those personal retrospective reflections. Most are not conclusions, but questions that need further exploration.

Inquisition or Quest Within?

We all have a tremendous capacity to embody contradictions within our beliefs and behaviours. Research can expose these contradictions, if we let it. I have long believed in participatory, yet I was totally unprepared for the way in which assumptions I did not even realise I held were dramatically challenged.

Questioning is a common and highly acceptable type of behaviour for people from the North. It is a trait which is actively encouraged in children, and applauded in students. In research, it is perceived as essential. Yet I often noticed that people in other cultures didn't really do it, except within the context of socially determined greetings and exchanges. In my Lesotho research, I began to ask questions myself about the values underpinning "questioning" and the extractive nature of knowledge acquisition.

This became very apparent in our experiences at the second school which was perceived as not being so successful. The teachers had told parents to come to the school to meet us, and we carried out the same type of semi-structured interviews with these parents as we had in the first school. Even though those who were conducting the interviews were using their mother tongue and had explained the purpose of the visit, the parents were obviously disturbed, distrustful, and fearful. The difference was that in this situation, the parents rarely had contact with the school, they were not welcome at the school, and their "inferiority" was constantly reaffirmed in relation to the educated staff at the school. A short explanation by a group of strangers was not enough to enable them to understand and feel part of our research experience. So, here was a very extreme power imbalance, and questioning was a type of exploitation. But even in situations where there was willingness and trust (as in the first school), I felt uncomfortable with the methods that involved direct questioning.

Questioning other people about their lives, particularly where the questioners have more power or are not trusted friends or family members, is a process of extracting personal parts of themselves for our own use and gratification. This is in line with traditional western approaches to many aspects of life: extracting what we want from the environment, dominating over other cultures, rampant consumerism. Do we have any right to do this? Very few people in situations of less power are likely to refuse to be questioned, and so "consent" is a poor excuse.

I also feel that there is a big distinction between the approach to gaining knowledge which is based on acquisition, which can be called 'acquiry', and an approach which is basically a quest within oneself, engaging the spirit, heart and mind, which can be called 'enquiry'. For me, the initial impulse towards questioning others gave way to listening to others, sharing their experiences, engaging with them, and questing within myself. Research becomes a process of placing oneself in a situation, engaging with it, and reflecting on what happens within oneself. The job of research facilitator becomes one of supporting others to engage in the same process of self-critical reflection.

I notice now that my own way of accessing knowledge about different cultural situations has changed dramatically. When I visit India, I rarely ask questions when I find myself in a puzzling situation. Instead I stay with the experience, I wait, I listen, I observe, and later, I reflect. I find I learn a lot more this way.

I'm Only Here to Learn!

Another variation of this extractive process is the "I'm here to learn" approach which so many of us flying in from the North say in order to demonstrate our humility in the face of the real knowledge of the people on the ground. After several days of "learning" during the Lesotho research, I began to feel that I was not pulling my weight. Everyone around me was working very hard sharing their experience, giving information, analysing and problem solving. I was careful not to give my opinions or to collude with their expectations that I might be some sort of "expert" because I was from London. I soon realised that this is a false and in a sense hypocritical stance to take. We all have skills and knowledge, and I was denying my 20 plus years of freely received education and privileged exposure to a wide range of situations if I did not believe I had anything to offer. The more tricky approach was to offer what was appropriate to offer, and to develop a real exchange which did not in any way undervalue one type of contribution against another. In my case, I found the balance was well established after I presented some straightforward teaching sessions on different aspects of research methodology.

Oral Cultures are Wonderful! Just let me write that down...

Another main area of my learning relates to examining another aspect of the cultural underpinnings of research; research in cultures which are predominantly oral.

In my own research, I had reservations about the extent to which my own insistence on written records, and my encouragement to others to write their experiences down, constantly undermined oral culture. Even those from the North who try to validate oral testimony do this by writing about it. The research challenged my assumption that the function of memory is to recall "facts". Another possibility was that memory was a creative process which gave "insights into how people make sense of their lives and social worlds" (Slim and Thomson, 1993).

In an attempt to find alternative means of accessing, storing and communicating knowledge, many of our methods focused on oral testimony, story telling, drawings and non-literacy based activities. The presence of the team member who was blind helped considerably in heightening our awareness of the richness of aural observations. Ideally, if the research did not have to be written up for an academic audience, it would have been more appropriate to present the conclusions in different media; drama, drawing, video, stories, songs etc.

Authors, Authority and Authenticity

It is no accident that the terms authority and authenticity come from the term "author". For me the notion of authorship became central. The primary authors of the experiences the research was addressing were the children, the teachers, parents, community members. It is to these authors that the research is primarily accountable. For me this presented a challenge in that I was intending to try to make this research accountable to an external audience many thousands of miles away with different notions of rigour. I had been unwilling to impose a Northern academic concept of rigour onto other participants in the research. Despite the vulnerability of staying with this process, not knowing what would emerge, by the end of the research my notions of what counts as "rigour" had changed considerably.

The rigour was the breadth and depth of self-critical awareness permeating the whole process. The authority of the research and its authenticity stems from acknowledging who the authors of the research are, and by letting their words, their perceptions, their analyses shine clearly through. This pragmatic rigour has its own validity.

From Capacity to Power, from Participation to Emancipation

The final key lesson I will share with your relates to the question, who can do research? My conclusion is that anyone who has some capacity to reflect on their own situation can be a researcher. This includes children with learning disabilities and people without literacy skills. I feel that a distinction needs to be made between "researchers" and the "research facilitator". Everyone involved in the research should be a researcher, and the job of the facilitator is to transfer research skills and enable people to become their own researchers.

Although everyone (maybe apart from some very severely mentally disabled people) has the capacity to do research, in situations of extreme poverty and oppression, people do not have the power. Oppressed groups include disabled people, children, women, and even with the opportunity to "participate", their participation will merely be the lubrication of someone else's research agenda unless they have the power to do so. The ultimate test of successful research is not the degree of participation, but the extent to which it leads to emancipation (Swantz and Vainio-Mattila 1988, p. 131)).

If you as research facilitator are serious about helping facilitate this, then be warned, you will have to allow your own research agenda to be transformed, you will have to lose control, but hold on tight to your self-critical perspective.

CONCLUSION – YOUR JOURNEY

I hope that this chapter has challenged your thinking about research. Don't believe what I have said, check it out in relation to your own experience and the unedited version of my thesis. If you don't agree, challenge my arguments and develop an alternative. Don't get stuck on details which do not make a difference to people's lives, this is a great academic distraction! Development is a continuum from the personal to the global; research can bring the two ends of this continuum together. Spend your time on finding better, more authentic, more integral, more rigorous approaches to research which result in greater social justice and emancipation for all.

SELECTED BIBLIOGRAPHY

BARNES, C. (1992), "Qualitative Research: Valuable or Irrelevant?", *Disability, Handicap and Society* 7(1), pp. 115-125.

BARTON, L. (ed) (1992), *Disability, Handicap and Society. Special Issue: Researching Disability* 7 (2).

BROKENSHA, D.W., WARREN, D.M. & WERNER, O. (1980), *Indigneous Knowledge Systems and Development*, Lanham, Maryland: University Press of America.

CHAMBERS, R. (1983), *Rural Development: Putting the Last First*, Harlow: Longman Scientific and Technical.

CHAMBERS, R. (1992), "Rural Appraisal: Rapid, Relaxed and Participatory", *Discussion Paper No. 311*, Brighton: Institute of Development Studies.

CHAMBERS, R. (1993), *Challenging the Professions: Frontiers for Rural Development*, London: Intermediate Technology Publications.

CHAMBERS, R. (1994), "All Power Deceives", *in* Davies (ed), *IDS Bulletin* 2 (25).

CONNORS, J. L. & DONNELLAN, A. M. (1993), "Citizenship and Culture: the role of disabled people in Navajo Society", *Disability, Handicap and Society* 8(3), pp. 265-280.

DAVIES, S. (ed) (1994), "Knowledge is Power? the use and abuse of information in development", *IDS Bulletin* 25 (2).

EDWARDS, M. (1989), "The Irrelevance of Development Studies", *Third World Quarterly*, 11 (1), pp. 116-135.

ENDA (1993), *Children's Participation in Action Research: Training Course for* Trainers, Harare: ENDA.

FEE, E. (1983), "Is Feminism a Threat to Scientific Objectivity?", *International Journal of Women's Studies* 4, pp. 378-392.

FINCH, J. (1993), "'It's Great to Have Someone to Talk to': Ethics and Politics of Interviewing Women", *in* Hammersley, M. (ed) *Social Research: Philosophy, Politics and Practice*, London: Sage Publications.

FREIRE, P. (1968), *Pedagogy of the Oppressed*, New York: The Seabury Press.

GLUCK, S.B. & PATAI, D. (1991), *Womens' Words: The Feminist Practice of Oral History*, London: Routledge.

GUIJT, I., FUGLESANG, A. & KISADHA, T. (ed) (1994), *It is the Young Trees That Make a Thick Forest: A Report on Redd Barna's Learning Experiences with* PRA, London: IIED.

HARRY, B. & KALYANPUR, M. (1994), "Cultural Underpinnings of Special Education: implications for professional interactions with culturally diverse families", *Disability and Society* 9 (2), pp. 145-165.

KISANJI, J. (1993), "Special Education in Africa" *in* Mittler, P., Brouillette, R. & Harris, D. (eds), *World Yearbook of Education 1993 – Special Needs Education* London: Kogan Page.

KRIEGLER, S. (1989), "The Learning Disabilities Paradigm: Is it relevant in the South Africa context?", *International Journal of Special Education* 4 (2), pp. 165-171.

KRIEGLER, S. & FARMAN, B. (1994), "Redistribution of Special Education Resources in South Africa: Beyond Mainstreaming Towards Effective Schools", *International Journal of Special Education* 9 (1), pp. 1-12.

LINCOLN, Y. & GUBA, E. (1985), *Naturalistic Enquiry*, London: Sage Publications.

MALINGA, J. (ed) (1991), "Integrated Education – the real thing", *Disability Frontline* 8, pp. 9-11.

MILTON KEYNES WORLD DEVELOPMENT CENTRE (1992), *Challenging a Disabling World*, Milton Keynes: Milton Keynes World Development Education Centre.

MITCHELL, D. & BROWN, R. (eds) (1991), *Early Intervention Studies for Young Children with Special Needs*, London: Chapman and Hall.

OAKLEY, A. (1981), "Interviewing Women: a Contradiction in Terms" *in* Roberts, H. (ed) *Doing Feminist* Research, London: Routledge and Kegan Paul.

PETERS, S.J. (ed) (1993), *Education and Disability in Cross-Cultural* Perspective, London: Garland.

REASON, P. (ed) (1988), *Human Enquiry in Action: developments in new paradigm research*, London: Sage.

REASON, P. & ROWAN, J. (eds) (1981), *Human Inquiry: a sourcebook of new paradigm research*, Chichester: John Wiley and Sons.

ROBSON, C. (1993), *Real World Research*, Oxford: Blackwell.

SCHON, D.A. (1983), *The Reflective Practitioner*, New York: Basic Books.

SCHON, D.A. (1987), *Educating the Reflective Practitioner*, New York: Basic Books.

SERPELL, R., MARIGA, L. & HARVEY, K. (1993), "Mental Retardation in African Countries: Conceptualisation, Services and Research", *International Review of Research in Mental Retardation*, Vol. 19, pp. 1 – 39.

SHAKESPEARE, P., ATKINSON, D. & FRENCH, S. (eds) (1993), *Reflecting on Research Practice: Issues in Health and Social Welfare*, Buckingham: Open University Press.

SLIM, H. & THOMPSON, P. (1993), *Listening for a Change: Oral Testimony and Development*, London: Panos Publications Ltd.

STUBBS, S. (1994), *A Critical Review of the Literature Relating to the Education of Disabled Children in Developing Countries*, London: Save the Children Resource Centre.

STUBBS, S. (1995), *The Lesotho National Integrated Education Programme: A Case Study on* Implementation, London: Save the Children Resource Centre.

THEIS, J. & GRADY, H.M. (1991), *Participatory Rural Appraisal for Community Development*, London: IIED and SCF.

VULLIAMY, G., LEWIN, K. & STEPHENS, D. (eds) (1990), *Doing Educational Research in Developing Countries*, London: The Falmer Press.

WERNER, D. (1994), "Child-to-Child as a Transforming Educational Process" *Newsletter from the Sierra Madre* 29, pp. 19-20.

Useful Organisations

The organisations listed below are just a few of the growing number of organisations involved in disability and development. Several have websites with links to other contacts and resources. A few produce newsletters and publications (e.g. Disabled Peoples' International, Disability Awareness in Action, ActionAid India, EENET – the Enabling Education Network).

Disabled Peoples' International (DPI) and *Disability International*
101-7 Evergreen Place
Winnipeg, Manitoba
CANADA R3L 2T3
Email: dpi@dpi.org
Website: http://www.dpi.org
"DPI is a grassroot, cross-disability network with member organizations in over 110 countries, over half of which are in the developing world. The main functions of DPI are Development, Human Rights, Communications, Advocacy and Public Education."
DPI produces a worldwide magazine: *Disability International*.

Disability Awareness in Action (DAA) and *Disability Tribune*
11 Belgrave Road
LONDON SW1V 1RB
United Kingdom
Email: DAA_ORG@compuserve.com
Website: http://ourworld.compuserve.com/homepages/DAA_ORG
DAA provides "an information network for disabled people and their organisations worldwide, to support their self-help activities and to ensure their equality of opportunity ... DAA produces and disseminates information, most of which is based on the direct experience of our readers in 158 countries". The newsletter, *Disability Tribune*, is available in many languages and formats, including from the website.

ActionAid
Hamlyn House
Archway
London N19 5PG
UNITED KINGDOM
Website: http://www.actionaid.org/home.html

ActionAid India Disability Division and *ActionAid Disability News*
ActionAid-INDIA, P.O. Box 5406
3 Rest House Road
BANGALORE – 560 001
INDIA
Website: http://www.actionaidindia.org
ActionAid Disability News is for planners, administrators, professionals, funding and implementing agencies involved in disability and rehabilitation. It is free of charge.

Action on Disability and Development (ADD)
23 Lower Keyford
Frome
Somerset BA11 4AP
UNITED KINGDOM
Email: ADD@GN.APC.ORG
Website: under preparation.
(See Barbara Frost's paper in this book for more information on ADD).

Asia Pacific Rehabilitation Journal
J-124 Ushas Appartments
16th Main, 4th Block
Jayanager
BANGALORE 560 011
INDIA

Disability Research Unit (DRU) and The Disability Press
Dept. of Sociology and Social Policy
University of Leeds
Leeds LS2 9JT
UNITED KINGDOM
Tel: (44) 113 2334414; Fax: (44) 113 2334415
Website: http://www.leeds.ac.uk/sociology/dru/links.htm
DRU runs undergraduate and postgraduate courses on disability studies and has a strong programme of research. The website details publications, DRU courses, links to relevant sites, including the international email discussion list "disability-research".

Enabling Education Network (EENET) and *EENET Newsletter*
Centre for Educational Needs
School of Education
University of Manchester
Oxford Road
Manchester M13 9PL
UNITED KINGDOM
Email: eenet@man.ac.uk
Website: http://www.eenet.org.uk
(See Susie Miles's paper in this book for more information on EENET).

HealthLink Worldwide (formerly AHRTAG)
Farringdon Point, 29-35 Farringdon Road
London EC1M 3JB
UNITED KINGDOM
Tel: (44) (0)20 7 242 0606; Fax: (44) (0)20 7 242 0041
E-mail: info@healthlink.org.uk
Website: http://www.healthlink.org.uk
HealthLink Worldwide publishes *CBR News* on disability issues and provision.

Hesperian Foundation (David Werner, author of *Disabled Village Children*)
PO Box 1692
Palo Alto
California 94302 USA

Inclusion International (The International League of Societies for Persons with Mental Handicap)
Galeries de la Toison d'Or
29 Chaussée d'Ixelles, 393/32
B-1050 Brussels
BELGIUM
Website: http://users.skynet.be/incluit/

Institute of Child Health
Centre for International Child Health
University of London
30 Guilford Street
London WC1N 1EH
UNITED KINGDOM
Email: cich@ich.ucl.ac.uk
Website: http://www.ich.ucl.ac.uk/
(CICH has a research programme and runs an MSc in Community Disability Studies for those working in community-based disability programmes in the majority world).

International Centre for the Advancement of Community Based Rehabilitation
Queen's University
Kingston, Ontario,
CANADA K7L 3N6
Email: icacbr@post.queensu.ca
Website: http://meds.queensu.ca/icacbr

Oneworld.net
Website: http://www.oneworld.org/
Oneworld.net is an internet community of 467 organisations leading the way for human rights and sustainable development worldwide, including on disability.

Oxfam (UK and Ireland)
274 Banbury Road
Oxford OX2 7DZ
UNITED KINGDOM
Website: http://www.oxfam.org.uk/index.html

Rehabilitation International
432 Park Avenue South
New York
NY 10016 USA

Save the Children Fund (SCF UK)
17 Grove Lane
London SE5 8RD
UNITED KINGDOM
Website: http://www.savethechildren.org.uk/

UNITED NATIONS SYSTEM – RELEVANT ORGANISATIONS
The official UN website (which has links to websites for UN organisations and partners) can be found at: http://www.unsystem.org/

IMPACT (An International Initiative Against Avoidable Disability) c/o WHO
20 Avenue Appia
CH-1211 Geneva
SWITZERLAND

ILO (International Labour Organization)
Vocational Rehabilitation Branch
4 Route des Morillons
CH-1211 Geneva
SWITZERLAND
Website: http://www.ilo.org/

UNESCO (United Nations Educational, Scientific and Cultural Organisation)
7 Place de Fontenoy
75700 Paris
FRANCE
Website: http://www.unesco.org/

UNICEF (United Nations Childrens Fund)
Unicef House
3 United Nations Plaza
New York
NY 100017 USA
Website: http://www.unicef.org/

UNDP (United Nations Development Programme)
1 United Nations Plaza
New York
NY 100017 USA
Website: http://www.undp.org/

WHO (World Health Organization)
20 Avenue Appia
CH-1211 Geneva
SWITZERLAND
Website: http://www.who.int/

Index